"This is a wonderfully important book which reminds
living well is not simply to eradicate pain, discomfort,
we truly value; a task that requires us to be open to
A real breath of fresh air at a time when our definition
treatments for mental illness have been overly
movement."

—**Brock Bastian, PhD**, professor in the department of psychology at the
University of Melbourne, and author of *The Other Side of Happiness*

"How many sunsets do you have left? Strong scripts, suggested exercises and homework, nuanced troubleshooting, and sticky metaphors all vividly show clinical methods
to build lives worth living. Surprisingly creative later chapters give even experienced
therapists new directions. This book is worth the investment."

—**Kelly Koerner, PhD**, author of *Doing Dialectical Behavior Therapy*

"Clients seek treatment longing for a better life. Even when unspoken, this longing is
an impetus to seek help and the factor that justifies the work inherent therein. This
book masterfully explains how values work can be implemented in various treatment
approaches. With deep clinical wisdom, readers are walked through various nuances of
clarifying and promoting valued actions. Importantly, common difficulties are presented along with practical ways to address them. Useful for experienced and novice
clinicians alike, this book will help you help your clients to live lives with the dignity
and vitality they seek."

—**Andrew Gloster, PhD**, professor at the University of Basel, where he
heads the division of clinical psychology and intervention science

"*Values in Therapy* is a wonderfully written testimony and practical guide on how values can help humans build lives of meaning and purpose, and in so doing, reduce their suffering. It is going to be an essential text in my clinic, and I have no doubt it will become essential to you, too. LeJeune and Luoma have enriched the book with clinical examples that show how values work has changed the lives of the people they have served, and their work comes alive on the page. You have in your hands a resource that will not be left on the shelf. Use it to help with the challenges of bringing values into therapy, to gently face the pain of not living as one hopes to, and to travel down the path of deep meaning that is a life with values at the center. This is a great book that will enrich your work and your life by helping you explore, build, and take action. I highly recommend it for anyone who cares to find the riches that lie in helping others."

—**Louise Hayes, PhD**, clinical psychologist and senior fellow at the University of Melbourne and Orygen Centre for Excellence in Youth Mental Health; fellow at the Association for Contextual Behavioral Science; and coauthor of *The Thriving Adolescent* and *Get Out of Your Mind and Into Your Life for Teens*

"Spend time with this book and it will change the way you interact not only with your clients, but also with yourself, your loved ones, and most likely all of your interactions. Filling life with meaning, connection, and curiosity is at the very heart of this well-written book. It is a great addition to your library no matter if you are early in your therapeutic career, or an experienced therapist. This book is a gold mine!"

—**Tobias Lundgren, PhD**, assistant professor and research group leader in the department of clinical neuroscience, and head of health care development at the Center for Psychiatry Research at the Karolinska Institute in Sweden; and author and coauthor of numerous research articles and books, including *The Art and Science of Valuing in Psychotherapy*

"*Values in Therapy* has changed the way I work with clients, and also my own inner life. The theory and practice suggested by the book are deceptively simple and very powerful. Jenna LeJeune and Jason Luoma have written an insightful, often surprising, supremely practical guide to helping counselors bring meaning and purpose to their own lives and the lives of their clients."

—**Martha Beck, PhD**, *New York Times* bestselling author of *Finding Your Own North Star*

"If you want to help your clients build richer, more meaningful lives, develop a sense of purpose and fulfillment, and find motivation and inspiration from deep within, then you need this book. The authors take you step by step through the use of values to enrich and enhance any type of therapy. Loaded with simple but powerful exercises and tools, and a wealth of case examples, this is a truly practical guide for helping your clients to harness the power of values and use it for profound transformation."

—**Russ Harris**, author of *The Happiness Trap* and *ACT Made Simple*

"Fresh, comprehensive, and clear, if you must choose only one book about values in therapy, choose this one. It covers every topic of importance with grace, never letting the authors' obvious sophistication get in the way of serving the needs of the reader. You will feel supported and empowered, and your clients will be uplifted. Whether or not you are an acceptance and commitment therapy (ACT) clinician, if you care about values work in therapy, this is the book you have been waiting for."

—**Steven C. Hayes, PhD**, Foundation Professor in the department of psychology at the University of Nevada, Reno; and codeveloper of ACT

"Jenna LeJeune and Jason Luoma have shared with us a book about living a meaningful life guided by values that comes from their hearts truly. This work matters to them, and you see and feel it in their writing. *Values in Therapy* is a clinician's guide designed to not only assist us in helping clients to imagine and engage their deepest purpose, it is also about imagining and engaging our own. The clinical examples are thoughtfully presented, and the self-directed 'inside out' work invites clinicians to be curious about their own values-based actions and the meaning they create. This is a must-read book for all therapists, not simply those interested in ACT. Learning what it means to be alive and creating—to live well and with vitality is the essence of this book."

—**Robyn D. Walser, PhD**, licensed clinical psychologist, author of *The Heart of ACT*, and coauthor of *The Mindful Couple* and *Learning ACT*

Values
in
Therapy

A CLINICIAN'S GUIDE *to* HELPING CLIENTS
EXPLORE VALUES, INCREASE PSYCHOLOGICAL
FLEXIBILITY & LIVE *a* MORE MEANINGFUL LIFE

JENNA LeJEUNE, PhD • JASON B. LUOMA, PhD

CONTEXT PRESS
An Imprint of New Harbinger Publications, Inc.

Publisher's Note

This publication is designed to provide accurate and authoritative information in regard to the subject matter covered. It is sold with the understanding that the publisher is not engaged in rendering psychological, financial, legal, or other professional services. If expert assistance or counseling is needed, the services of a competent professional should be sought.

Distributed in Canada by Raincoast Books

Copyright © 2019 by Jenna LeJeune and Jason B. Luoma
    Context Press
    An imprint of New Harbinger Publications, Inc.
    5674 Shattuck Avenue
    Oakland, CA 94609
    www.newharbinger.com

Cover design by Amy Shoup

Interior design by Michele Waters-Kermes and Tracy Carlson

Acquired by Tesilya Hanauer

Edited by Melanie Bell

All Rights Reserved

Library of Congress Cataloging-in-Publication Data on file

Printed in the United States of America

21 20 19

10 9 8 7 6 5 4 3 2 1   First Printing

Jenna would like to dedicate this book to her parents, Jerry and Jo Ann LeJeune. Thank you for your unwavering love and support in helping me live out my values. I can't imagine having better role models than you for what it means to live a well-lived life.

Contents

Acknowledgments

All the knowledge I have and everything that I have written here is simply the accumulation of everyone who has influenced me: my family (my parents, Josh, Monica, Josephine, and Michael), friends, mentors (Drs. Duhamel, O'Connor, Arnkoff, Rayburn, Bonanno, and Myers), colleagues, trainees, and, most importantly, my clients, who have patiently shaped me over the years. I have been incredibly fortunate to be surrounded by so many wise, generous, and inspiring people from whom I have learned so much over the years. I would like to thank the people at New Harbinger for encouraging me and giving me the freedom to write from the heart even if that is somewhat unconventional for a professional book. A big thank-you to Aki Masuda, PhD, Rebecca Pasillas, PhD, and Matthew Skinta, PhD, who graciously shared their expertise and gave us invaluable feedback related to the cultural issues discussed in chapter 8. Finally, and most importantly, I would like to thank my coauthor, husband, and partner in all things, Jason. This book would never have happened without you. Thank you for your relentless faith in me and your constant reminders to return to my own values and let those guide me in this process. You see and bring out the very best in me.

—JTL

Thank you to my parents, who first taught me the importance of values. To my brother, who showed me the importance of centering your life around service to others. May your memory live on in all those you touched with your life. Big heart, open wide. To all my trainees and supervisees over the years for letting me test out new ideas with and on you and for teaching me so much. To my clients, from whom I've learned so much. To Steve Hayes, for your openness in allowing this unknown person to join your lab all those years ago and for your example of values-guided leadership in all the years since. To Robyn Walser, coauthor, mentor, and friend, for your friendship, warmth, and guidance. To Tobias Lundgren, for your relentless easygoingness, humor, and modeling of how to put values first. To Kathy Schuetz, my model in living simply, with warmth and connection to the earth. To Kelly Koerner, for teaching me how to think more clearly, understand more deeply, and act with more intention. And finally, to Jenna, for allowing this glorified editor to contribute to her unique and special book.

—JBL

Introduction

Therapy oriented solely toward reducing suffering misses something essential about humans. Put someone in a coma and they do not experience pain. However, it's also apparent that there is something missing from that life as well. The vitality is gone. Human life involves action, purpose, pursuit, direction, and an orientation toward doing something that matters. We don't just act randomly. We don't react based only on instincts. No, much of what we do has *purpose*. And we yearn for meaning, for a sense that our actions have a purpose that goes beyond just this moment, this person, and this situation.

Yet, often these meanings and purposes are not deeply considered. We can easily lapse into mindlessness, reactivity, and habit—into deeply ingrained patterns of living that may not align with what we would choose. In short, we lose touch with our values. This happens to all of us.

If you are a therapist, think about your clinical work. How often do you have conversations about what is most important to your clients? How often do you talk with them about what they truly, most deeply want their life to be about? If you are like most, these kinds of conversations often take a back seat to addressing more acute forms of suffering or simply the daily problems that pop up in clients' lives.

What about yourself? When was the last time someone asked you what you really wanted your life to be in the service of and actually listened? When you get to the end, what do you want your life to have stood for? What more important questions could there be? And yet, these conversations seem to be exceedingly rare.

This is a book about how we, as therapists, can have conversations about meaning and purpose with the people we serve, conversations that connect our clients to the bigger picture of what they want their life to be about. These are conversations about values. I wrote this book because I wanted to offer a guide for therapists who want to help their clients reconnect with the bigger picture of what, even in the midst of all life's suffering, is most important to them, what would be a life worth living. I wanted to help facilitate these conversations about meaning and purpose. But I wrote this book not just for the humans that happen to be in the role of "client" at this moment in time, but also for we humans who inhabit the role of "therapist."

Each time we as therapists invite a client into our therapy room, we are inviting suffering into our lives. And yet we do this willingly! Why? I believe most of us are willing to sit with suffering in this way because we have a sense that our work is about something more than our mere comfort. And yet, in the dailiness of our work, conducting session after session, we can lose contact with the bigger picture of why we do this difficult work and what we would choose our effort to be in the service of. And so, I also wrote this book to help with that. This book is aimed at helping you reconnect with your values as a therapist, your why for doing the work you do, and helping you engage with work in a way that is most deeply meaningful to you. That contact with your central purposes will sustain your motivation and give you a sense of direction as you spend the years of your career. To this end, each chapter in this book includes an inside-out learning exercise where you can apply these concepts in your own life. We also end the book with a chapter on helping you reconnect with and utilize your own values in your work. Therapy is most powerful when both people in the room, client and therapist alike, are clear on what they want their time to be spent in the service of, what is most meaningful and important to them.

Why Put Values at the Heart of Therapy?

Placing values at the heart of therapy means we are putting what is most important at the forefront of our work. It clarifies the purpose of the work we do. By orienting our work around values, we help our clients connect with what is most meaningful to them even in the midst of their suffering. In doing so, we orient the therapy around helping them create for themselves a well-lived life rather than simply attempting to minimize their pain.

To denote this idea of situating your therapy in terms of values and seeing your work through the lens of values, we have adopted the term "values-guided therapy." This is not to imply that this is a new kind of therapy. Heaven knows we don't need yet another brand of therapy! Rather, it's simply a name for describing this process by which therapy is ultimately used as a means to serve your clients' values, and the process of mindfully reflecting on what is most important as the context for what you do in therapy.

You already have a tremendous amount of training and wisdom (and if you're a seasoned clinician, loads and loads of experience) to guide your therapy. This isn't meant to replace that, but rather add to it—using values to supercharge your work. There is a mountain of data out there about what interventions are most helpful for various kinds of struggles. As someone who is interested in utilizing what science suggests are the most effective methods for helping individuals, I would urge you to do those things. But we also know that a life worth living is about more than just alleviating symptoms or reducing suffering. Grounding the work that you are already doing in values allows you to also address these bigger issues of meaning and purpose. Thus, even though you still may be using many of the same interventions, values can offer a different "why" to guide your work.

About This Book

In this book I'm going to be speaking to you from where my heart lies, as a therapist. That is how I spend the vast majority of my professional life, working one-on-one with clients with the aim of helping them live lives of meaning and purpose. However, in my role as clinical psychologist, I also train other therapists who want to incorporate more of a values focus into their work. Over the years I can't tell you how many times I have heard colleagues say things like, "I love the values stuff in ACT, but I don't really know how to put it into practice." My goal is to respond to that request. This book is meant to be practical and easily applicable rather than theoretically precise or comprehensive. The theory that I'll cover in this book (which is largely restricted to part 1) is there only to the extent that it is needed to effectively guide the work, while the vast majority of the book (part 2) is dedicated to practical application. There are other excellent resources (for example, Dahl, Lundgren, Plumb, & Stewart, 2009) if you are interested in getting deeper into theory. But in this book, I tried to write as if I were talking to a supervisee or chatting with a colleague who shared my enthusiasm for values.

With that in mind, if what would be most helpful to you is a highly technical book that dives deep into the theoretical underpinnings of values work, well, I'm glad you took the time to read this introduction (which of course you did because you're probably a very thorough, detailed person who wants to really understand it all!). However, if that is what you are looking for, I would humbly suggest you return this book, because this is not that book. Trust me, I tried to write that book. When I was first approached to write a book on values, I immediately fell into some old, well-honed, but largely unhelpful patterns. I started valuing "looking smart" over speaking from my heart. I painfully slogged through writing a couple of dense, intellectual chapters that I thought were pretty darn good; I was feeling *very* smart. Then I gave it to my partner and coauthor, Jason, to read. Being one of the most kind and loving people I know, he said the following with as much gentleness and kindness as possible: "Uh, Jenna, what *is* this? This isn't your book. You're trying to write someone else's book. You need to write *your* book!" Oops. I definitely felt a little less smarty-pants after that! Of course, he was right. In trying to write the book in the service of "looking smart," I had lost what was most important for me to share. This is often what happens when we lose contact with our values, and it happens to all of us! So, I started again, this time trying to follow those values I would choose to make important rather than my ego. The result is a highly personal, though somewhat unconventional, professional book that I hope, in the end, will be useful to therapists doing this work.

This book is a reflection of both my own values and how I am in my therapy practice. You'll see me in this book. It's personal. Both writing a book and doing therapy in such a personal and transparent way feels risky, but frankly, I don't know how to be effective any other way. As you'll see in this book, values aren't just something for our clients. I truly believe that in order to do good values work, we as therapists need to be living out our own values in the therapy room and in our lives.

You will also notice that unlike most professional books, this book is written in the first person. It's my (Jenna's) voice you are hearing. Jason has been an invaluable coauthor and this book is infinitely better because of his influence. We worked together throughout this book and the result is a combination of how we both approach this work. However, we felt that presenting one consistent perspective would help the reader get a better sense for the feel of doing values work and its radically personal nature.

All of the clinical cases in this book are based on actual clients I have worked with, though names and identifying information have been changed to protect their confidentiality. In addition, in an effort to be inclusive in my language, I have chosen to use nonbinary pronouns throughout the book (such as they/their rather than she/he or his/hers). This, too, was a values-based decision.

I also want to acknowledge that what is written here is but one possible way of understanding and approaching these profound issues. It is not *the* way, nor is it any more or less true than any other way of understanding values. What is written here is highly influenced by our (Jason's and my) own cultural context, with us both coming from predominantly white, Anglo-American cultures in which we are, in general, members of majority identity groups. We also come from a context in which understanding the world through the lens of science is generally accepted. Thus, my perspective is inherently limited. Mine is but one perspective and it is with great humility that I share my thoughts on values as *a* perspective, not *the* perspective.

Based on ACT, but Applicable to All

This book is grounded in the theory emerging from acceptance and commitment therapy (ACT) and contextual behavioral science (CBS). However, though I come to this from an ACT perspective, this isn't a book about how to do ACT. In fact, you don't need to know anything about ACT to be able to use what is in this book. Instead, it's a book about how to have powerful and effective conversations that can help orient clients toward what matters most to them.

I, personally, have found ACT to have the most comprehensive theory and set of techniques for working with values of any therapy I have encountered. ACT has a long and rich history of focusing on values in psychotherapy. The values component of ACT is also the reason why many clinicians, including myself, got interested in ACT in the first place. In addition, ACT offers a unique psychological flexibility model that incorporates values that I find indispensable in this work (more about this in chapter 2).

However, ACT doesn't have a monopoly on values and meaning. Humanistic and existential therapies, most notably logotherapy, have long focused on the human struggle to live lives of meaning and purpose. Leaders in other various psychotherapies, from psychoanalysis to cognitive behavioral therapies, have also advocated for the importance of incorporating values-specific work into their interventions (Cameron, Reed, & Gaudiano, 2014; Grumet & Fitzpatrick, 2016; Holmes, 1996; Neff & Germer, 2013; Wong, 1997). Values can guide your therapy no matter your approach, and I hope this book will be useful regardless of your theoretical orientation. So, if you're an ACT therapist, great! If you're a gestalt therapist, great! If you are a psychodynamic, somatic, cognitive-behavioral, emotion-focused, or eclectic therapist, great! As long as your ultimate goal is to help your clients intentionally construct and live out well-lived lives, however they would personally define that, then this book is intended to give you new tools for doing so. And really, what could be better work than getting to help people do that?

PART 1

Fundamentals

CHAPTER 1

The What and Why of Values

True happiness...is not attained through self-gratification but through fidelity to a worthy purpose. —Helen Keller

How many breaths do you think you have left in your life?

How many sunsets have you stood in awe of this month? How many more sunsets do you think you have left?

How many times have you told your best friend that you love them recently? How many more "I love yous" might you have left to give this person?

Consider further that most things in our life aren't equally spread out across our life span. If you have parents or siblings, think about them. You used up the vast majority of the time you're ever going to spend with them before you were eighteen. During that time, you may have spent nearly every day with them. Now, even if you still see them quite often, you probably have 5 percent or less of your total time with them left. Would you be doing anything different if you were in more regular contact with how precious little time you had left with them?

Endings often sneak up on us and we often have less time than we think. Loved ones die unexpectedly, friends move, our health suddenly deteriorates, or a crisis happens and along with it goes our sense of security. Any of these crises can happen to us at any moment and for many of us, they have. If something like this has happened to you, then I'm guessing it gave you pause to reflect.

Crisis and loss often have a way of clarifying what is most important to us. Once we (Jason and I) had made the decision that it was time to let our sweet twenty-two-year-old dog Dalai go, we wanted a few more days to really soak up all that we could with her. We took time off from work. We drove up to see my family so they could say goodbye to her. We went for long car rides where she could hang her head out the window and took her for one last hike on her favorite trail even though Jason had to carry her most of the way. We didn't want to waste any of the final days we had with her. Then, when it was time, Dalai got to die peacefully at home, in our arms, after finishing off a piece of German chocolate cake. Now that's a good ending to a good life. May we all be so fortunate.

It often takes a crisis or significant loss to make us stop the autopilot of our lives, focus on what really matters, and live life with vigor. But what if it were possible to live with that kind of clarity of purpose and values without something terrible needing to happen? No, I'm not talking about ending every day with a big slice of German chocolate cake or giving up your career to spend every moment with your dog. What I am talking about is living with the intentionality that often only comes to us in times of crisis. The months and days leading up to Dalai's death created an urgency that allowed me to be incredibly intentional about how I chose to spend my time and how I chose to be in my interactions with her. I had a clarity about what mattered to me and how I wanted to be that can easily get lost in the daily routine of life. Although those were some of the hardest days of my life, they are also some of the ones I feel most proud of. I wish I were more often as gentle, kind, and compassionate as I was with Dalai during those final months and days. That, for me, would be a life I would be proud of having lived when I get to my last sunset.

Living a values-based life is about living with intention, consciously choosing to live out a well-lived life, whatever that means for you personally. We don't know how many breaths we have left to breathe or how many "I love yous" we have left to say. All we know is that it is fewer than we had yesterday. Living a values-based life is about making the most of each of those breaths in this one life we know we have to live.

What if your work were about helping people do that? What if, through your work, you could help people pause and ask themselves what really matters, to help them develop the clarity of purpose and meaning that all too often only comes to people through a crisis? That is what this book is about. This book is meant to give you the tools to help your clients put their deepest values at the core of their lives so that they don't need to wait for a crisis.

What Are Values?

Acceptance and commitment therapy (ACT) and the research paradigm that underlies it, contextual behavioral science (CBS), has a rich history and extensive body of both clinical and empirical work regarding values. From an ACT perspective, we might say that values are "freely chosen, verbally constructed consequences of ongoing, dynamic, evolving patterns of activity, which establish predominant reinforcers for that activity that are intrinsic in engagement in the valued behavioral pattern itself" (Wilson & DuFrene, 2009, p. 64). Or put (somewhat) more simply, values are "verbally constructed, global, desired, and chosen life directions" (Dahl, Wilson, Luciano, & Hayes, 2005, p. 61). Both of these definitions are eloquent, comprehensive, precise, and, at least for me, a little daunting. So instead, I usually prefer to simply think of values as how you are living when you are living a meaningful life.

I'm not going to spend time here unpacking the technical definitions of values; there are many other resources that do an excellent job of that (e.g., Dahl et al., 2009;

Wilson, Sandoz, Flynn, Slater, & DuFrene, 2010). Since this book is meant to be a practical guide for how to actually use values to ground and strengthen your therapy work, this chapter will leave the technical definitions aside and instead focus on some of the main qualities and features of values that are important to keep in mind as you do values work. This includes the following:

1. Values are behaviors. They are ways of living, not words.

2. Values are freely chosen. They are not the result of reasoning, outside pressure, or moral rules.

3. Values are life directions, not goals to achieve. They are always immediately accessible, but you'll never complete them.

4. Values are about things you want to move toward, not what you want to get away from.

In this chapter, I'll also cover some of why I think values are important and how they function. Finally, at the end of the chapter, I'll loop back around to definitions, but I'll focus on simple, practical descriptions that you might actually use in your work with clients.

Values Are Behavior

From this perspective, values aren't really a thing at all. Values are the ways of living and being in this world that are important and meaningful to you. They are ongoing patterns of action. There is no "value" in the absence of action.

One way to talk about values is to say that they are a combination of verbs and adverbs, rather than nouns. They describe what you are doing (verb) and how you are doing it (adverb). Caring (verb) for sweet old Dalai committedly and compassionately (adverbs) was what was meaningful to me, and thus my "value" was shown through the quality of my caring in a committed and compassionate manner.

Values aren't about words. They are found in watching what people actually do with their lives, where they invest their time, energy, and focus. The goal of exploring values in therapy is to help build a person's ability to contact and experience the patterns of living they might choose. Ultimately, I don't actually care so much if my clients are able to identify specific values words they would espouse (such as "I value compassion and commitment"), nearly as much as I want to help them develop a sense of the lived pattern of behavior that would be most meaningful and vital to them, in other words, what they would do if they were living compassionately and committedly. You might come up with a word for it, or a metaphor, or some other way to describe it that points to that lived pattern, if that is helpful. But don't let those words, metaphors, or images take the place of the actual journey. The *process* of valuing is what is important.

Values Are the Qualities of Action, Domains Are the Arena

"I already know my values. I value my family." "Spirituality is my highest value." "I really don't value my health." If asked about their values early on in therapy, clients will often give these types of statements. But if values, as I am describing them, are qualities of behavior, then things like "family," "spirituality," and "health" don't really fit that way of speaking about values. To further complicate matters, much of the psychological literature and assessment measures related to "values" also tends to focus more on what I would call "valued domains" than values in the sense of qualities of action. While on one level, these are just words we're making up, I also think it can be helpful to make a distinction between values (as I'm using the term) and valued domains.

If values are qualities of action, then you could describe valued domains as being the arena in which those values are enacted. Valued domains are broad categories or areas of living that many people find to be important, though individuals differ in terms of how important each domain is to them. For example, the Valued Living Questionnaire-2 (VLQ-2; Wilson & DuFrene, 2009) is a core ACT values assessment measure that assesses valued living in the following twelve values domains:

- Family (other than marriage and parenting)

- Marriage, couples, or intimate relations

- Parenting

- Friends and social life

- Work

- Education and training

- Recreation and fun

- Spirituality

- Community life

- Physical self-care (diet, exercise, and sleep)

- The environment (caring for the planet)

- Aesthetics (art, literature, music, beauty)

When doing values work with clients, especially in the initial phases, it can often be helpful to focus your exploration within one or two high-priority valued domains. Because values tend to be relatively consistent across domains, exploration of values in one domain will likely provide useful information about what that individual would choose to value in another domain. The domains you start with could be those in which your client already has some sense of clarity regarding their values or those in which they feel they are already living in line with their values. Alternatively, you may decide to choose a domain that the client says is very important to them, but in which they feel they have lost contact with their values. However you decide to use them, valued domains can provide a useful way to focus your values exploration. Just make sure that you are clear that these broader areas such as "family," "friends," "work," or "health" are not the values in themselves, but rather are potentially important areas in which the client might like to target valued living.

Values Are the Directions, Goals Are the Markers

You can also describe values as being the direction you want your behavior to move you toward. Like a compass, values provide you with a consistent sense of direction for your life. Values are not a destination, an outcome, or some goal to achieve. They are the direction you choose for your journey.

As guiding directions, values are always immediately available and inexhaustible. If you have chosen to head east, the great thing is, no matter where you are, east is always there. You don't need to get anywhere else or have anything be different in order for you to turn toward east. At the same time, no matter how far east you go, you will never get there; you'll never reach "east." As long as you have a journey in front of you, there is always more east you can move toward. This allows life to have purpose and meaning in the here-and-now, rather than always looking toward some future accomplishment or milestone to offer that meaning.

If values are directions, goals are milestones to reach or things that can be accomplished or obtained. Ideally, values establish the direction you want your life to head and goals serve as markers to help you navigate and let you know whether you're still on course. Goals are helpful to orient us, but they are not the point of the journey. Applied to the therapy context, it is values that guide the therapy, and only after that direction has been established do we move on to selecting workable goals that might move our client toward their chosen direction.

Values allow for more flexibility than goals. To continue with the analogy of values as directions, there are many goals that would take us east. For example, if you were in California, you could head east by setting a goal to go to New York. But if, along the way, the roads to New York became blocked by a massive snowstorm, you could continue on your journey east by shifting goals and heading to Florida instead. Your life's direction has not changed. But if you were only focused on the goal of getting to New York and lost the ability to go to New York, then you'd be stuck. In this way, a life that is guided by values is more flexible and helps us pivot as needed when the inevitable curveballs of life come our way.

Helping our clients learn to remain focused on the value behind a goal and develop the flexibility needed to stay on course if one route gets blocked is an essential task in values-guided therapy. Here's a real-world example from Jason's life. In his twenties,

Jason developed chronic back pain that made it difficult for him to ride his mountain bike, something he loved to do. It was so painful that he eventually gave it up, along with many other physical activities. On the other side of grieving these losses, Jason was able to reflect on what was important to him about riding. He realized it allowed him to enjoy the outdoors while caring for his body. Realizing that mountain biking was but one way to live out those values, he started experimenting with different ways to live them. After much trial and error, he learned that he could ride a particular kind of recumbent bicycle, which now allows him to live out his values around nature and health during his daily commute. Same direction, different route. Similarly, when our clients suffer major losses, it can be useful to work with them to identify the overarching values underlying the loss, which can then lead to new ways to live out those values.

Rigid attachment to goals can also create problems when the function of a goal changes in a way that no longer serves one's values. For example, for my client Ann, running went from being a way to care for her body (values-consistent for her) to a way to punish her body in an attempt to control her weight and body shape (values-inconsistent for her). These shifts from one function to another may have important consequences, but may not be noticed if all we are attending to is the form of the behavior rather than its function. This can result in persisting with behaviors that may at one time have been linked to values, but end up moving an individual away from their values and generating more suffering.

In addition, while values are always immediately available and inexhaustible, goals are always in the future (see chapter 7 for more on this, including an experiential exercise). Goals create a sense of discrepancy between where we are now and where we want to be (the goal), which can feed further entanglement in judgment, evaluation, self-criticism, and blame. This can end up sabotaging the very behavior changes or goals the person set out to achieve in the first place (Bell, Salmon, Bowers, Bell, & McCullough, 2010; Duarte et al., 2017; Powers, Koestner, Zuroff, Milyavskaya, & Gorin, 2011).

Values don't depend on outside consequences, circumstances, or situations to work; they are the end in and of themselves. In contrast, behavior focused on outcomes (goals) often has a more instrumental quality—it's more of a means to an end. A goal such as working to obtain money or dressing a certain way in order to be admired by others often functions as a means to an end, rather than something important in and of itself. Ultimately, a life filled with behavior that is experienced as a means to an end often ends up feeling empty and unsatisfying. The singer-songwriter Harry Chapin (1988) illustrated this idea in the following recollection of something his grandfather told him as he was nearing the end of his life:

> Harry, there's two kinds of tired. There's good tired and there's bad tired… Ironically enough, bad tired can be a day that you won. But you won other people's battles; you lived other people's days, other people's agendas, other people's dreams. And when it's all over, there was very little you in there. And

when you hit the hay at night, somehow you toss and turn; you don't settle easy… Good tired, ironically enough, can be a day that you lost, but you don't even have to tell yourself because you knew you fought your battles, you chased your dreams, you lived your days and when you hit the hay at night, you settle easy, you sleep the sleep of the just and you say 'take me away'… Harry, all my life I wanted to be a painter and I painted; God, I would have loved to have been more successful, but I painted and I painted and I'm good tired and they can take me away.

Living a life in line with our own, personally chosen values, rather than pursuing others' goals that may not be connected with our values, gives our life honor, meaning, and purpose. That is the well-lived life that ends with good tired.

In sum, by keeping our primary focus on values, rather than being overly attached to specific goals, therapy (and life) becomes more flexible, workable, sustainable, and just plain rewarding. For all these reasons, in values-guided therapy, the emphasis is on the journey (the value), not the checkpoints along the way (the goals). The goals we set with our clients need to be flexible and responsive to their values, not set in stone as inherently "good" things in and of themselves.

Here's a clinical example to illustrate how therapy can shift focus from rigid goals to more flexible and immediately rewarding values.

CLINICAL EXAMPLE: JOSÉ

When he came to work with me, José was singularly focused on finding a wife and having children. He believed his life's mission was to be a loving husband and father. But José was focused on the goal part of that statement, being a father and a husband (getting married and having children are things that can be accomplished and thus are goals). José saw this as a stepwise process. He had to 1. get married and have children and then 2. he would get to start living a life in line with his values by being loving toward said wife and children. The only problem was, despite his best efforts, José hadn't been able to find the life partner he was looking for. He went on anywhere from three to five dates a week, always hoping the next date would be "the one." As soon as he realized that whoever he was out with wasn't "the one," he would dump her, often in a callous and unkind fashion. His focus wasn't on how he was treating the person he was currently with, but rather on moving as quickly as possible to the next woman in case she might turn out to be the eventual wife he longed to treat lovingly. She never was.

José had become despairing due to what seemed to him an impassable barrier to living out his mission. He also didn't like himself much. He had sought therapy on several occasions, which had mainly focused on changing his approach to finding a partner, either by focusing on social skills training or adjusting his expectations. He learned useful things from these experiences, but still felt stuck, blocked from being able to live the life he wanted to live.

José and I took a different, values-based tack. What if the problem wasn't that he couldn't find a wife? What if the thing that was resulting in José's despair was that he was not living out his values in the here-and-now with the life and people he had in front of him? He was so focused on getting someplace else that he didn't even realize he was treating the women who were in his life right now in a way that was very inconsistent with his stated values, which resulted in him not being proud of the man he was being. We shifted focus from the goal (getting married and having kids) to the value (caring lovingly). José and I worked together on identifying how he would be living his life now if he were being that loving person he would like to eventually be to a wife and children. "Loving," or more precisely, relating to others in a loving way, became the direction his life was heading in.

This focus on values as a direction helped free José up from his narrow focus on one particular outcome. Rather than dating being solely a frustrating means to an end, it became a life-affirming way to live out who he most wanted to be in his present, non-ideal circumstances. Every date, no matter whom he was with, became an opportunity for him to live out his core values *now*. His focus shifted from some future destination he just couldn't seem to reach, to a journey he could live on a daily basis, regardless of whether or when "Ms. Right" did eventually show up. While he still hoped that someday a wife and children might also be part of his path, they were no longer a precursor to him living the "loving" life he wanted to live. Living his valued life now gave him a sense of purpose and honor to each day, as each day became part of being that loving man he felt was his life's mission to be.

Other Important Characteristics of Values

There are also some other key characteristics of values that are worth highlighting. For one, they are experienced as *freely chosen* by those who hold them; also, they are *appetitive*—that is, they are what people are drawn to moving toward rather than focused on moving away from.

VALUES ARE FREELY CHOSEN

A core characteristic of values is that they are experienced as being freely chosen. Similar to what Harry Chapin's grandfather was speaking of in the story above, it is essential that people connect with the values that they would take personal ownership of, that they would stake a claim to as being *their* values. Values, from this perspective, are not chosen based on "shoulds." They are not mandated by some external entity (such as a person, government, religion, or advertising agency) as being the "right" values to choose. In this way, values are distinct from what we usually think of as "morals." Morals are "standards of behavior or beliefs concerning what is and is not acceptable for them to do" (*Oxford Dictionary*, n.d.). Morals tend to be highly connected to our history of how others have responded to us when we have behaved in particular ways, resulting in our sense of right versus wrong. In contrast, values follow the immortal words of many a wise mother; they operate on the "just 'cause" principle. Why would I choose to live a life in which I value being loving? "Just 'cause." It's my life and I get to choose what would make it a well-lived life for me. I choose loving.

In this way, values are also not based on reasons. While we can come up with reasons or justifications for our chosen values if asked, each of these reasons appeals to something else as the measure of what's important. For example, if you said you valued being loving because it makes people happy, then does this mean that you really value making other people happy, rather than being loving? If asked why you valued making other people happy and you said it was because it made you happy, then does this mean that the underlying value is your own happiness rather than making other people happy? This process of justifying values by appealing to other metrics can go on forever. The way out is to recognize that we need to start somewhere and say that we choose to make something important "just 'cause." Thus, valuing relies more on things like choosing, creating, assuming, and dreaming than it does weighing out a list of pros and cons (Luoma, Hayes, & Walser, 2017). This doesn't mean values are haphazard or chosen at random. Hopefully, deep intentionality and reflection go into choosing what we want our lives to be in the service of, which is something that values-guided therapy can facilitate. But what you choose to value can't ultimately be justified by logical arguments or reason.

"Freely chosen" also means that our choice of values has not been limited in any way, including by our current circumstances, life events, or our histories. The entire array of possible values one might choose to live out is available to everyone at all times. This idea was at the heart of Viktor Frankl's seminal work *Man's Search for Meaning* (1946/1984), in which he writes of humans' ability to find meaning and purpose even amidst the most horrific of circumstances, the death camps of the Holocaust. There are no life circumstances that can rob us of the ability to live lives of meaning, which I would call values-based lives. Just stop for a moment and think about how powerful that idea is. Values might be one of the few places, possibly even the only place, where we're all on a level playing field. We *all* get to choose among *all* the options when it comes to valued lives, and nothing that has happened or can happen to you can take that away. Just imagine what an incredibly powerful and empowering idea that could be to many of the people we serve!

I am not making a claim that it is "True" with a capital "T" that values are freely chosen and not heavily influenced by our learning history. If values are behavior, then of course our values are influenced by our history, our current context, and our biology. However, in a values-guided approach to therapy, we seek to create a context in which the individual *experiences* their values as having been freely chosen, because that is useful when our aim is to help people consistently live lives that are aligned with their values in a sustainable way.

Let's return to José from the clinical example above. Certainly, José's culture and history had shaped him and influenced his commitment to family. However, José didn't experience his value of lovingly caring for those he was in relationship with as something externally imposed upon him, but rather something that he freely chose. He wouldn't have said that his religion made him choose to value being a loving family man; instead, he saw being a member of the Church of Jesus Christ of Latter-Day Saints (LDS) as supportive to him as he lived out this valued life he had freely chosen. From his perspective, he chose to be a member of the LDS church in part because it supported his values, not the other way around.

VALUES ARE APPETITIVE (I.E., STINKY CHEESE-LIKE)

Although I usually try to steer clear of using technical jargon with clients, I make an exception when it comes to describing values as "appetitive." One of the reasons why I think this works is because, as its shared roots with the word "appetite" are so apparent, the word "appetitive" can serve as something of a metaphor.

A technical term used in behavior analysis, appetitive comes from the root words *appétitif* (French) and *appetitivus* (Latin), meaning "seek after." Simply put, an appetitive is any stimulus/consequence/reward that an individual will seek out because it satisfies some need or urge; it is something the individual has an "appetite" for, if you will. An "aversive," by contrast, is any stimulus/consequence/punishment that an individual will attempt to avoid or escape. Thus, describing values as being "appetitive" simply means that the individual is inherently drawn to move toward values. You don't need some external reward or prize to sustain valued behavior; connecting with our values *is* what is rewarding/reinforcing.

To get less technical, values are directions you seek to move *toward* rather than being about something unpleasant you are trying to get *away* from. You can simplify this with clients by talking about the distinction between "toward" and "away" moves (Polk, 2014). "Toward" moves are behaviors oriented around moving toward something you want (including values), whereas "away" moves are things you do in order to get rid of or away from something you don't want (such as painful thoughts or feelings).

I often use metaphors to get across a somewhat complex point without getting overly technical. But metaphors have to be apt to the particular person you're talking to. Because I live in Portland, Oregon, where great food is a big part of the culture, a metaphor that often works in my context is talking about how appetitives are like stinky cheese, such as in the example below.

Clinical example: Orienting toward appetitives. The following clinical example demonstrates how I might talk about appetitives as a way of orienting therapy toward, rather than away from, something. This might occur in a first session as part of the treatment planning process.

Therapist: Have you ever seen those experiments where the scientist is trying to teach a rat to move through the maze or something like that?

Client: Sure. We read about those in my Psychology 101 class.

Therapist: Great. Well, as you might remember, there are two basic ways you can get the rat to go through the maze. One way is to do something that the rat finds unpleasant, like shock the rat. The rat will quickly move away from the shock and thus will move through the maze to wherever the shock isn't. The rat's behavior is dictated by the shock. The rat isn't really trying to go toward anything so much as it is trying to get away from something.

But there's a second way to get the rat to move through the maze. You can put a big hunk of stinky cheese at the end of the maze where you want the rat to go. Guess what will happen?

Client: The rat will run to the cheese.

Therapist: Yep, every single time. In fact, if the cheese is good and stinky enough, you can make the maze really, really hard, and put up all sorts of difficulties for the rat, and the rat will still persist in moving toward the cheese. We call the stinky cheese here an "appetitive," you know, kind of like the word "appetite." Saying something is an appetitive just means that it's something that is very appealing to you and you'll seek it out the same way the rat will seek out the stinky cheese. In this case, it's the stinky cheese, rather than the shock, that is guiding the rat's behavior.

Client: That makes sense.

Therapist: We humans aren't all that different from rats in some ways. We can either be focused on trying to get *away* from something unpleasant—an aversive—or moving *toward* something: an appetitive. One of the things we can explore in our work together is what you want to guide you as you move through this life of yours—the shocks or the stinky cheese? We've already talked a fair bit about some of the things you're trying to get away from, like your feelings of anxiety and thoughts of being worthless—the shocks. But it seems to me that we also need to keep our eye out for your stinky cheese because I'm guessing you don't want your whole life to be oriented around the shocks.

Client: That sounds good, but the problem is I don't know what my stinky cheese is.

Therapist: Of course not. Whatever your stinky cheese is will be unique to you, and you haven't had much of a chance to explore that yet. You've been working so hard on getting away from the shocks, and so of course you haven't been able to focus much on what might be your potential stinky cheese. I don't know what your specific flavor of stinky cheese is yet either. Figuring that out can be part of what we do together. My word for whatever that stinky cheese in your life would be is "values." Values are whatever would make for a meaningful, well-lived life. Because the ultimate prize at the end of the maze of life, the ultimate stinky cheese, is to be able to have said that your journey was in pursuit of what mattered most to you and that that's what guided how you moved through this world. Would that be something you might be interested in exploring here in therapy with me?

Values and Language

The appetitive motivation involved in values depends heavily upon language and cognition. Language and cognition are the very medium of meaning, purpose, and valuing. Thus, in relation to values, language and cognition can be used strategically to harness and strengthen the influence of certain types of languaging and thinking.

As just one example of how language and cognition can be constructive when it relates to values, let's examine how thinking, remembering, and imagining have the ability to bring "there" and "then" into the "here" and "now." Through language, an imagined future or a remembered past can be experienced as if it were happening right now. On the one hand, this can lead to a lot of suffering. For example, take a moment to think of one of your dearest loved ones dying. Just thinking about that can bring some of that suffering to you now, even if your loved one is currently healthy and safe. On the other hand, these same abilities can be very useful when it comes to values, as this is what allows us to contact the consequences of living out our values in the present moment even when those consequences aren't literally here. For example, imagining, thinking about, or talking about my values of wanting to be loving and playful as I relate to my niece and nephew allow me to contact some of the consequences of being that loving and playful auntie, even though Josephine and Michael are currently 8,000 miles away. Those consequences and feeling some of what it's like to be that auntie can then influence my choice of behaviors now. This is essentially the same thing that happens when your friend says, "Gee, wouldn't a pizza taste good right now?" and suddenly you find yourself craving pizza. Language allows you to "taste" the value, which then might affect what you select to do next. Connecting with the bigger picture of what we want our lives to be about shifts what is reinforcing and may even allow us to overcome patterns of behavior related to avoidance or escape that we tend to get stuck in.

CBS uses the term "augmenting" to refer to this way in which language affects what is reinforcing for us. From this perspective, values can function as "augmentals" in that they can support and reinforce values-consistent behavior (Törneke, 2010). These terms are part of a theory of language and cognition called relational frame theory (RFT; Hayes, Barnes-Holmes, & Roche, 2001), upon which much of ACT is based. Although covering RFT in any detail is beyond the scope of this book, much of what is written here is based on RFT principles. You don't need to understand RFT in detail to do excellent values work any more than you need to know engineering to be an excellent car driver. However, if you are interested in learning more about RFT,

I would suggest *Learning RFT: An Introduction to Relational Frame Theory and Its Clinical Application* (Törneke, 2010) as an excellent and relatively approachable resource. And if you really want to dive deep, *Relational Frame Theory: A Post-Skinnerian Account of Human Language and Cognition* (Hayes et al., 2001) is considered the seminal book on the topic.

Why Values?

In addition to having a sense of what values are (and are not), it may also be helpful to take a look at some of the reasons why orienting toward values can be helpful in therapy.

Values Create Meaning

When I look at the larger context of my clients' lives, beyond the symptoms they report, many suffer with being disconnected from a sense of meaning or purpose, which has been linked to both physical and psychological well-being (Creswell et al., 2005; McCracken & Yang, 2006). Meaning is one of the curses and benefits of language. Language allows us to ask ourselves questions like, "Does any of this mean anything?" and feel despair. But language also allows us to think about our highest ideals for a well-lived life or remember our greatest heroes and thereby be inspired to rise to the challenge even in the most difficult of circumstances. As Joseph Campbell wrote (Osbon, 1995, p. 16), "Life is without meaning. You bring the meaning to it. The meaning of life is whatever you ascribe it to be." Through values we choose what would, for us personally, be a meaningful life and then, through the process of living out those values, we create meaning. Meaning is constructed in moments when we are connected with what matters, when we are in contact with a life we would define as being worth living (Luoma et al., 2017). The therapist who is guided by values works with clients to build lives of meaning and purpose by helping them have more and more moments connected with what matters most.

Values Provide Consistency and Sustain Behavior

Think about a recent interaction you had with a colleague, your partner, your friend, or someone else who matters to you. It doesn't have to be a big or important interaction, just some recent interaction you had. How did you decide how you wanted to behave in that interaction? Most of the time these decisions are made without much thought. We just react on autopilot. Very often our response is in reaction to some momentary thought or feeling we are having. If you were feeling loving or appreciative or caring in that moment, it's likely that your behavior reflected those feelings and things probably worked out well for the person you were with. But what happens if the feeling or thought that is present happens to be a difficult one like anger, frustration, jealousy, or fear? In those cases, having our behavior guided by those thoughts and feelings may take us down a very different path, one that may not be consistent with how we would ideally choose to behave. Thus, it can be helpful to have a more reliable guide than our momentary thoughts and feelings, something that helps us see the bigger picture of who we want to be in our lives. Values provide that guide. While our thoughts and feelings are largely out of our control and change rapidly from moment to moment, our values tend to be more consistent and thus can provide a more reliable guiding beacon even during turbulent times.

Returning to the story of our dog Dalai might help illustrate this point. Although I loved that little pup dearly, during the final months of Dalai's life, most of the time when I was with her, I wasn't feeling tender loving feelings. I was primarily feeling fear, tremendous sadness, and also, though this is difficult to admit, frustration (she had dementia and so would keep us up much of the night barking at things that weren't there). Nearly every time I interacted with her, I wanted to get away from those painful feelings and thoughts, which would also mean getting away from her. Pausing to connect with my values, which include qualities of patience, commitment, and compassion, allowed me to remain consistent with these values, even when what I felt like doing was running away. In addition, what made that pause useful was that it had that quality of free choice to it that I identified earlier as an essential component of values. In those moments I wasn't scolding myself about what I "should" do. Values aren't shoulds, and such scolding would have just been adding more aversives to an already painful situation. Instead, in the pause I was bringing the reinforcing properties of values into that painful moment so that I could choose something I wanted (the "stinky cheese" of caring compassionately and patiently for this little critter that I had loved for nearly twenty years) rather than only focusing on what I didn't want (the "shock" of fear and sadness at her impending death).

Values also provide consistency in that they can serve as a kind of verbal glue that links our actions and goals together to create a larger whole. Instead of life being a series of disconnected moments or accomplishments, values can be seen as part of a larger pattern or purpose. Each valued action is like a link in a chain or a key part of the plot of an important story. This connection to a larger context can help with the motivation to continue the valued pattern. It provides a kind of robustness in the face of momentary thoughts, feelings, or urges. For example, when I can see the thread of love and service I have woven into the thousands of therapy sessions I have conducted, this connects me to a sense of wholeness and motivation to lean in and open up my heart to the next client even if in that moment I'm feeling something other than the desire to lean in and be open. That next session then continues and further strengthens the larger pattern that, taken as a whole, creates a meaningful and purposeful work life.

Values also provide consistency in that they are, arguably, an inexhaustible source of motivation. This can be contrasted with motivation based on aversive control strategies. Have you ever walked out of a doctor's office swearing that you're going to lose weight/eat better/floss your teeth more? I certainly have! In those times, our motivation is usually based on fear or shame or some other unpleasant feeling. But time passes, and with it so does that unpleasant feeling; and thus the motivation that was sustaining our behavior evaporates. We often need to be re-exposed to a motivator in order for that stimulus to continue to serve as a motivator and thus sustain behavior. This is the strategy my client Beth used when she would stand in front of the mirror before every meal telling herself how fat and disgusting she was. She wasn't trying to be cruel to herself; she was actually trying to motivate herself to change her eating. But she was doing it through aversive control strategies. Many of our clients try to motivate themselves using such strategies. When it fails, they often conclude that they didn't have enough motivation and increase the self-reprisals or fear or whatever their aversive of choice is, hoping that will do the trick. Values provide a more compassionate alternative, and, based on data from mediational analyses of ACT, a more effective strategy when it comes to sustaining behavior change (Gregg, Callaghan, Hayes, & Glenn-Lawson, 2007; Lundgren, Dahl, Melin, & Kees, 2006).

Values Tell You What Works

We all want to know whether or not our efforts are successful. Our clients want to know whether what they are doing is "working," and we as therapists also need to know whether our interventions are effective. But we can't know if we are making progress until we know what we want to progress toward. Values provide that metric. They are the chosen ends. They are the ultimate outcome measure. If what a client is doing is moving them toward their values, then it's working. If it isn't, then regardless of any other side effects (such as a decrease in symptoms or an increase in something pleasurable), as a values-guided therapist, I would say that what the person is doing ultimately isn't working.

At a fundamental level, values *are* the why. My clients' values anchor everything I do in therapy. That is not to say that values-guided therapy only involves values exploration and clarification. We also need to focus on other repertoires that support valued living rather than only talking directly about values (chapter 2 is all about these other repertoires). But even when my immediate focus is on something else, as a values-guided therapist, my interventions are ultimately intended to serve valued living. Framed in this manner, exposure therapy can be about valued living as opposed to anxiety reduction (Thompson, Luoma, & LeJeune, 2013), dialectical behavior therapy skills can ultimately be in the service of valued living rather than decreasing self-harm being the end goal in and of itself (Cameron et al., 2014), and behavioral management of diabetes can be about more than just staying alive and instead be about having a life well lived (Gregg et al., 2007). Values organize and give a sense of integrity to the whole therapeutic enterprise regardless of the individual techniques you are utilizing.

Keep It Simple

It is important for therapists whose work is grounded in values to have a deeper understanding of the essential qualities of values and how they function in the therapy room. Thus far, this chapter has focused on laying that foundation. However, when talking with clients about values, I usually think it's best to keep it simple. Remember, values aren't words, and sometimes values can lose their essence when we start putting too many words around them. So, when talking with clients, try to keep your descriptions of what you mean by "values" simple, focusing on building curiosity or inspiration rather than trying to be comprehensive or "right." The following are potentially useful, if incomplete, definitions you might try with clients.

Values are:

- What a well-lived life would be for you personally

- How you are living when you are living a meaningful life

- Those qualities that, when you get to the end of everything, you want to have embodied in your life

- What you want your life to stand for

- What is meaningful and what you would want to matter to you

- The journey you would choose for this one life you know you have to live

- What you want the journey to have been about once you get to the end of this life

- The kind of person you want to be as you move through this world

- The qualities of living that would lead you to say, "Ah, now that was a life well lived!" once you have gotten to the end of it

- Intentionally constructing a well-lived life

PRACTICE: Your Definition of Values

Now you give it a shot. If you had to define what *you* mean by the term "values" in a sentence, what would you say to a client?

_____

_____

_____

Values and Culture

Values-guided therapy focuses on the process of helping our clients choose well and helping them discern what is important to them from inside their own unique lived experience. It does not focus on the *outcome* of what our clients choose to value. This also entails an essential core assumption: a radical respect for the client's values. Part of this stance is strategic—I want to be able to offer my clients the choice and freedom to live the life that *they* would choose. A lack of pressure, whether overt or covert, from me supports their freedom to choose. But the other part of this stance is based on humility—a recognition that my experience and my cultural background are only one of many in this world, and that I am fallible, no matter how certain I think I am about some things. Thus, I believe it is essential that any therapist who works with values be aware of the reactions that emerge from their own cultural background, as these reactions may influence their client's freedom to select what *they* would want their life to be in the service of. This is an important topic that we will discuss in much more detail in chapter 8. However, recognizing the importance of context and culture is such an essential concept in values-guided therapy, it is important to bring that into the conversation even as we are just beginning to lay the groundwork for this approach to therapy.

Takeaways

- Values are behaviors. They are ways of living, not words.

- Values are freely chosen life directions. They are always immediately accessible, but you'll never complete them.

- Goals are markers to show that we're on course, but they aren't what is important in the end.

- Values are the ultimate in appetitive motivation, the "stinky cheese."

- Through language, we can bring the consequences of valued living into the here-and-now.

- Values create meaning, provide consistency, and sustain behavior.

- Values *are* the "why" of therapy.

- Keep it simple! When talking about values, focus on opening up curiosity, possibility, and inspiration over total comprehension.

- Be aware of your own cultural lens. Be curious and humble when it comes to your client's cultural perspective.

Next Steps: Values-Guided Therapy Self-Assessment

Much like I end most of my therapy sessions, I'll end each chapter in this book with some exercises for you to work on. In subsequent chapters, there will be suggestions for things you can practice in your work with clients. There will also be numerous "inside-out learning" suggestions that you can apply to yourself. (Values work isn't just something for your clients!) But since we're just getting started on this journey together, it might be a good idea for you to get a sense of where you are starting from. In Appendix A you will find a Values-Guided Therapy Self-Assessment form. I'd encourage you to fill it out and take some time to reflect on what your responses might tell you about what you already know and what you have to learn.

In addition, as you are reflecting on these questions, you might also consider how your values might guide you as you approach this book. Imagine you were a client or a loved one that was choosing to take a look at some of their strengths and also potential areas of weakness they might want to work on. Knowing that such self-reflection can be hard, how would you want to treat that person during their process? In your ideal world, how would you want to support or encourage that person in their growth and self-exploration? How would you want them to treat themselves as they go about and potentially struggle with learning new skills and discovering new things about themselves? Given the values you would want to guide your interactions with others, how might those same values guide how you would choose to treat yourself as you go through this self-reflection process? In this way, you can be living out your values even as you go about the process of evaluating your own connection with values.

CHAPTER 2

Valued Living Requires Psychological Flexibility

The good life is a process, not a state of being… The direction which constitutes the good life is that which is selected by the total organism, when there is psychological freedom to move in any direction. —Carl Rogers (1961, pp. 186–187)

Humans are amazing creatures. Like most other animals, we are motivated to avoid unpleasant experiences and seek pleasant experiences. However, unlike most other animals, our advanced capacities for language and cognition also allow us to look beyond our own immediate comfort, pleasure, or even survival, if doing so can serve some higher purpose (Wilson, 2015). Consider my client Ken, who, as he was going through the painful process of dying of liver cancer, decided to value appreciating and caring well for nature over focusing primarily on trying to alleviate his pain. He chose to spend the short remaining days of his life picking up garbage on his favorite hiking trail rather than in a hospital receiving more treatments. Or my colleague Kate, who chose to value compassion over avoiding grief. She intentionally adopted a fifteen-year-old dog that was in the final stages of his life as a way to live out her value of compassionately caring for "the forgotten ones" even though she knew that doing this would bring her profound emotional pain. Or my own father, who, at age seventy-seven, willingly chose physical and psychological discomfort when he spent two weeks with me in a tent in remote Africa. In doing so, he chose to move *toward* his values rather than away from the pain of anxiety and the aches in his body. Each of these choices was guided by values that allowed the person to transcend their immediate pain and suffering to do what was part of living a good life for them.

What Values Guide Your Therapy?

Most therapy approaches are implicitly guided by some set of values. The problem, from a values-guided therapy perspective, is that the values promoted are often assumed in therapy. Perhaps the most common assumption is that the main purpose of therapy is to alleviate pain, suffering, or symptoms (Katz, Catane, & Yovel, 2016). Implicit is the idea that alleviating distress and symptoms will then make living a meaningful life more possible for our clients (Arch & Craske, 2008). While alleviating pain and symptoms can be valid aims, there are two problems with this. First and foremost, it doesn't put the client in the driver's seat of what their therapy would be in the service of. And second, as we'll talk about more in this chapter, trying to alleviate symptoms does not necessarily lead to a well-lived life full of meaning and purpose.

Opening Up Choice Beyond the Alleviation of Pain

In a values-guided approach to therapy, clients are encouraged to explore and choose whatever they might value, including values that might be in addition to, more encompassing than, or instead of avoiding pain or reducing symptoms. Therapy that puts values at its heart does not make assumptions about what our clients would choose to value; rather, it openly and explicitly explores what each client would choose to orient their life around. The therapy then is focused on *that*. This to me, is fundamentally respectful of our clients' autonomy and their capacity for growth.

Maybe you are saying to yourself, "Yes, but my clients are coming to me saying that they want to get rid of their depression/anxiety/insecurity/shame/self-loathing" (in other words, they are specifically saying they want therapy to decrease their psychological suffering). Of course they are! So are most of my clients. When I myself have sought out therapy at different points in my own life, it invariably has been prompted by some suffering I was struggling with. None of us wants to suffer. This isn't a problem; it's just a part of what it means to be human. However, what does tend to be problematic is when people aren't aware of what they are choosing to orient their life around or are not even aware that there is a choice at all. When someone's life becomes so caught in the pursuit of pleasure, or, even more frequently, the avoidance of pain, it can lead to a narrowing of options for what their life *could* be about. A life that revolves around feeling good and not feeling bad to the exclusion of all other possible valued activities tends to generate a lot of suffering (Chawla & Ostafin, 2007). Indeed, data suggest that decreases in suffering during therapy do not predict subsequent increases in valued action, while valued action does predict subsequent decreases in suffering (Gloster et al., 2017).

The act of valuing the alleviation of pain is usually happening without awareness; it doesn't occur to the person as a choice. Especially for our most stuck clients, they often feel like their lives depend on controlling, containing, solving, fixing, alleviating, soothing, or otherwise reducing the pain that they are experiencing. They, like all of us, want to live a good life. However, for many of us, including many of the people we serve, the cultures in which we operate have sold us the message that a good life comes through not suffering; in other words, the key to living well is feeling good. As the brilliant author and activist bell hooks so eloquently said:

One of the mighty illusions that is constructed in the dailiness of life in our culture is that all pain is a negation of worthiness, that the real chosen people, the real worthy people, are the people that are most free from pain. (hooks, 1992, p. 52)

It's no wonder that so many of our clients come to us with the implicit assumption that a valuable life is one that is free of pain and thus, believe getting rid of pain must be a necessary precursor to living the meaningful, well-lived life they long to live.

Values-guided therapy helps clients become aware of what they are valuing, recognize when their behavior is in the service of escaping pain, and notice when/if they might choose to value something else. By anchoring therapy in values, we seek to help people transcend whatever suffering they experience, bring meaning to the process of living, and experience their response to pain (as well as other situations) as a choice in which seeking escape is but one option.

Valuing as a Process

In a values-guided approach, the primary function of therapy is to facilitate clients' ability to choose what they would want their life to be in the service of and then help them organize their behavior such that it serves those ends in a consistent, holistic, and sustainable way. Notice that there are two parts to this; first, there is the choosing part, and then there is the living or the action part. Most approaches to values tend to focus on the first part, identifying or clarifying core values. However, in a values-based approach, being able to identify one's values is not the end goal in and of itself. Instead, therapy needs to give clients the tools to live a valued life outside the therapy room, which necessitates an emphasis on supporting a *process* of valuing. Thus, we need to also focus on helping clients develop the behavioral repertoires and capacities that allow them to engage in activities that, when taken in totality, will result in what they would regard as a well-lived life—a life with purpose, meaning, and integrity. The aim is to help clients learn a new process of valued living that they can carry forward into their life even after therapy ends.

Psychological Flexibility and Valued Living

When we consider valuing as a process, it becomes apparent that knowing what we would choose to value is not enough. Research shows that knowing what is important to us doesn't typically improve our lives, but acting in line with what is important to us does (Bramwell & Richardson, 2018). Thus, knowing our values is necessary, but not sufficient. Living our values is what makes the difference. Even if we know what is important to us, all kinds of obstacles arise on the path and pull us off course. We get caught up in the nonessential, overly focused on our suffering, trapped in a limited and separate sense of self, lost in the future and past, or wrapped up in our stories about ourselves, others, or the world. All of these responses distract us from living the life that we would choose for ourselves. Thus, living a life guided by values depends on having the flexibility to respond to all of these psychological obstacles in ways that allow us to repeatedly reconnect with the direction we would hope for our lives and take the steps that are part of manifesting that direction in our lives. One term for this capacity is "psychological flexibility" (Hayes, Strosahl, & Wilson, 2012).

The remainder of this chapter will focus on how various psychological flexibility repertoires are essential to exploring values and sustaining valued living. Unlike the rest of this book, much of this chapter is somewhat didactic and technical, though I've tried to minimize that as much as possible. Having an intellectual understanding of these concepts isn't typically necessary (or even helpful) for clients, but having a solid understanding of theory is useful for therapists, as it can help guide what we do. As a therapist doing values work, it's essential to be aware of some of the psychological processes that can get in our clients' way. It's also important to understand what client repertoires may need strengthening. Theory provides the guide for what to do with this information. Thus, for this chapter we're going to broaden our focus beyond values so that we can have the background needed to discuss how to address barriers that arise while working with values.

What Is Psychological Flexibility?

Many of you are probably familiar with the saying, often attributed to Albert Einstein, that psychopathology is "doing the same thing over and over again but expecting different results." While perhaps overly simplified, inside this saying is an important truth that has been borne out now by thousands of studies—inflexibility and rigidity are at the heart of psychopathology (Chawla & Ostafin, 2007; Spinhoven, Drost, de Rooij, van Hemert, & Penninx, 2014). We need to be able to be flexible and responsive in order to adapt to life's changing demands. Psychological flexibility is a way of talking about the capacity to respond adaptively to the challenges that life presents in ways that fit with our values. More technically, psychological flexibility has been defined as "the ability to contact the present moment more fully as a conscious human being and, based on what the situation affords, to change or persist in behavior in order to serve valued ends" (Luoma et al., 2017, p. 16). Figure 1, which was inspired by an image created by Forsyth & Forsyth (2015), is one way to illustrate this concept of psychological flexibility.

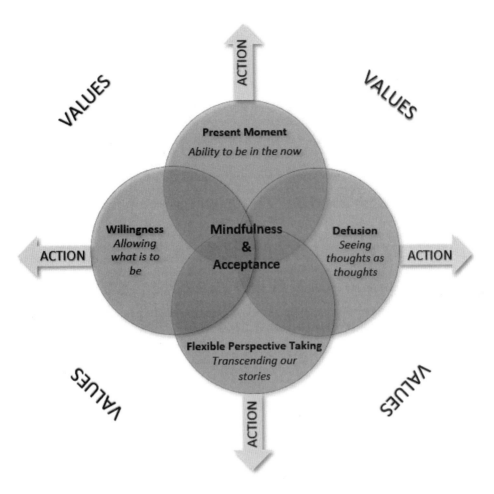

Figure 1. Inspired by Forsyth & Forsyth (2015). Values are the foundation or context for all that we do as therapists. The four flexibility processes that are part of mindfulness and acceptance give us the flexibility to take effective action that enacts our values.

From this perspective, values are not just a part of a psychological flexibility model, they are the very foundation of psychological flexibility. Values are the why, the ultimate purpose, the context that guides all the other work we do with our clients. As depicted in the above diagram, values form the ground on which the other psychological flexibility processes lie. The arrows represent how our values are reflected through effective action, or where we focus our time and our effort. In the center of the diagram are the processes or capacities that allow us to respond adaptively to the internal (thoughts, feelings, sensations) and external (situations and people) environments of our lives. These four processes are in the middle because they allow us to have the flexibility to return to what really matters (our values) and take action on it. These central processes can also be thought of as forms of mindfulness and acceptance. Opening up to and embracing our experience as it is, what we call *willingness*, frees us from struggling with the pain that is an inevitable part of life. This struggle often distracts us from our values and can paradoxically increase suffering. *Cognitive defusion* refers to those aspects of mindfulness that involve learning to watch our thinking without so much attachment, to view words as simply words and images as simply images. We can get so caught up in our thoughts that the world as directly experienced ceases to exist. Defusion frees us from the virtual world structured by our thoughts, allowing us to return to our values and pragmatic action guided by them. Attending to the *present moment* in a way that is flexible, fluid, and voluntary opens up possibilities for us to learn from our current experience and to see new options for action. The present moment is where learning occurs and where our values are lived. Finally, *flexible perspective taking* involves learning to take multiple and varied perspectives on ourselves, as well as being able to contact a transcendent sense of self as a conscious observer that is greater than the content of our stories about ourselves, others, and the world. This helps temper the effects of our self-limiting and self-defeating stories that can constrain our ability to put our values into action. All of these other flexibility repertoires are needed in order for us to be able to take action toward our values.

Flexibility Repertoires That Facilitate Valued Living

As depicted in the diagram above, there are four main mindfulness and acceptance processes involved in psychological flexibility: 1. Willingness (also called Acceptance), 2. Defusion, 3. Present Moment, and 4. Flexible Perspective Taking (also called Self-as-Context). Each of these processes, described in detail below, are needed for us to be able to freely choose what we would value in our lives and have the flexibility to live out those values even in the midst of the obstacles that life (and our minds!) will inevitably throw our way. What follows is only a brief introduction to these other psychological flexibility repertoires focusing on their relationship to values. For more on these concepts, see more comprehensive ACT resources, such as Hayes, Strosahl, & Wilson (2012).

WILLINGNESS/ACCEPTANCE

Human beings are almost certainly the best problem solvers that have ever walked the face of the earth. Problem solving is essentially the ability to detect problems or threats and find ways to get rid of them. The human mind has evolved over millennia to become an exquisite problem-solving machine, and no other species on the planet is better at this than we humans. Our species was once cold and hungry, so we figured out to how to create fire. We developed shared languages, transportation, and eventually the Internet, allowing a level of cooperation and interdependence that eclipses that of all other animals. And now that we have cooperated to threaten the destruction of our home planet, we're busy problem solving how to live on Mars. This problem-solving ability, along with the language and cooperation skills it has facilitated, has allowed us to dominate the planet. But, like so many things, this amazing strength has also become our downfall.

The problem with problem solving. Don't get me wrong, problem solving is great! I love being able to have shelter and cook my food and talk to my loved ones while I am halfway around the world. But difficulties tend to arise when internal experiences like our thoughts, feelings, and sensations become the problems we are trying to solve. When the highly attuned "problem/threat detector" that is our minds focuses inward, it reacts to painful thoughts, emotions, and sensations as if they were actual physical threats, problems to be solved. We then spring into action, struggling against (fight) or attempting to run away from (flight) these painful parts of ourselves. However, unlike external threats and problems, the way language and cognition works means that there is no place we can go where these thoughts, emotions, and sensations won't follow. As the saying goes, "wherever you go, there you are."

This understandable tendency to try to get away from our painful internal experiences (thoughts, memories, sensations, feelings, and so on), even when this action causes harm, is called "experiential avoidance." Experiential avoidance (EA) is a transdiagnostic variable that has been shown, now in hundreds of studies, to be central to the myriad of ways humans suffer, ranging from depression (Mellick, Vanwoerden, & Sharp, 2017), to substance use (Forsyth, Parker, & Finlay, 2003), to PTSD (Tull, Gratz, Salters, & Roemer, 2004), to anxiety (Spinhoven et al., 2014), to self-harm behaviors (Chapman, Gratz, & Brown, 2006; Howe-Martin, Murrell, & Guarnaccia, 2012), among others. In addition, EA has been shown to have deleterious effects beyond recognized psychopathology, including learning difficulties (Harper, Webb, & Rayner, 2013), burnout (Vilardaga et al., 2011; Hinds, Jones, Gau, Forrester, & Biglan, 2015), and overall lower quality of life (Hayes et al., 2004). Like the example of the rat under aversive control in chapter 1, when we become oriented around avoiding painful thoughts, feelings, or other internal experiences, our lives get smaller and we don't function as well in the process. My client Linda offers an example of how EA can shrink one's life and drain any sense of meaning from it.

Clinical example: Linda. Like many of the people I serve, Linda had a history of extensive and prolonged abuse and victimization as a child by several people she trusted. Given this history of interpersonal trauma, it was totally understandable that, as an adult, whenever Linda would get close to someone, particularly if it involved sexual intimacy, painful memories would come flooding back in from her previous abuse and she would have an overwhelming urge to flee.

The most effective solution Linda had found to getting rid of these painful experiences was to avoid any situation that posed even the possibility for intimacy. When she was avoiding intimate relationships, she didn't feel as vulnerable and didn't have nearly as many painful flashbacks. Her avoidance worked, at least in terms of decreasing her acute symptoms. This decrease in acute distress and lower symptomatology had led some of her previous therapists to proclaim that her therapy had been "successful," even though her "progress" had come at a very high price. Her previous therapies seemed to have started from an assumption that the alleviation of pain would be what Linda would choose to most value in her life if she were free to choose. However, that assumption seemed to have led them astray. Although Linda was experiencing relatively little in terms of acute distress when I first started seeing her, she was actively contemplating ending her life because to her, the constricted and rigid life oriented around avoiding pain she had created wasn't really a life worth living. Linda was caught up in a cycle of avoidance that was working well in the short term, insofar as limiting her acute pain, but she was paying for it with her life—at least the life she would want to live. When it came down to it, what Linda wanted more than anything else was to be able to be loving, vulnerable, and intimate with the people she cared about. But as long as her life was ruled by EA, a life that included such intimacy was not available to her. In her case, Linda *knew* what was most important to her—interacting with trustworthy others in a loving, vulnerable, and intimate way—but she didn't have the psychological flexibility needed to respond effectively to the painful psychological experiences that inevitably showed up as soon as she started living out her values.

Willingness as an alternative to experiential avoidance. In order to live a life aligned with our values, we need the ability to be with the difficult thoughts and feelings that arise as part of our journey. As soon as Linda started taking steps on her chosen journey toward being intimate and loving in her relationships, her internal dialogue was filled with painful thoughts like, "What if he hurts you?" or "Don't be stupid. You know you can't trust any man!" or terrifying memories and feelings from her past. She would then metaphorically pull over to the side of the road, abandoning her journey until those painful experiences subsided. But the whole time she was on the side of the road, she wasn't getting to be on the journey she wanted for her life. Acceptance, or as I prefer to call it, willingness, offers an alternative to putting our life's journey on hold.

Willingness is choosing to be with what is without struggling or attempting to run away from it. It isn't liking it, resigning to it, or putting up with it. It is simply allowing our thoughts, feelings, and sensations to be whatever they happen to be at the moment. Much of our thinking and emotion is rooted in our history and thus you can also think of willingness as allowing your history to be what it already is. In this way, willingness is the opposite of EA; instead of trying to avoid or get away from painful thoughts or feelings that show up, in willingness we open up to our experience, making room for whatever shows up in order to continue to move forward in our valued direction. Through willingness, we can develop a less adversarial posture toward our history and our experience. Our history and the experience that results out of it are not seen as the enemy. Through willingness, they are no longer a barrier between us and the life we would want to live.

"Just make room for it." "Just allow it to be there." Sound easy? If so, then you should be grateful because you probably haven't experienced the kind of stop-you-dead-in-your-tracks panic Linda experienced every time she allowed herself to be touched by someone she was trying to develop an intimate relationship with. And you probably don't know how convincing my client John's thoughts are when they tell him he is evil and that he does not deserve to live, let alone experience compassion. Or maybe you've never experienced the swirling black hole feeling of emptiness that torments my client Jenny, from which cutting is her only escape. When I'm talking about willingness, I'm not just talking about being willing to feel uncomfortable. I'm talking about the incredible courage and commitment my clients have in being willing to have *all* their experience that shows up as they move toward their values. They are willing to do this because they have chosen that there are more important things to them than their pain.

Willingness in the service of valued living. I care deeply about the people I serve and have no interest in asking them to suffer more than they already have in their lives. I see no value in needlessly experiencing discomfort or pain. Life is hard enough as it is. It is only willingness *in the service of living a valued life* that is honorable. Willingness isn't emotional self-flagellation or wallowing. It's something much more empowering.

The reason I generally choose to use the term "willingness" rather than "acceptance" in my work is, in part, because of the connotations the word acceptance has for many of the people I serve. Many of them have been told to "just accept it" for much of their lives. They have been told to "accept it and move on" by society, by the people who have victimized them, by people who care about them and want them to suffer less, and by their own minds. I do not want to be one more voice in that "just accept it" chorus.

Willingness, on the other hand, to me implies an action they can take, rather than a letting go or resignation. It's a choice, *their* choice. They are saying, "I would be willing to experience X (if X is whatever pain happens to show up) if that means I get to have a life in the service of Y (if Y is whatever would be most meaningful to them personally, their values)." Values give honor and dignity to our suffering, and willingness makes valuing even in the presence of extreme pain possible. It is because Linda had chosen to value intimacy that she willingly made room for her panic sensations. John wanted more than anything else to live a life of compassion, which he decided in the end also meant extending compassion to himself. Because of that, we needed to help him develop different ways of relating to the self-loathing thoughts that inevitably showed up as soon as he started allowing compassion in. And Jenny chose a life of boldness and courage. So, she opened up to learning how to be at peace with her "black hole," not bracing against it or giving into it. Instead, she learned to open up to it and even explore it by allowing the sensations and thoughts that it brought with it. All of this was in the service of getting to live a bold and courageous life.

That is what willingness is. It's not some wimpy resignation or petulant tolerance. It is taking back choice over what your life is oriented around. In choosing willingness, my clients are saying that *they* get to decide what their life will stand for—not someone else, not their history, and not their pain. Willingness allows the free choice that is essential in valued living. Without willingness, we will inevitably get pulled off our valued path as our suffering takes the reins.

COGNITIVE DEFUSION

"The mind is its own place, and in itself can make a heaven of hell, a hell of heaven" (Milton, 2007, p. 76). Milton's quote from *Paradise Lost* captures how the mind can become so powerful that it can start to create our reality. We can become so caught in the content of our thinking that we lose contact with our lives as actually experienced through our senses. ACT uses a made-up word, "cognitive fusion," to describe this process. Like two pieces of metal that can become fused into one, our thoughts about the world and the world as directly experienced become fused together so that we can only perceive the world as structured through thinking. Our ordinary state is to be so unaware of our thinking that our thoughts about the world, who others are, and who we are become our reality rather than simply being seen as thoughts. We take our thoughts as literal "truths" and fail to see them as experiences we are having in a given moment and context. When my client John is thinking that he is evil, he's not experiencing that as, "Oh, there is that thought again that I'm evil," but instead his mind creates his reality such that he *is* evil. Linda doesn't notice herself thinking that all men will hurt her and can't be trusted; that's just how it *is* and she responds accordingly, despite actually being surrounded by several trustworthy and caring men. In this way, our thinking can narrow our options and lead to inflexible and rigid ways of responding. Our curiosity to explore, be skeptical of our thoughts, and learn from our direct experience is thereby limited.

The problem with being fused with our thoughts does not lie in the accuracy/rationality or inaccuracy/irrationality of those thoughts. Instead, the problem lies in our inability to see thoughts as thoughts and thus the failure to evaluate the workability of those particular thoughts in a specific context. This is where values come in. Rather than focusing on the accuracy or rationality of our thoughts, we can focus instead on what works to facilitate valued action in our lives. As I tell my clients, I don't have some pipeline to the ultimate "truth" in life and I'm skeptical of the arrogance of anyone who says they do, including my mind and their mind. I want us to focus on what works and leave the battling for competing "truths" to others—we've got more important work to do!

This process of being able to look at thoughts and evaluate them in terms of their workability, rather than being caught up in what they present themselves to be—literal truths about the world—is called cognitive defusion. If fusion implies a lack of separation from our thoughts, in defusion, we undo fusion by separating from, becoming less attached to, or distancing from our thoughts. Said more simply, we move from seeing the world *from* our thoughts, to looking at or observing our thoughts. Defusion frees us, even if just briefly, from the virtual reality of the mind that Milton is referring to in *Paradise Lost*.

Defusion creates the space for valued living. Mindfulness traditions throughout history have touted the benefits of being able to notice thoughts as thoughts, learning to dispassionately observe them come and go as they do. From a values perspective, defusion is needed because it offers us the freedom to choose the life we would want to live. In fact, there is data to suggest that mindfulness interventions function, at least in part, by increasing values-based action (Christie, Atkins, & Donald, 2017). We need the capacity to observe our thinking and not be so rigidly caught up in our thoughts, in order to have the space to choose a life in line with our values. In a quote that is often erroneously attributed to Viktor Frankl, Rollo May said: "Human freedom involves our capacity to pause between stimulus and response and, in that pause, to choose the one response toward which we wish to throw our weight" (May, 1975, p. 100).

Defusion opens up the infinite possibilities of what our lives can be about when they are not constricted by our mind's programming, which is largely a product of our learning history and thus out of our control. Through defusion, we take our thoughts less literally, seeing them as one piece of input that is coming from one source, our minds. It's not that our minds are "wrong" or "irrational," but rather that they have evolved to detect threats and problems, not to create vital, meaningful lives. Observing our thoughts gives us the freedom to decide whether or not it would be workable for our agenda of living a values-based life to follow those particular thoughts. Defusion is what creates the space that Rollo May's quote refers to, the space that allows us the power to choose our response and thus how we will best live out our values.

ABILITY TO BE IN THE PRESENT MOMENT

Despite there being nowhere else but the present moment, we often spend much of our life in a conceptualized past and future. The tendency to get caught up in worries about the future or rumination about the past is pervasive. This kind of mental time travel is evident in many of the difficulties we see as therapists, from anxiety disorders with pervasive worry about the future, to ruminative depression with its regret, bitterness, and brooding about the past. No wonder so many treatments emphasize the importance of teaching clients to mindfully return to the present moment. This is where life happens and where flexibility is fostered.

When we are caught up in the future or past, we lose contact with both our internal and our external worlds. We are not aware of what we are thinking, feeling, or sensing in the moment, and as a result, we lose important information. We are unaware of the external environment and therefore are less responsive to what it might afford in terms of valued behavior. When absorbed in the future or past, our behavior is largely controlled by our conditioned thoughts and reactions; new possibilities are foreclosed. Our attention is more rigid and inflexible, as is our behavior.

Valued living occurs in the now. Valuing is happening right now; it occurs in the present. Right now, you are valuing something by your choice to read this book, but you may only have become aware of that in this moment when I drew your attention to it. We need to be able to come into the present moment in order to track what our behavior is in the service of. We need to be present to notice the consequences of our behavior and how it affects us and those around us. And we need to be present in order to notice what it feels like to live moments of life that align with who we most want to be. Without presence in those times, we are likely to lose out on the rewards that can be there, turning valued action into drudgery or another "have to" or "should." When we are able to return to the present, we can notice what we are valuing in the here-and-now, pivoting as necessary. Valued living requires the ability to be present and pay attention to what is most important to us.

FLEXIBLE PERSPECTIVE TAKING (SELF/OTHER-AS-CONTEXT)

Ever since you were an infant, you have almost certainly been trained to tell stories about who you and others are and why you do what you do. What's your name? What do you like? What do you feel? What are they like? Why did you do that? These are questions you have been asked and have answered countless times since acquiring language. We get reinforced for telling consistent stories that explain and justify our behavior, and we get corrected if we tell stories that are inconsistent or don't make sense to the people around us. For example, a child who repeatedly says they like trucks, but then one day says they hate trucks, will likely get some correction such as, "No, Emma, remember, you like trucks!" Over time we learn to tell more and more consistent stories that seem to describe ourselves, others, the world, and how all these things work.

The stories that others tell about us and those that we tell about ourselves are interwoven to form an interlocking tapestry of meaning that is very robust and slow to change. We learn that we are an "angry person" or a "girl" or an "American" or "good at writing." Without our awareness, we strive to act in line with our self-concept and avoid acting against it. When the consistency that is fostered is helpful, then these stories work great. But these stories can also be like glue that binds us to old ways of being when what we really need is change. For example, consider how a person who tends to think poorly of themself (i.e., has "low self-esteem") typically responds when someone else tries to tell them that they are actually a "good person." Do they think, "Really? Wow, I never thought of that!" and from then on believe they are a worthwhile person? That outcome is so unlikely as to seem absurd. No, instead their mind will probably generate arguments (either out loud or privately) about their worthlessness. They are fighting to maintain consistency in their story. This thinking, this defense of one's story about oneself, is the self-concept in action.

This process of "selfing," of constructing a self that seems to have qualities just like an object has qualities, is a wholly normal process and largely adaptive. This powerful language-based process results in what ACT refers to as the "conceptualized self" or "self-as-content" and occurs largely outside of our awareness. Rather than being able to observe these stories as what they are—attempts to explain and understand ourselves and the world that are necessarily incomplete and limited—we see ourselves and others from the perspective of these stories and thereby become controlled and constricted by them.

The problem with being overly attached to a conceptualized self isn't that these stories are always negative or are wholly inaccurate. Negative or inaccurate stories can actually be helpful at times. Likewise, even "positive" stories we might have about ourselves can constrict our behavior in unhelpful ways. Jason's client Doris was faced with just such a problem when she was trapped in her positive self story of being someone who "always looks on the bright side."

Clinical example: Doris. Doris was highly attached to seeing herself as being eternally optimistic and someone who always saw the best in people. Her frequent refrain was, "I always see the bright side!" This may not sound like a bad way to be. The problem was, rigidly clinging to this story resulted in her disregarding important information, including her own experience. In her case, Doris was unable to see how incredibly abusive her partner was, despite repeated physical, sexual, and emotional attacks. Always looking for the "bright side" of her relationship kept her from taking steps to change what was unworkable. Instead, she needed to be able to shift perspective and also see the darker, more harmful side, in order to make the changes necessary to get out of her dangerous and unworkable situation and back on course with a life focused on what would matter most to her.

The problem is not in the content of the story, but rather our relationship to the story. Our options for how to behave become constricted when we treat these stories as if they were the whole picture and don't see them as stories told from one perspective. Seen from only one perspective (ours), these stories can never be as multidimensional or complex as we actually are. It would be as if you were looking at an intricate sculpture but only seeing it from one perspective. Even if your observations were "accurate" from where you stood, they would be wholly incomplete and limited if you didn't walk around the sculpture, looking at it from all sides, and even taking a step back to take it in as a whole piece of art. Each of us and each of our lives is much richer and more complex than any story we could tell about ourselves.

Valued living requires shifting perspectives. The power our stories have is rooted in our inability to see alternate perspectives, or even notice that we are seeing from a perspective at all. The ability to notice the presence of the stories we have about ourselves, others, and the world, and subsequently take on various perspectives, is what allows us to transcend our stories, to be more than the content of our history. This transcendence allows us to create lives based on our values rather than following a predetermined story plot.

Perhaps the ultimate perspective shift is to be able to contact perspective itself— that is, the perspective of oneself as observer. Writings about mindfulness from many traditions have described this sense of perspective using terms like "pure awareness," "the silent witness," "original nature," "pure consciousness," or "the observing self."

From this observer perspective, we can contact a sense in which we are not any of the stories that our mind spins, but instead the place, the arena, or the context where life unfolds. Mindfulness practices of many sorts help us contact this sense of pure awareness that allows us to detach from these limiting stories, and can therefore be helpful in fostering valued living and psychological flexibility in general.

But there is also another, more commonsense way in which flexible perspective taking can be helpful. We can learn to see ourselves and our experiences from different vantage points, whether in space, in time, or even from the perspective of other people. Being able to shift perspective in this way can help free us up to see new possibilities for how to respond in our lives. It can open up a space for new choices for what we might value in our lives that is unconstrained by the stories we tell. Below is a clinical example that illustrates how fostering flexible perspective taking and stepping outside the content of the stories we have about ourselves can facilitate valued living.

Clinical example: Ben. Ben was a seventy-year-old single widow who came to therapy in a state of persistent depression. He rarely left his house except to come to therapy, which he had been in and out of many times over the years. A film buff, Ben spent most of his time in bed watching movies. He appeared disheveled and did not attend to his personal hygiene, reporting, "I just don't have the energy." Despite his isolation, Ben had several people who cared a great deal for him and visited him frequently. Most of these people were longtime buddies from days long ago when Ben was a fighter pilot in the Air Force. I remember being quite taken by how committed and loyal this handful of guys were to Ben. One of them even called me shortly after I started working with Ben to say, "All of us guys [Ben's buddies] wanted you to know that if there is anything at all we can do to help with Ben, you just let us know and we'll do it no matter what."

As I was getting to know Ben, he would say things like, "I've always been a depressive" and "I'm not the kind of person that people want to be around" and "Sometimes I can fake it, but if people knew the *real* me, they would hate me." Ben had developed this very rigid, unidimensional story about who he was, and he was attached to the idea that this version of himself was the *real* Ben.

It wasn't that Ben's story about himself was wholly inaccurate. He had been in a state of clinical depression for much of his adult life, and many people did find it difficult to be around him, including, at times, even his friends who seemed to be growing increasingly frustrated with the narrow and dim life he was living. Thus, the problem wasn't in the inaccuracy of the story, but the fact that it was told from a very limited perspective, one that wasn't helping Ben live out his values.

Unlike many of the people I work with, when Ben came to see me, he already had some clarity around his values. To him, living a life that was about loyal comradery and selfless service would be an honorable life. He was very clear on this. The problem was, while he was in bed and disengaged from the world, he wasn't really living out those values.

The way I saw it, a core block to Ben's ability to live out his values was his rigid attachment to a unidimensional and unworkable story he had about himself. Thus, for Ben, although values still anchored everything we did in our work together, the therapy needed to focus directly on helping him develop more psychological flexibility through learning to transcend his self story and expand his perspective-taking abilities. The following transcript is based on a session early in our work together.

Therapist: You seem to have a pretty strong sense of who you are and what your life is capable of being.

Client: Yep. I've had a lot of therapy, so I know myself pretty well. I guess, if nothing else, I've developed a lot of self-awareness through all my years of therapy.

Therapist: It certainly does seem like you know some versions of you really well. But if you were writing a screenplay for a movie and I was your editor, I'd tell you that the character of "Ben" doesn't seem very well developed. *(I chose this metaphor given Ben's strong interest in movies. The goal of the metaphor was to foster an observer perspective on his story.)* He's kind of unidimensional in how you present him. If he were a character in a movie, I'd say he was a bit cliché.

Client: What do you mean? I'm just describing what I'm like.

Therapist: Well, you're only telling the story of Ben from one vantage point. *(Here I am continuing to refer to "Ben" in the third person in order to facilitate his ability to look at the character of "Ben" that he has created from an outside perspective.)* It's like the movie is shot with only one camera that is focused at the base of Ben's bed. It only ever shows Ben as lying in bed, unshowered, and feeling suicidal. Sure, that guy doesn't look like the guy that his friends can count on and he doesn't look like he's capable of being of service to others.

Client: But I just can't get myself to do those things because I'm so depressed.

Therapist: Yes. That is the movie that's playing from your perspective. It's a continuous shot of that scene. But you know why they don't shoot movies with only one camera angle? Because it makes for a boring movie. We need to be able to see the characters and the scenes from different perspectives to get a full picture of what is going on and what is possible. You're only seeing the movie of "Ben" from one camera angle and it makes for a pretty boring and meaningless story. But come over here. *(I ask Ben to come sit in my chair and look at the couch where he was just sitting to further facilitate this outside perspective.)* Can you see that from this angle Ben isn't lying in bed thinking about ways to kill himself? This camera is capturing a Ben that is in therapy, talking about how he really wants to be there for his buddies, to be able to be depended on, to be of service. In fact, *this* movie shows a Ben who, even though he hadn't left the house in five days, dragged himself out of bed, put on clothes, and took a bus to get here in the service of being a good friend to his buddies. *(Here I am pointing out and reinforcing the values-consistent behavior he was engaging in at that moment.)* This camera angle adds some important information. It makes for a much more interesting story, one with more possibilities. I'm not saying this version of the story is the "true" one. All the different camera angles only tell part of the story and maybe all of them are true to a certain extent. I'm just saying that, if you want to be able to live your *whole* life, one that includes being able to be loyal to your friends, to be of service, to live a life that is honorable, it might be helpful to learn how to see that life from several different camera angles.

This was just the start of our work together expanding the ways in which Ben saw himself and what was possible for his life. We spent several months working on perspective-taking skills, including daily mindfulness practices, that allowed him to take a more transcendent view of himself at times. We continued to utilize the movie metaphor throughout therapy to facilitate this perspective taking. For example, I could interrupt when Ben was getting caught up in rigid or unworkable stories by simply saying, "What camera shot are we looking at now?" or, "Now tell me that same scene but from the perspective of what another camera captured." We also worked on defusion skills that allowed Ben to take a step back and notice the thoughts he was having about himself as thoughts, rather than as literal truths.

In the end, Ben didn't stop seeing himself from the position of "a depressive" lying in bed thinking of ways to kill himself. But that became only part of the story. He was also able to step outside of that view and notice when he was engaging in valued action. That noticing allowed him to contact the reinforcing properties that are inherent in valued action, resulting in him spending increasing amounts of time engaged in those activities. In other words, he didn't stop being "a depressive" in his mind, but his story about himself expanded to also include being a loyal comrade who served his community by regularly volunteering at his local veterans' organization, and a whole host of other experiences.

Flexible perspective taking is an essential tool for fostering the psychological flexibility that people need in order to contact and live their values. For me personally, it's probably the one I rely on most in my values-focused work. You will see that many of the values exercises offered in this book utilize perspective-taking strategies. The ACT literature offers a wealth of techniques, exercises, and metaphors for fostering a sense of self (often called self-as-context) that is larger and more encompassing than the stories we tell about ourselves. If you are interested in learning more about this process, I might recommend chapter 5 from *Learning ACT*, called "Building Flexible Perspective Taking Through Self-as-Context" (Luoma et al., 2017), and the book *The Self and*

Perspective Taking: Contributions and Applications from Modern Behavioral Science (McHugh & Stewart, 2012) as great resources for learning more about this important process.

Effective Values Work Includes Psychological Flexibility

Although ACT explicitly targets psychological flexibility, and the term "psychological flexibility" comes out of a contextual behavioral science perspective, we know from research that other therapy approaches besides ACT can also increase psychological flexibility, though they may use different language for the process. For example, there is evidence that DBT (Neacsiu, Lungu, Harned, Rizvi, & Linehan, 2014), CBT (Arch et al., 2012), and mindfulness-based stress reduction (MBSR; Labelle, Campbell, & Carlson, 2010) all function in part by increasing psychological flexibility, which includes people's ability to know what they value and put those values into action. You simply aren't going to be as effective addressing issues of values and meaning with clients if you aren't also attending to things like whether or not the client is willing to feel the difficult feelings that will inevitably arise in that work (willingness), consider alternative stories for their lives as opposed to being rigidly attached to the stories that are keeping them stuck (flexible perspective taking), detach from rigid and judgmental thinking that interferes with choice (defusion), or attend to what is being valued in the here-and-now (present moment). So, whether you come at values work from an ACT perspective or some other tradition, whether you call these processes psychological flexibility or something else, doing effective values work also includes paying attention to these related repertoires.

Focusing on Values Without Psychological Flexibility May Be Counterindicated

Attending to psychological flexibility is an essential component to values work regardless of the client. In the absence of psychological flexibility, bringing up the topic of hopes and dreams, aspirations, life goals, important relationships, and meaning can elicit old and tired judgments, evaluations, stories about oneself, and lots of pain. I imagine you've seen it with some of your clients. In addition, there is also data to suggest that, at least with some clients, it may be clinically counterindicated to attempt more in-depth and explicit values-focused work in the absence of attending to other psychological flexibility processes such as defusion, acceptance, perspective taking, and present-moment contact (Villatte et al., 2016). This may be particularly true for people who present with more intense PTSD symptoms (Twohig, 2009). Although empirically it is still unclear why this may be the case, one hypothesis is that individuals who have had some of their core assumptions about the safety, predictability, and controllability of the world shattered through trauma (Janoff-Bulman, 1992) may need more help finding a secure place from which to work before they can effectively explore such core topics as values.

This isn't to say that you can't do values work with people who have acute PTSD or other people who have similar difficulties. It's just that people vary in terms of how much psychological flexibility they already have and how much more they may need to develop in order to have more directly values-focused work be effective. Some clients can dive right in and others need more preparation. However, even when it would be most useful to first focus more directly on other flexibility repertoires, values still anchor those interventions because they are the "why" you are doing them in the first place.

Inflexible Valuing Isn't Valuing: Why Psychological Flexibility Is Needed

It is essential to pay attention to how clients are engaging with work on values as it unfolds in session—whether in a flexible or an inflexible manner. Ultimately, inflexible valuing gets us stuck. If you as a therapist don't take a step back and also attend to the other repertoires involved in psychological flexibility, your values work is likely to get derailed in a myriad of ways, as I discuss below.

Values work without willingness is not sustainable. Conversations about what matters often bring up difficult emotions—shame over past failures, sadness over past losses, fear of the future, or envy of others' circumstances, to name just a few. Our values make us vulnerable. For example, as soon as you stake claim to valuing intimacy, you will encounter the fear of losing that intimacy and connection with others. Thus, honest and real conversations about values require willingness to feel whatever shows up and accepting contexts that make that possible. To be able to engage openly in values work in therapy, we (both the client and the therapist) need to be able to embrace the vulnerability and pain that comes with the journey, or else be deflected from the path.

Values work without defusion is rigid. Clients usually come to discussions about meaning, purpose, and values with lots of ideas about how the world works or what "should be." Some clients may completely deny that anything matters to them or that they even have values. Other clients will quickly turn freely chosen values into rules or standards they *should* live by. As a result, values work can easily lose a sense of choice and quickly become a "have to." Although it may be culturally dependent, data suggest that in general, once people lose a sense of personal choice and an action is seen as a "should" or "have to," they are significantly less likely to persist in that behavior over time (Sheldon & Elliot, 1999). Thus, without being able to step back and notice the thoughts that arise when talking about what matters most, values work shifts from being vitalizing and freeing to aversive and rigid.

Values work without flexible perspective taking is constricting. When clients begin thinking and talking about what matters to them it often elicits stories linked to their self-concept. Thoughts like "It's too late for me" or "I'm not capable of that" or "I'm not that kind of person" are likely to show up. They can get caught up in perceived flaws, inabilities, and limitations that restrict what seems possible for them. If we are unable to help our clients take a step back from these self stories, to contact a sense of self that is larger than all these labels, reasons, and evaluations, then they are likely to become increasingly trapped by them, thus restricting what is possible for them in life. Our clients are larger than their limited perspective of themselves and their worlds, and unless they can be helped to see that, their lives will be constricted in ways that they cannot even guess.

Values work without present-moment awareness is lifeless. Thinking about what matters to them can draw some clients into obsessive rumination about past failures or losses, potentially leading them to completely abandon whole domains of living. Worrying about all the potential obstacles or how to move forward can exhaust anyone's energy and make values dry and lifeless. In addition, values are lived in the here-and-now. Therefore, if we aren't present and aware, we won't receive the benefits that come from living our life in a way that is true to our hearts. While values work will often include a focus on the future, it needs to be interspersed with mindfully attending to clients' present-moment experience while engaging in these valued patterns of action.

Finally, values work without action is empty (and not really valuing at all). When we begin to think and talk about what's important, we begin to see possibilities for how we might put these ideas into action. Ultimately, values are not thoughts, but the actions we take in our lives. Simply talking about values or simply knowing what is important to us isn't effective (Bramwell & Richardson, 2018); we need to live out our values. Thus, clients may need help in learning how to translate their values into specific, concrete goals and actions, and ultimately to string these together in larger patterns and habits.

Thus, while values are at the heart of everything we do in values-guided therapy, we also need to monitor these other repertoires essential to psychological flexibility (willingness, defusion, flexible perspective taking, present-moment contact, and effective action) as they unfold in session and work to strengthen these repertoires when rigidity interferes. Although these processes are often presented as discrete, they actually interact and work together to facilitate psychological flexibility. To see how the different flexibility processes can be combined in one exercise, you can read about the Content on Cards exercise and an accompanying clinical example of how the various flexibility processes can be used in the service of valuing at http://www.newharbinger.com/43218.

Takeaways

- For many, living a good life entails more than simply feeling good. Values-guided therapy is about giving them that choice!

- Valued living requires more than just knowing what we value. Psychological flexibility repertoires enable us to live out our values even in the midst of potential barriers.

- Willingness is what allows us to take back choice over what our life is oriented around.

- Defusion creates the space needed for valued living.

- Stepping outside of our stories and taking on different perspectives frees us from the limiting stories of what our life can be.

- Valued living is occurring now. Pay attention to what is actually being valued.

- There is no such thing as values in the absence of action.

- Doing values work without also attending to other psychological flexibility processes is incomplete and very likely ineffective.

Next Steps

- Select a client who is persistently focused on trying to avoid/get rid of painful thoughts, feelings, memories, or sensations (in other words, someone who is struggling with significant EA). With that client in mind, reflect on the following:

  · What do you imagine they might most long for if their suffering subsided? Have you explicitly asked them about this?

  · If that person could choose between a) having a life that was filled with what was most important to them but also included the suffering they currently have or b) having a life devoid of their suffering but also devoid of meaning, which do you imagine they might they choose?

  · Is it possible that there are ways in which you have limited this client's free choice by assuming that the alleviation of pain would truly be what they would most want to focus on in therapy (and their life)? Is there anything you'd like to do differently in this regard?

- Read the Content on Cards exercise at http://www.newharbinger.com/43218. Ask a friend or colleague to role-play with you as you practice guiding the exercise.

- **Inside-out learning: How is your own psychological inflexibility getting in the way of your valued action?** Consider something you've been wanting to take action on for some time but with which you have had difficulty staying on track. Choose something that is a valued action, something you would actually choose to make important rather than a "should" or "have to." Consider the following in regard to this action:

  - What thoughts show up as soon as you consider taking this action?

  - What sensations do you notice?

  - Do you have any urges?

  - Do any memories show up?

  - What do you do when these show up? Do you do anything to avoid these thoughts/sensations/urges/memories when they show up? Consider both internal emotional control strategies (such as distraction, worry, problem solving, and justifying) and external emotional control strategies (such as eating, avoiding situations, substance use, shifting to another activity, and so on).

  - How much has avoidance of these experiences gotten in the way of you taking the action you indicated you want to take?

PART 2

Practical Application

CHAPTER 3

Orienting Clients Toward Values

A journey of a thousand miles begins with facing in the direction you want to go, over and over and over again. —Anonymous

"When do I begin doing values work with a client?" "How do I introduce it?" "Where do I start?" These are questions that frequently come up for therapists looking to incorporate values work into their therapy. These are good questions that I hope to address in this chapter. However, these questions also all seem to imply that values work is a "thing" to do in therapy, a technique or set of techniques. Yes, there are lots of values exercises and techniques you can do, and many are outlined in this book, but those techniques aren't the sum of what it means to have values guide your therapy.

Whether implicitly or explicitly, your values and your client's values are already guiding what is happening in the therapy room. By talking more explicitly about values, this process of valuing can occur with intention and a sense of choice. Values work is not simply a task to complete in therapy ("I need to help my client identify their values"), but rather an ongoing process that lays the foundation for the treatment plan, informs case conceptualization, guides when to select which interventions and for what function, and serves as the ultimate measure of treatment progress. Similarly, values do not simply guide *what* to do in therapy, but they also inform *how* we choose to relate to those we serve (see chapter 9 for more information on therapists' values). This chapter is about how to begin the conversation around values and orient our clients to this kind of work.

Introducing Values

When should you introduce the idea of values when working with a client? While, of course, the answer to that depends on the client and the context, I'd argue that it is often important to introduce values very early in your work with a client, even in the first session. There are a few reasons why I usually find it helpful to start off therapy with an explicit discussion of values.

Values Inform and Motivate the Rest of Therapy

I see values-consistent behavior—that is, behavior that aligns with what is most important to the client and what they wish to embody—as being *the* crucial outcome measure in therapy. Thus, without having at least some vague sense of what your client would choose to value, it is difficult to come up with a comprehensive treatment plan and goals. After all, you can't know if you're making "progress" if you don't know what you're supposed to be progressing toward. And it's your client's values that set the direction; what *they* would choose to have their life be in the service of is the end goal. Assuming that we can know what our clients would choose to value without asking them about it directly seems to me to be arrogant, and I often find those assumptions to be inaccurate as well.

Another reason I like to begin values work as soon as possible is that therapy is hard! What we ask of our clients is often very difficult. It's tough to look at the areas in our lives where we are stuck or feel helpless or hopeless. Those are exactly the areas where we are most vulnerable. It's no wonder most clients come to therapy with some fear or ambivalence. Data suggest that connecting with values helps clients persist with difficult or painful tasks (Grumet & Fitzpatrick, 2016; Páez-Blarrina et al., 2008) and can help with treatment adherence (Forman, Butryn, Hoffman, & Herbert, 2009; Woods, Wetterneck, & Flessner, 2006). Thus, bringing values into the picture early can connect clients to a source of motivation that can help them through the difficult process of making important life changes. Meaning motivates. Think of all the difficult, painful things people go through when it's in the service of something they care deeply about (just ask any parent, or marathon runner, or political activist!). Values provide the reason to stick with it when things get difficult.

But it isn't just our clients who struggle with motivation. Therapy can also be difficult for us therapists; at least it is for me. Spending all day every day connecting with and being emotionally available to my clients in the way that I do takes a lot out of me. I am absolutely willing to pay that cost, but I darn sure want to know what it's in the service of, what I'm playing for. Values tell me what my client and I are playing for. When the stakes are high, when I'm playing for something really important, I give it my all, as do my clients. And what could be more important than the possibility of creating a life worth living? So, in this way, having values discussions early in therapy can also help *you* with motivation. There is also data to suggest that connecting with our values as therapists can help with things like burnout (Vilardaga et al., 2011), which I'll talk more about in chapter 9.

This is not to say that you "should" start right off with in-depth values work. Some clients may need more extensive preparation, including working directly on other psychological flexibility repertoires, before they are likely to be capable of more in-depth values exploration. For example, clients who are highly entangled with judgmental thinking may need to learn how to observe their thinking with a bit more detachment (defusion) before they can fully consider their values. Others may need to learn how to make room for the painful thoughts and feelings (willingness) that are likely to show up when they start discussing what really matters to them. For others, you may need to first work on perspective-taking skills (self-as-context) in order to loosen their attachment to self-limiting stories about themselves and others that unduly restrict what they might choose for their lives. Still others may need to get better at noticing their own feelings, desires, or bodily experiences (present-moment awareness) before they can know what they want. And many people may need more time for a trusting relationship to develop before being vulnerable in the ways that values work requires. However, even when work on these other repertoires is necessary before we can begin more in-depth values work, I have found that it is still important to have values present from the outset, as it is values that provide the foundation for the therapy. For these reasons, I start talking about values and how they direct the rest of our work together as early as the first session, even if we are going to focus on something besides values work initially.

From the moment I begin talking with a potential client, I am listening for hints of values. I am listening for places where vitality shows up or where there is a sense of willing vulnerability as clients are speaking with me. Values are a part of what we are talking about in the very first session when we're just starting to explore treatment planning. I have found over and over again that if my client and I are not having those conversations early on, we're often missing something very important. Let me give you an example.

CLINICAL EXAMPLE: HEATHER

Heather burst into tears during our very first session when I brought up values with her. She had spent the first twenty minutes of our intake session running through her litany of "problems" for which she had been in and out of therapy, both inpatient and outpatient, for much of her life. It was a compelling story in many ways, and she had experienced tremendous suffering. But as she repeated the story I could tell she had retold countless times to countless other therapists, there was something dead to it. And so, as she went on, I was intentional about displaying mild boredom on my face. (I learned pretty early on, though probably not early enough, that when you're as emotionally expressive as I am, it's best to at least be intentional about the emotions you're expressing because the "blank slate" thing probably isn't going to work for me!) Heather was confused by my apparent lack of interest in all the ways in which she had suffered and was continuing to suffer. For many clients, having that suffering validated by being listened to and really heard is exactly what is needed. But not for Heather. I could hear it in her voice and see it on her face; she had told this story and had it heard countless times before. Her story was worn and tired and lifeless. So, I tried to reflect that lifelessness through my nonverbals.

Finally, I responded:

Therapist: Why should I care? Why do you care?

I didn't speak in a confrontational or cruel tone, but rather my tone was one of lifelessness and resignation. The goal was to use my tone of voice to help Heather contact the life-sucking quality of her struggle to get rid of her pain. Suffice it to say, don't use this blunt tactic unless you know enough about yourself as a stimulus that you know you can pull it off. I am a five-foot-two middle-aged woman who frequently gets mistaken for a kindergarten teacher. "Intimidating" is not the first word that comes to people's mind when they encounter me. But this is my hidden superpower! My "cute" dresses and Mary Jane shoes allow me to get away with a lot more than many therapists could. Most of the people I serve grant me the benefit of the doubt, and so I can, at least in the right context, get away with saying something as evocative as "Why should I care?"

That said, even little ol' me needs to follow up a statement like that with some display of vulnerability and care. So I continued:

Therapist: I am incredibly fortunate to get to work with the people I work with. I care deeply about and am totally committed to those people. *(Here I'm modeling how values work by putting my own values into the room.)* My heart is in the work I do. But if I'm going to invest something as precious to me as my heart, I want to know it is for something really, really important. Look, you've seen a lot of great therapists and *(said bluntly, but not unkindly)* yet here you are, still cutting, still burning, still purging, trying whatever you can to take away the tremendous pain you feel, pain that you came by honestly from an incredibly painful history. But I don't have a magic power none of those other therapists had that will take all this pain away. But you know what I do have? I have heart. I'm willing to give one hundred percent to something if it is important enough. And if you want to work with me on something that really matters, a life that really matters, then I'm all in.

Client: *(Somewhat intrigued, if reticent, but engaged)* I don't know what that would be. I don't know what a "life that matters" is. This is all I know.

Therapist: I don't know what it will be for you either. But I have a sense that it's something bolder, more expansive, more vibrant than just a life without cutting. Would you say that all the horrific suffering you've endured and all the hard work it will take to work through all that history would be worth it if all you got in the end was a life without cutting? ... I'm guessing not. Let's play for something bigger if we're going to do this together.

That's when she burst into tears. Knowing me, I'm sure I did as well. That is an example of using values to increase motivation, both for the client and for the therapist.

Heather and I had the privilege of getting to work together for quite some time. When we stopped working together, everything wasn't perfect for Heather, but she hadn't self-harmed in over a year. She had found and then survived the loss of a healthy, loving relationship, the first of her life. However, the real outcome of importance was that Heather's compass orientation had been reset. She could catch it when she was going back to focusing on what she didn't want, when she was trying to get "smaller" in reaction to the pain of her life. She told me several times that our first session was the most important one we had; that conversation about therapy being about creating a bold, expansive, vibrant life was what had set the shift in motion.

Opening to Possibility

The above vignette illustrates what I think is the key element in introducing the topic of values to clients. When values are first introduced, the conversation should aim to open up a sense of possibility or curiosity, rather than attempt to move quickly toward certainty or resolution. The goal isn't to have the client start clarifying their values. The aim is to create a sense that therapy (and their life in general) could be focused on something bigger or more encompassing than their struggles.

A recent experience I had may serve as a metaphor to illustrate what I'm talking about in terms of initial values conversations creating a sense of possibility, curiosity, or even wonderment. Recently, I was fortunate enough to visit the largest dark sky reserve (an area that restricts the amount of artificial light pollution) in the world, which is in southern New Zealand. Most of the time I look up at the night sky with well-established expectations of what I'll see up there. But this time I looked up at the limitless expanse that stretched before me and realized that what I thought I knew was only one tiny bit of a whole universe. I looked up at that endless wonderment and couldn't help but be awestruck. "Wait, *this* is what has been there all this time and I just couldn't see it? And if I can see all this now, what else might be out there?" It was as if I saw an infinite possibility for the very first time, even though it had always been there. That is what it was like for me on that clear night at the bottom of the world. And that's what I'm going for when I introduce values to a client. They often think they know the limits of their life, of what changes are possible. And so, when they come into therapy, they usually only talk about those changes they think might be possible. I want to create a dark sky reserve experience for them, but instead of the sky, it's their life that opens up, even if only for a moment, and they experience a sense of the vast possibility it holds and the curiosity to explore it.

When introducing your client to the idea of having values guide your work together, a key aim is to help the client move from a place of "I know what this [my life/my struggle/the solution] is/can be" to one of curiosity and possibility. You are essentially trying to interrupt the story the client has bought about their life (defusion) and help them see that their ordinary perspective is only one of an infinite number of perspectives they could have on themselves and the possibilities for what their life could stand for (self-as-context/flexible perspective taking). This opening up to possibility is central and lays the foundation for the exploration process that is to come. Heather didn't break down in tears because she had some sense of clarity about her values. Her tears were because, for the first time in many, many years, a sense of possibility opened up for her as she saw the dark sky reserve of her life.

Incorporating Values into Treatment Planning

Explicitly bringing in values during the very early stages of therapy, while you are still deciding what therapy will be in the service of, makes treatment planning and goal setting more collaborative and broadens the possibilities for therapy. This is important because the client's ideas about what they think is the problem and its solution (or their certainty that there is no solution) is often part of what keeps them stuck. Thus, in order to open up a new sense of possibility, values work needs to be introduced in a way that steps outside the client's normal frame of reference. To do this, it's helpful to understand and validate our client's perception of their problems, but also find a way to disrupt it or reconceptualize it in some way before introducing values work as an option.

There are many different ways to bring values into the treatment planning process and open up the possibility for what your client's life and your work together can be about. You've seen one example above in the case of Heather. Of course, I am certainly not suggesting that the evocative approach I took with Heather would be the best way to start your average values conversation with a client. That approach was only workable because of the very specific context that both she and I presented. We need to be flexible and contextually sensitive in how we introduce values. In general, effectively introducing values into the treatment planning process often includes two key elements:

1. Summarize the struggles and initial goals your client has identified thus far in therapy. Be sure to check with your client about whether your understanding is accurate.

2. Present therapy as an opportunity to step back from their presenting problems, to look at the bigger picture of their life and the context in which their difficulties are situated.

Below are a couple of examples of how you might use these general guidelines when introducing values for the first time. First, let's talk about the kind of things you might say to a client who presents to therapy with a primary goal of reducing their experienced pain, whether that is depression, anxiety, chronic pain, or any other emotional state. This is probably the most common presentation we encounter with clients. Their focus on reducing pain to the exclusion of other purposes for their life has often restricted their life tremendously, and yet they usually are requesting their therapist join them in their struggle to reduce their pain (in other words, to help them get away from the "shocks" as discussed in chapter 1). We need to sidestep this trap if we are going to create the space to explore new possibilities for that person's life. For example, here is what I might say to a client looking to get rid of their depression:

Therapist: We've talked for a bit now about your depression and how much you've struggled with it. As we go along, we'll spend more time exploring your depression and what you've been doing to deal with it. At the same time, you are more than just your depression, even if it feels like that's all there is sometimes. When we are suffering, we can get so caught up in that pain that we lose contact with the bigger picture of what gives our life meaning and what we might want with the time we have on this planet. It's like we miss the forest for the tress. So, what I'm suggesting is that part of what we may need to do is take a step back, maybe way back, and look at the bigger picture of your life: for example, what you really want your life to be about. These are the kinds of things that make life worth living. I imagine this might be pretty difficult to do or may even feel impossible. Yet I would argue it's worth doing. Because it's not really enough to just focus on keeping you alive; I want to help you have a life that is worth living. What could be more important than knowing what you want really want for this one life you know you have to live? How does that sound as something to include in what we do together?

The next example relates to clients who come to therapy with goals that appear to be more clearly linked to values. For example, they may want to focus on relationships, work, parenting, or their health. In these cases, it's important to incorporate the goals the person has already stated into the initial introduction. Below is an example of how I might introduce the idea of orienting therapy around values with a client who comes in wanting to get help with their parenting:

Therapist: I really get from what you've said that your relationship with your kids is important to you. I've also heard a lot about what you think isn't working in that relationship and things you'd like to change. This relationship is extremely important to you, so important that even though you probably have lots of other things you're struggling with, it's this relationship you came to therapy for. If this work is going to be most helpful, then we need to get a sense of what is most important to you in being a parent, what you'd most want if you could choose anything. Because, given how important this is to you, I'm guessing that what you'd most long for that relationship to be about is more than just a lack of the current problems you're having with your children. My guess is, if you could choose, you'd want that relationship to be about something profoundly meaningful to you. So, would you be interested in exploring that, in having our work be about helping you move toward what is most important to you with your kids rather than only focusing on getting rid of what you don't want in the relationship?

Both of the above examples incorporate the two general guidelines for introducing values into your treatment planning. These general scripts and guidelines are only a starting point. You will need to find your own way to do this that helps the client open up to the sense of possibility that we are looking for as we introduce values in this early stage. You will need to incorporate your client's personal experiences and history in a way that displays empathy for the unique struggles of your individual client. This is their own unique dark sky reserve you want to help them see. Below is an example of how it might look in a real session that incorporates the above two key elements, while at the same time, I hope, also conveys the sense of opening up to possibility that we're seeking to create during this process.

CLINICAL EXAMPLE: SHASTA

Shasta, a married mother of three young children, was a stay-at-home mom. She had long-standing struggles with worry and rumination, including body image and other "self-esteem" issues. Shasta came into therapy because she wanted to work on her body image, which she felt meant finding the right diet solution so that her body changed into one that she had more positive feelings about. Throughout the intake she repeatedly mentioned feeling "bored," described herself as "boring," and stated that her life just wasn't "meaningful." The following conversation came toward the end of our intake session after I had already developed a basic understanding of Shasta's own conceptualization of her struggles and perceived solutions.

Therapist: It sounds like there are several things you're struggling with and would like to be different in your life. You've been feeling badly about your body for quite some time and would like to feel better about it. It also sounds like you experience a lot of worry and anxiety that is very distressing to you. And, you'd like to be less preoccupied with what other people think of you. Your hope is that through our work together we'll be able to help you make changes so you feel better about your body and also reduce your anxiety and worry, especially about what other people think. Does that sound about right? (*Here I'm summarizing the client's conceptualization of their problems and proposed solutions and checking in with the client about whether it's accurate.*)

Client: Yep, that about sums it up.

Therapist: Is it possible that that's part of the problem? (*While the context didn't call for me to be as provocative as I was with Heather, who was much more entrenched in her suffering, I still wanted to say something that could interrupt Shasta's story in a useful way.*)

Client: What?

Therapist: You said that your struggles with body image and your worry "sums things up." Is that how you'd want it to be? I guess I'm wondering, if you could choose, are those the things that you'd like to "sum up" what your life is about?

Client: (*still a bit confused, but curious*) I'm not really sure what you mean.

Therapist: What if you are feeling your life doesn't have much purpose or isn't very meaningful because it's largely focused on things that, well, frankly, you don't find to be very meaningful, like your body image and other similar worries? What if the solution isn't about solving those problems, but rather shifting so that more of your energies are focused on the things that would actually be more meaningful to you? (*Shasta's particular context allowed me to use this more straightforward way of introducing values than I might use with some clients.*)

Client: I don't know what that is, I mean, other than my kids. Being a good mom is really important to me, but my whole day is already spent doing things for them. (*Here, I see in Shasta the tendency to define herself by her roles, "mom," "wife," "school auction chair," and so on. I want to introduce the idea of values as being more related to qualities of action than outcomes or particular roles.*)

Therapist: Absolutely! I can tell you really care about your kids and being a great mom to them. But, I'm not really talking here about *what* you're doing as much as I am about *how* you are doing what you are doing and what those things are in the service of. That's what I might call your values. (*I'm also educating a bit here about what values are.*)

Client: And that would help me feel like my life was more meaningful? (*She's still focused on an outcome, her life feeling "meaningful," versus the process of living a meaningful life.*)

Therapist: Values actually define what would be a meaningful life for you. Living a values-based life, by definition, means you would be living a meaning-filled life.

Client: How do I figure out what that would be?

Therapist: Maybe that could be at the heart of our work together? Rather than focusing primarily on the stuff you don't want to have, stuff that I think you're saying isn't very meaningful to you, therapy could be focused more on the stuff that is meaningful, on supporting you in exploring, choosing, and moving toward what you would want to have your life be about. Would you be interested in doing *that* work together?

From this place of curiosity and possibility, we were able to work on exploring Shasta's values and what would make for a meaningful life for her. By the end of therapy, she was significantly less distressed by and preoccupied with her thoughts about her body. While her actual body image never in fact changed very much (she still would have said she really didn't like the shape of her body), she was actually caring well for her body in a way she had never been able to sustain before. But because our work focused on values, those actions, which included how she nourished and exercised her body, were seen as a way for her to live out her values of caring for her family (she was able to develop the perspective of seeing herself as a member of her family) in a committed, consistent, and nurturing way rather than as a way to change how she thought or felt about her body. The result was more lasting and, importantly, more meaningful change for Shasta.

Tool: Values Card Sort

Once you and your client have elected to have values guide your work together, a Values Card Sort is an excellent exercise to start the exploration process. I like to start with this exercise because it's straightforward, interactive, and clients tend to really like it.

In this exercise, the client is presented with a set of cards on which various potential values words and a brief definition are written. The client then goes through several rounds of sorting the cards according to what is most or least important to them. I often use this tool during the very early stages of values exploration. It can be especially helpful for clients who have had little or no practice with the concept of values, have a limited vocabulary for describing their values, don't already have a strong sense of what might be important to them, or have difficulties articulating moment-to-moment preferences, wants, or needs. I have also found this exercise to be a helpful way to reorient clients who respond to values questions with statements about goals (such as "I want to travel" or "I would value being a dad") to start thinking in terms of values as directions rather than outcomes.

One thing to keep in mind is that the Values Card Sort is not meant to be the means by which clients will identify their values once and for all, even though clients (and sometimes therapists) often approach the exercise this way. It is pretty unrealistic to think that this simple ten- to fifteen-minute exercise is going to allow your client to walk away with a lasting and clear sense of something as complex and profound as what they would want their life to stand for. The Values Card Sort is a wonderful tool, but it isn't magic. Instead, I see the Values Card Sort task as an introductory sampler, a taste-tester if you will. It is an initial exercise to help introduce the client to both the concept of values and the practice of choosing, as these are often unfamiliar to many people. It can also be helpful for clients to simply see some of the things that people might choose to value, just to get some sense of what we're talking about. It's as if you were going to learn to paint but had very little exposure to art. Looking at a palette filled with different types of paints (oils, acrylics, watercolors) in many different hues and saturations might give you ideas about some of the possibilities for what you might paint.

Focusing not so much on *what* the client chooses, but rather *how* they approach the task makes the Values Card Sort a very useful assessment tool. Are they thoughtful and reflective as they go through the exercise? Do they become ruminative, paralyzed by a desire to get it "right," or, conversely, haphazard as they sort the cards? Many clients don't have much practice with choosing at all. For these clients, the Values Card Sort can be a helpful way to have them start practicing that important skill of choosing.

INSTRUCTIONS

There are many variations of this exercise you can experiment with. For most clients, I tend to use a series of three rounds of sorting the cards. It can be helpful to begin with some discussion of the distinction between values and goals or morals/"shoulds" (see chapter 1 for more on this topic). Then, invite the client to consider the values cards and which ones they might choose to be most important to them. You may want to begin with an invitation like, "Imagine you are at the end of your life looking backward. Pick the words that would describe a life you would have been proud to have lived if it was totally up to you." Depending on the client, you may want to take some of the pressure off by saying something like, "Imagine what you might choose if no one would ever know what you chose." Regardless of how you do it, a key component is that you want to help the client contact a sense of freely choosing, a sense of possibility.

Here is a sample script you can use to introduce the activity. You can download a set of values cards to print out at http://www.newharbinger.com/43218.

Therapist: I want to get a better sense of what might be most important to you if you were totally free to choose. We'll call these your values. One way to think about values is that they describe the kind of person you'd want to be or what you'd want your time on this earth to be in the service of if you were totally free to choose. In other words, when it's all said and done, what would having lived a "well-lived life" mean for you personally? Would you be interested in doing an exercise that might help you explore this a bit more? *(Pause for client answer—choosing to explore values is a kind of valuing.)*

If the client agrees, you're ready to give the instructions.

Therapist: Great. On these cards are some words that reflect some of the things that people choose to make important in their life. It's not an exhaustive list and we can certainly add to it if there are other words that seem to fit better for you. But this will at least give us a place to start. You'll be sorting these cards into different categories based on how important you would want each of these things to be in your life. This isn't what you feel you're prioritizing right now in your life or what others would say you should value or even what you think you should value. Right now, I'm just interested in what you would want to make important in your life if you were totally free to choose.

(If you have a sense that a client might be more stuck in experiential avoidance or focused on what they don't want rather than what they do want, you might want to add something like the following.) Sometimes things feel important to us because they help solve our problems, for example, we hope that they will reduce our suffering. Other times things feel important to us because, like tools, they help us get the things we want. However, tools are usually a means to an end and not really something we would care about in and of themselves. And while solving the problems you have may feel important, right now we want to just focus on what you would find meaningful and satisfying in and of itself. So, you might pretend, just for the moment, that all your suffering has ended and that you have no more problems. What would you still find meaningful and worthwhile? What would you seek, even if there were no problems and no obstacles? That's what I want you to keep in mind when you're choosing these cards.

(If you have a sense that a client might be overcontrolled or might have a tendency to stifle themselves with overthinking, self-criticism, or perfectionism, you might want to add something like the following to help them "loosen up" a bit with the activity.) Also, this doesn't have to be the end-all-be-all of your values. We're just starting out here. So don't overthink it. You don't have to get it "right." You'll have several different rounds to go through and we can even come back to this activity and do it again later on if you feel like you want to change how you responded. Right now, we're just starting to explore here. So, let's see if we can have some fun with this. Okay?

Once you have oriented the client to the idea of values as being freely chosen, you can start with the card sort. As the above script indicates, it's often useful to do more than one round of sorting the cards. Here is a suggested sequence of three rounds I often use.

Round one.

1. Have the client sort all the values cards into the three categories ("Very important," "Important" and "Not very important") based on what they would choose to value if no one were to find out, allowing for as many cards as they want in each of the categories.

2. As they are going through the task, periodically remind the client to focus on what they would choose if there were no right or wrong and no one would know.

3. Debrief: Once they have sorted all the cards, ask for any observations the client noticed. Questions could include:

   · What was it like for you as you tried to sort these cards?

   · What did you notice yourself thinking or feeling as you were doing it?

   · Was it easy for you to know what you would want to make important in your life?

   · Did you feel pulled to give what you thought were "right" answers? Who determines what those "right" answers are?

   · How did you go about your sorting? How did you know to put a card in the "Not very important" pile versus the "Important" pile or the "Very important" pile?

Round two.

1. Take the cards the client put into the "Very important" category in round one and discard the rest.

2. From those "Very important" cards, ask the client to select only ten cards they would choose to make most important. Most clients pick significantly more than ten cards for the "Very important" pile in round one, but if they don't, then just have them select a number that is significantly less than they initially put in that pile. The point is to help the client contact the process of choosing what they would make important.

3. Debrief: Ask for any observations the client noticed. Questions could include:

   · What was it like for you as you tried to choose just ten (or whatever number it was) among all these values that were all very important to you?

   · What did you notice yourself thinking or feeling as you were doing it?

   · Was it easier or harder for you than round one?

   · How did it feel for you to discard the ones you decided not to include?

Round three.

1. Set the client's top ten cards from round two out in front of them.

2. Ask them to choose their top three by saying something like, "Now, if you could only choose three to focus on in your life, assuming there were no right or wrong answers and that you were completely free to choose, which three would you choose? Remember, these values aren't just the things you'd like to accomplish, have, or what you'd enjoy the most. Rather, values are those ways of being in the world that you would most want to dedicate your life to. They are the ways of living that would be most meaningful for you personally."

3. Debrief: Ask for any observations the client noticed. Questions could include:

   · How did you choose your top three?

   · Do these three have anything in common with each other?

   · As you look at these three cards, would you say that a life in service of these would be a life well lived?

   · If someone observed your life today, would they be able to know what you chose here as your top three values?

WRAP-UP AND HOMEWORK

In ACT, just like any other experiential therapy, any exercise is also an assessment. So, after your client has gone through the various rounds of the Values Card Sort, be sure to follow up by asking about their experience of the exercise. While you may get some information about what they would choose to value, what you are most interested in is learning more about their process of valuing, for example, how they choose or what thoughts or feelings show up for them when they do choose to value something. I'll often ask things like:

- What was that task like for you? Was it easy? Was it harder than you thought?

- What did you notice about how you made your choices about which words to put in which piles?

- Did you notice any particular feelings come up during any parts of the exercise?

- If you had to do it again, would you do anything different?

- Did you notice any differences or similarities between what you chose to put in the "Very Important" category and what you tend to make important in your daily life?

- What do you think it would be like if you did something like this exercise each day, something that reminded you what you wanted to make important in your life?

As a way to extend the exercise outside the therapy session, I almost always give my clients a copy of their round three top choices. Sometimes clients will take a photo of them. But I also typically write them down. I frequently give my clients an index card at the end of each therapy session on which I write something to summarize the session (a metaphor, an idea, a question, and so on) along with a homework assignment for them to do that week. For a session that included the Values Card Sort exercise, some examples of homework I might write on that index card would be:

- Read out loud these top three values you chose at the start of every day. Then, at the end of the day, take one minute to write down anything you noticed about your day that you think was influenced by having read the values at the start of the day.

- Choose one word each day from the above and do one thing that day to intentionally reflect or embody that value.

- Have a conversation with a loved one reflecting on your experience of doing this exercise today.

- At the end of each day, rate on a five-point scale how much you felt you embodied each of these three qualities during the day.

OTHER VARIATIONS

Described above is just one variation of the Values Card Sort exercise. Depending on the function you're wanting the exercise to serve and what kind of data you're looking for, consider using some of these other variations:

- Record the results of "round one." For "round two," have the client sort all the cards again according to one or more of the following instructions:

  · What they have been taught by others/society to value or what they feel they "should" value.

  · What they have been valuing with their actions over the past week.

  · What they might have valued ten years ago.

  · What they think they might value in twenty years when they are a bit older and wiser.

  · How they think someone they really admire would sort the cards. (For example: If you were X, how do you think you would sort these? What does X's life really seem to stand for?)

Then ask the client to talk about any similarities or differences between what they chose in the two rounds.

- If they are in a relationship, do the exercise with their partner focusing on sorting the cards based on what they both would want their relationship to stand for.

- Take the cards from "round one" and ask the client to chunk them into groupings to come up with possible overarching values.

TROUBLESHOOTING THE VALUES CARD SORT

While this exercise is generally straightforward and rarely goes awry (which is one reason I like to include it early on in therapy), there are a couple of common places where I see therapists getting stuck with the exercise.

Using the Values Card Sort as a values identification tool. The most common misstep I see with this exercise is when the therapist and/or client views the exercise as an all-powerful, one-and-done values identification tool. Both therapist and client can become focused on the outcome of the task, as if it holds the answer: "Look, I did it. I've identified my values. They are these three words. Now what?" Be careful you don't fall into this trap. At this stage in therapy, values work is about encouraging the client's curiosity and a sense of possibility rather than naming or pinning down their values.

You might think of Values Card Sorts as kind of like speed dating; it's a great place to start, you can get some really interesting information, and it can tell you what you might want to further explore, but you probably don't want to make any lifelong commitments just based on the outcome of it. To troubleshoot this tendency, during the wrap-up and debrief part of the exercise I'll often remind clients of the exercise's function, sometimes even using the speed dating metaphor (though a younger and significantly hipper client recently let me know that I may need to update my metaphor as speed dating is apparently *so 2012!*).

Some clients need help learning the process of choosing. Some clients have a history of abuse, neglect, or chronic invalidation wherein they were never encouraged or supported in learning about their own preferences, wants, desires, or needs. They get what they prefer confused with what others prefer, what they have been told they prefer (but actually don't), or internalized rules about what they should prefer. They forget to take into account their current state, for example, whether they are hungry, angry, sad, anxious, or tired. They may mislabel what they feel based on what others have told them, or they may not even know what they feel in a given moment. They may totally ignore themselves, their preferences, and experience, responding instead based on rules or "shoulds," and thereby lack compassion for themselves.

Suffice it to say that if a person never got to practice figuring out what they prefer, they might need help with that process of noticing their preferences as part of the foundation for later values work. For these clients, jumping into the "freely chosen" aspect of values work can be not just daunting, but totally foreign. It would be like never hearing music before and then being asked if you prefer Bach or Mozart. So, for folks with this kind of difficulty, you probably want to start with some basic practice learning about the process of preferring and choosing before jumping into an exercise like the Values Card Sort, which may overwhelm the client with too many options. You can read more about helping clients learn the process of choosing and practice noticing preferences in chapter 7. In addition, you can find the clinical vignette of Charlotte that demonstrates one way to help clients with these difficulties gain more practice with noticing preferences and choosing at http://www.newharbinger.com/43218.

Other Tools for Assessing Values

Other tools are also available to begin the process of exploring values. Two such tools are the Valued Living Questionnaire-2 (VLQ-2; Wilson & DuFrene, 2009) and the Bull's-Eye Values Survey (BEVS; Lundgren, Luoma, Dahl, Strosahl, & Melin, 2012), both of which are free to use. The VLQ-2 identifies twelve values domains and asks clients to rate their sense of possibility for change, importance, consistency of action, satisfaction, and concern about each domain. The Bull's-Eye measure is simpler, covers fewer domains, and uses a visual metaphor of an archery target on which clients can mark how "on target" they feel they are living in terms of their values. Both the VLQ-2 and the BEVS are fairly brief, easy-to-use tools that can provide valuable information for where to focus, especially at the onset of therapy. They can also be used to assess change over time.

A tool I tend to use when I want to do more in-depth exploration is the Personal Values Questionnaire (PVQ; Blackledge, Ciarrochi, & Bailey, 2006). The PVQ is pretty long, and for that reason I typically give it to my clients to complete between sessions. The PVQ asks clients to describe what they value in each of nine domains and rate their sense of importance and success in living out their value in each domain. In addition, the PVQ provides information about pliance (whether the supposed value is tied to how the client feels others would view them) and experiential avoidance (whether engaging in the supposed valued action is a way to get rid of some painful emotion, such as shame, anxiety, or guilt). Discussing the client's responses can be extremely useful in providing information about other psychological flexibility repertoires, particularly willingness and defusion, that are likely to come into play in your values work. In general, whenever you choose to use a values assessment process, it's important to discuss the results with the client to facilitate collaborative treatment planning and to ensure that you understand what the client meant by their responses.

There are numerous other values measures available, including ones tailored for specific populations, including adolescents (Ciarrochi, Blackledge, & Heaven, 2006), those struggling with substance use (Miller et al., 2016), and those living with chronic pain (McCracken & Yang, 2006). There are also promising interactive apps clients can use to track their values behavior (see, for instance, O'Connor, Tennyson, Timmons, & McHugh, 2019).

Clinical Indicators of When to Shift (or Return) to Values Work

Values are never very far out of sight in my work with clients. They are always a part of what I'm doing because they are the *why* of what I am doing. But throughout therapy, there are times when it's useful to bring values to the forefront. Three of the most common are:

1. When a client is ambivalent or "unmotivated,"

2. When a client is numb, disconnected, or disengaged, and

3. Before engaging in difficult goals or actions.

In Times of Ambivalence or a Lack of Motivation

Therapy is hard! Of course clients experience ambivalence or what might look like a lack of motivation, "resistance," or even "laziness" at times. Maybe they cancel sessions, don't complete their homework, or tend to spend the session chitchatting about their week. While these things can be frustrating for therapists, myself included, I don't find it very helpful to conceptualize these as being the result of some character flaw in my client. Rather, when I see a lack of action on their part, it's more helpful for me to assume they simply aren't in contact with the catalyst required for action. Values are a key catalyst. When I'm talking about this with trainees, I'll often use the metaphor of the grandmother who finds superhero strength to lift a bus under which her grandchild is trapped. You wouldn't ever call the grandmother who isn't normally lifting buses "resistant" or "lazy." You'd just say that that strength was only available to her when it was needed to save her precious grandchild. Sometimes our clients can feel like we're asking them to lift the bus. We need to make sure they see the kid (values) trapped under it if we want them to be able to do the heavy lifting we're asking of them.

When Clients Are Numb, Disconnected, or Disengaged

We all want to avoid suffering. For many of us, including many of our clients, our lives can become oriented around avoiding pain (experiential avoidance). Sometimes experiential avoidance can be incredibly effective at reducing pain. Avoiding social events can help someone not feel social anxiety. By avoiding relationships, a person isn't likely to feel the fear of rejection, loss, or hurt that are seemingly inevitable parts of being in relationships. But it's often the case that we can't be very selective when it comes to which feelings we get to avoid. Experiential avoidance often results in more pervasive numbness, disconnection, and disengagement (Chawla & Ostafin, 2007).

Moving toward values can help clients become more aware of the cost of their experiential avoidance. Shifting the focus to values intentionally moves the client into the pain they have been "successfully" avoiding. This will often come with a sense of loss, sadness, regret, or shame when they contact the discrepancy between the life they are living and what they would choose to have their life be about. This pain, when embraced—a task made easier or at least honorable by a focus on the values the client is seeking to live out—can help move them toward change. For more on experiential avoidance and connecting with the values that can be found in pain, see chapter 5.

Before Beginning Something Difficult

Clients put their faith and trust in us. They trust us to guide them into very painful and dark places. We do this, hopefully, with the humility that this incredible honor deserves, and with the understanding that it will be worth it in the end. But we can't know what would be "worth it" to our clients without knowing what they would value. It is *their* values that define what would be worth it. When my client and I are approaching something very difficult in our work together—an exposure task, an emotional risk, a big life change, a commitment to some action in service of values that is likely to bring pain—I don't always need to know the perfect route through the darkness and pain. Instead, my most important job is to help us stay focused on the guiding light of values we're moving toward. If I lose sight of that, we're both lost. I can't expect my client to always be able to keep their eye on that light when they are in the midst of doing something very difficult. Instead, it's *my* job to point to the guiding light of the client's values.

Revisiting values before or during something difficult can be a way to remind both you and your client what the hard work is in the service of. It gives honor to the hard journey you're both on. That reminder can help you both find your way in the darkness.

Pitfalls in Orienting Clients Toward Values

As you begin this process of orienting your client toward values, there are some potential pitfalls to look out for. Two of the most common are (1) moving too quickly to naming or identifying values and (2) difficulties around pliance or "shoulds."

Trying to Identify Values Too Quickly

One of the most common trouble spots in these early stages of values work is the drive to identify values too quickly. Clients often want to "figure it out" and it can be tempting for us therapists to go down that path. But doing so too soon can often result in the inflexible behavior that happens when we get attached to particular concepts or words, that is, when we get fused. Clients may jump quickly to identifying their values because they think that's what you want them to do or what they should be able to do. I can't tell you how many times I've had a client say, with a sense a shame, something like, "Isn't it pathetic that I don't know what my values are?" In reality, nothing could be further from the truth. Many of us have had a fair amount of practice identifying goals (though some not even much of that), but little if any support in identifying our values. So, of course most people don't have a clear sense of what would make for a well-lived life for them!

All in all, I am much more interested in clients coming away from a values conversation with a sense of possibility and curiosity than I am in them being able to articulate any specific phrases, statements, or qualities. In fact, I'm often a little leery when a client comes out of an early values conversation with too much certainty about their values. It may be an indication not of values clarity, but rather that they may be approaching the change process just as rigidly and inflexibly as they approach their life in general.

Pliance and "Shoulds"

Some clients have a history that was heavily focused on shoulds and shouldn'ts, leading to behavior that tends to be in reaction to those sorts of external rules. As a result, they may be rule followers, or conversely, react against what they think others expect of them. In values work, these folks will often generate words or phrases that sound like values but are really more about pliance or what they think they *should* do. Pliance and its opposite, counter-pliance, are technical terms from behavior analysis that basically mean that a person's response is determined by what they have learned will please or displease someone else.

This behavior can be tricky to catch, especially when a client is responding based on what might be pleasing to you. While some clients will actually use words like "should" that make it easy to notice the pliance, it's often the case that this rule-governed behavior is more subtle and can only be observed by reading between the lines. For example, I'm often curious when my clients who struggle with body image and food difficulties claim "health" to be a very important value, as more often than not, I've found that this is mostly linked to external messages about things like beauty and desirability, especially since for so many of them "health" seems to be synonymous with weight loss and being thin. Similarly, you may want to probe a little deeper when clients purport to value something that you have indicated you hold dear, as your disclosure may trigger your client to respond out of a desire to please you. For more on working with pliance/counter-pliance in values work, see chapter 7.

Takeaways

- When should values be a part of the work? Hopefully always. It's an ongoing process that informs the rest of therapy.

- Don't focus on trying to "figure out" a client's values. In the early stages, focus more on increasing curiosity, a sense of exploration and possibility, and openness to the idea of choice.

- The Values Card Sort is a great tool to begin to explore the topic of values, but don't rely on it to give you the "answer." Remember, values aren't words; they are ways of living.

- Values aren't "shoulds." Be on the lookout for pliance.

Next Steps

- Pick one client whom you think could benefit from a more values-focused approach. Practice saying out loud how you might introduce the idea to that client. Or, better yet, ask a colleague or friend to role-play the client while you introduce the idea of values.

- Download the values cards from http://www.newharbinger.com/43218. Read through the values and descriptions listed on the various cards, making any changes or additions you feel would be best for how you work. (Remember, these things aren't set in stone. Use whatever would work best for you and the people you serve.) Then, print out the cards.

- Do a Values Card Sort with a friend or colleague, practicing how you might do it with a client. Be sure to ask for feedback that could help you deliver the tool more effectively with a client.

- **Inside-out learning:** Practice doing a Values Card Sort with yourself, focusing on your work-related values. What did you notice about your process of choosing? Do the cards you selected tell you anything about something you might like to change or work on?

CHAPTER 4

Becoming a Truffle Dog:
Guiding Values Exploration

It's a magical world, Hobbes, ol' buddy... Let's go exploring! —Bill Watterson
(The last line of the final *Calvin and Hobbes* comic strip, published December 31, 1995)

I think of doing values exploration as a little like going truffle hunting. Truffles (not the chocolate kind) are an incredibly precious and expensive fungus that can transform even the most ordinary of dishes into something amazing. Truffles are found underground, usually buried under leaves and dirt and other muck, so you can't just go wandering around in the woods and expect to stumble across them. It takes work. You need to know where to look and be familiar with the signs that suggest a truffle might be hidden nearby. One of the best ways to find truffles is with the help of a truffle dog (or pig, but calling myself a truffle pig just doesn't have the same appeal. So, I stick with the truffle dog analogy). Truffle dogs are highly trained and singularly focused on sniffing out truffles. They know where to start digging, can smell and see things that the human truffle hunter can't, and can help guide the truffle hunter to the prized stash.

Values, like truffles, are incredibly precious. They can transform even the most difficult of lives into something extraordinary and profoundly meaningful. But, just like truffles, values are often buried under a lot of muck—pain, fear, or even just the unimportant stuff that can swallow up whole lives. So, it can be helpful to have a guide in our values exploration, someone who is highly trained in sniffing out where the truffles/values might be buried. My job, as a values-guided therapist, is to be like that truffle dog. I don't have all the answers, but I do have enough experience and training in working with values that I know where they tend to be buried and how to help guide my clients to potentially fertile ground. My clients and I work together as a team, exploring the terrain of the client's life in our hunt for what would make that life meaningful.

This chapter is going to focus on training you to be a truffle dog so you can help guide your clients toward living what for them would be a well-lived life.

Two Points of Entry into Values Work

Just as you can find truffles by going to France, Italy, or Oregon, there are different entry points into doing values work. This chapter will focus on helping clients contact their values via the positive, reinforcing properties inherent to values. In this strategy, the goal is to facilitate the client's ability to contact potential instances of values-congruent living by taking them into places in the past, present, or future that are associated with some of the positive feelings many people experience when they are in contact with their values, including tenderness, pride, joy, awe, and more. The positive affect route is usually the most direct and obvious route to values work. You might want to consider this entry point with clients who generally:

- Are able to express and experience positive affect

- Are sensitive to reward or positive reinforcement

- Are at least moderately emotionally expressive

- Are able to access a sense of being at ease, safety, belonging, and/or content-ment, at least in some contexts

- Are *not* profoundly emotionally flat or disconnected, even if they may be emo-tionally guarded or self-protective

- Have been in contact with their values at some point in the past but who have lost contact with those values

Keep in mind that values aren't always associated with warm fuzzy feelings, and this isn't the only route to exploring them. The second entry point into values work is through emotional pain. In the next chapter, I'll talk about how pain can also be a gateway to values work. For now, though, just keep in mind that while the general principles and qualities that guide values exploration remain consistent regardless of the point of entry, some clients may not respond as well to specific strategies that depend on positive feelings as they may not have as much access to those types of experiences.

What Truffles Smell Like: Qualities of Effective Values Conversations

In order to be an effective values explorer, you need to know what contacting values feels like, sounds like, and looks like. One of the biggest stumbling blocks I see in many of the therapists I work with is that they tend to pay a lot of attention to *what* is being said (the content) but not as much attention to *how* it is being said (the process), such as the pace, vocal tone, responsiveness, body postures, and facial expressions. For example, a client may be using words that suggest a goal rather than a value, but if their voice carries a sense of vitality and vulnerability, it may be best to stick with that and dig a little deeper, as there is likely a value underlying that goal that you can uncover. Conversely, a client may be saying words that sound like values, such as, "I want to be patient and loving toward my partner," but if they are said in a resigned manner, monotone voice, or with little accompanying facial expression, you might have more of a "should" on your hands rather than a freely chosen value, and thus you might need to move elsewhere to find more authentic values. Thus, when facilitating values conversations with clients, I often try to pay more attention to the quality of the conversation than the content of the conversation. In fact, sometimes I'll encourage my trainees to watch videotapes of their sessions, if they have them, with the sound off, seeing if they can notice instances when values were more or less present in the room just from the nonverbals. You may even want to try this out with your own sessions.

Because it is the qualities, rather than the content of the conversation, that usually tell you whether you're on the right track in terms of values, this chapter is going to focus on tuning in to those qualities. As a starting place, I'm going to focus on four key qualities very often present in effective values conversations: vitality, present focus, willing vulnerability, and choice (Luoma et al., 2017). These four qualities can be thought of as the primary scent profile of the values truffle. Keep in mind, though, that it is difficult to know what effective values conversations look/sound/feel like without actually experiencing them yourself. That's part of why I have included the "Inside-out learning" suggestions at the end of most chapters. Knowing how to do effective values-guided therapy requires experiential learning as well as intellectual knowledge. It's tough to know what a truffle really smells like or tastes like just from reading descriptions of it; you actually have to spend time smelling and tasting truffles.

Vitality

If you find yourself having a conversation with a client and it feels like they are saying things they have said a million times before, or if it feels boring or rote, then move on; there are likely no truffles to be found there. Values lie in conversations that have a quality of being "alive." They are conversations that have energy or vitality to them that, if you pay close attention, is almost palpable. This doesn't always mean they are pleasant or filled with joy or hope. Sometimes the energy is one of deep longing, sorrow, or loss. But there is a vitality to it regardless of the valence.

The vitality present in effective values conversations also tends to have an expansive quality. There may be a freshness or sense of ongoing discovery. In values exploration, you are exploring what the person would hold most dear, their hopes and dreams, or conversely, what is behind their deepest fears and regrets. This is the stuff of meaningful, vital, vibrant conversations.

This life-filled quality of values conversations also means they are generally not overly intellectual—you aren't caught up in thoughts, or trying to "figure it out." If your values exploration is feeling constricted, overly intellectual, or too much like "problem solving," it's not quite where it needs to be. Back up and go to the last place you sensed some vitality and restart your search there.

There are several nonverbals I look for that signal the presence of vitality in values conversations. Changes in voice inflection and pace (as opposed to being more monotone or having a uniform cadence), a hesitant or exploratory quality characterized by pauses, and even changes in breathing (either holding breath or slightly more shallow, rapid breathing) may all indicate an alive quality to the process. Depending on how emotionally expressive your client is, you'll also often be able to track the vitality in the conversation by your client's affective display, which can include anything from joy, excitement, or pride, to fear, loss, sadness, or longing.

Observing your own reactions can also help you assess the presence or absence of vitality in a values-focused conversation. For example, if you were to watch a video of me during a values conversation that was high in vitality, you'd likely see things like me sitting at the edge of my seat, with an intense expression of interest or curiosity on my face, and you'd probably see my eyes welling up many times.

Present Focus

As noted in chapter 1, values are always immediately available. You don't need to get someplace else or achieve something first before you can start taking action on your values. To value something means you are valuing it now, not in some other time, place, or context. In this way, values conversations are always present focused. We are interested in what the person is valuing and would choose to value in this moment— not at some other point, under other conditions.

Values conversations often tap into the past or the future, but effective ones also have a sense of emotional immediacy. Questions like "What did you dream about for your life when you were young?" or "When you imagine looking back on your life at the end of it, what kind of life would you be proud of having lived?" can be very useful to help with values exploration. But the key to making these questions about the past or future "alive" is to make use of perspective-taking strategies—shifts of perspective in terms of time, place, or person that use language to bring that past or future into the present. By using the tools of language and perspective taking in this way, you can shift from asking the client to simply recall the past or think about an imagined future to a place where the "then/there" is "here/now," one in which you can explore together in the present.

It can be helpful to attend to the tense used in the conversation. Pay attention to whether you and your client are talking in the past, future, or conditional tense (that is, speculating about a possible past/future and using if-then statements). Notice the difference between the following three examples:

Therapist: Think back to that time we talked about before, during college, when you said you felt more alive and life was more meaningful to you. See if you can put yourself back there. If that person were talking to me, what would they say were some of the things that matter to them? (*In addition to shifting the time perspective by asking the client to put themselves back in another time, referring to the client in the third person facilitates a shift in the person's perspective.*)

Example A: Present tense.

Client: I'd say that I really care about making a difference. I don't really know exactly how, but I know my life means more than just making money. More of my time is spent doing things I think have a positive impact rather than just trying to get ahead.

Example B: Past tense.

Client: I used to care about making a difference. Back then I used to spend a lot of time doing things I thought would make a positive impact even if they didn't really get me ahead in the world.

Example C: Conditional tense.

Client: Back then I would have liked to have made a difference if I had known how.

Can you tell the difference in how each of these conversations would feel in the therapy room? In example A, the client is speaking from the "now" even though it is about something that occurred in the past. Sometimes even coaching the client directly to speak in the present tense can bring things more into the present moment.

A lack of present-moment focus can also be signaled by talk of some imagined future. This is often accompanied by the use of the conditional tense (if/then), and frequently an "away" agenda (experiential avoidance) starts creeping into the conversation. When you see this happen, it can be helpful to bring the conversation back to the present by helping the client notice what they are actually valuing in the here-and-now. Here's an example of how that conversation might go. We'll pick up the conversation after the client has already identified living a life of "courage" as an important direction:

Therapist: I can really see that living courageously is something that you would choose.

Client: Absolutely! That's the reason why I'm here to work on my anxiety.

Therapist: Sorry, you lost me there. You were talking about how important it would be for you to focus on living courageously, but then it seemed like you were saying you wanted to focus on living without anxiety. Can you help me see how those things are related to you?

Client: I want to get my anxiety under control so then I'll be able to be more courageous. *(They are now using the conditional tense by saying they would like to value courage if/when anxiety is under control.)*

Therapist: So, it sounds like, if you could choose, you think you would want to live courageously at some future point, after other things have hopefully happened. But right now, in the life you actually have, you would instead choose to value anxiety, or more specifically, getting rid of anxiety, over valuing courage? Is that right?

In this brief example, the client engages in a relatively subtle, but common shift out of valuing in the present moment. By asking questions that help the client observe what they are valuing right now, you can bring the conversation back to the present. If values are patterns of behavior, then it is important to help the client learn to track what they are actually valuing through their actions in the present so they can evaluate whether or not that aligns with what they would choose to value.

Willing Vulnerability

Where are you most vulnerable? Think about the times in your life when you have been most hurt. I can almost guarantee that it involved something or someone you cared deeply about. I know that's certainly the case for me. Caring deeply opens us up and exposes our most tender parts. If someone is in contact with something they care deeply about, they are vulnerable, and that vulnerability will be present in the conversation. Life is contained in that vulnerability. There can be an incredible tenderness in those moments. It can be bittersweet, especially if the person's behaviors are not fully in line with what they would want to matter to them. For example, it's bittersweet to contact how much you care about being present for your children when you are also faced with the fact that you rarely see them because you are working eighty hours a week.

The vulnerability that is present during effective values conversations is a particular kind of vulnerability: it's *willing* vulnerability. In that willingness is often an incredible power, courage, or fierceness. Most of the people I serve, and probably many of your clients as well, have been deeply harmed in their lives. They have been victimized and exploited. They have been taken advantage of and have felt intensely helpless. That kind of vulnerability comes from being in a position of powerlessness and my clients don't need any more practice with that kind of vulnerability. *Willing* vulnerability is something altogether different. I'm talking about the fierce, powerful, "Hell yeah, let's do this!" kind of vulnerability that comes when someone is willing to do whatever it takes to stand up for what is most dear.

This kind of vulnerability is awe-inspiring to me. As Brené Brown said, "Vulnerability is our most accurate measurement of courage" (Brown, 2012). I am privileged to get to work with some pretty damn courageous people. My client Katie was just such a person.

CLINICAL EXAMPLE: KATIE

Katie's history of intense abuse and neglect had taught her that you can't rely on anyone to stick around or be kind to you, let alone love you. For the first many months of our work together, she was consistently surprised when I showed up to session and didn't "fire" her. With those intense fears of being unlovable and "disposable," you can imagine how difficult it was for her to be in intimate relationships.

At some point during our values-guided therapy together, Katie decided that she was going to start the training to become a foster parent. And she didn't just want to be any foster parent. She planned to be a foster parent to older kids and teenagers. When I asked her why teenagers, she said, "Because those are the ones who need to be loved the most." Get that—here was a woman who had come to me because she was so terrified of being rejected and unlovable, and now she was *willingly* committing to a life in which she was pretty much guaranteed to feel, at times at least, rejected and the object of anger and resentment (I mean, have you ever met any teenagers?). And she knew this. She had no illusions about the process. We had long conversations about what it would be like for her when a foster child she had been caring for left. She also knew that many would have difficulties with attachment or effectively showing their love. Yet still, her value of lovingly caring for these kids was way more important to her than making sure she never felt rejected. How could you not feel awe in the face of that? That is the kind of power and courage that is evident in willing vulnerability.

It's important to remember that the quality we are looking for is *willing* vulnerability. Vulnerability in the absence of willingness is probably more a sign of powerlessness than it is an indication of valued action. Katie's decision to willingly open herself up to feeling the very things she was most afraid of feeling came from a place of power. She wasn't just recreating old patterns of being in relationships with others who weren't able to show her love. Rather, her decision was the result of her reclaiming power in her life by choosing to act on what was most important to her and she was willingly, in the "*Absolutely!*" kind of way, allowing herself to experience the vulnerability that comes with that.

The willing part is key because values are about behavior. The vulnerability is the experience and willingness is the behavior. We might have a sense we could be hurt, that something painful could happen, and yet we freely accept that risk in the service of something that is greater, more encompassing, or more important. Our values create this more encompassing experience and motivate the choosing of vulnerability. Therefore, willing vulnerability is a sign that values are present.

When looking for the quality of willing vulnerability, you might also examine your own reactions for clues. For example, if the willing vulnerability has a more tender quality, I will typically notice feeling compassion or, in cases where the willing vulnerability is more bittersweet, sadness is often present for me. But the most common reaction I have when there is willing vulnerability in the room is one of awe, humility, and inspiration. How could you not be in awe of courageous willing vulnerability like Katie's and that of the countless other clients I have the privilege of serving?

Choice

When my niece Josephine was a toddler, I used to make up stories for her. She got to choose the genre, the setting, and the main character (which, unsurprisingly, was often "a young girl named Josie") and then I would craft a story based on her criteria. I loved watching the look on her face as she thought about what she wanted her story to include—anything was possible to her. It's the same look kids have when they are allowed to dream big. It's as if life presents itself as an infinite array of possible options from which they can have free choice.

Then over time, life tends to shrink us. We begin to limit what we think our lives can be about, what we imagine is available to us, who we imagine we can be. This happens very early on for some, while others of us get to bask in "anything is possible for me" a little longer. It's often subtle and we usually don't even notice it's happening, but it happens all the same.

That "dreaming big" look Josephine used to get on her face is the look I'm searching for during values exploration. It's a look of "What, you mean if *anything* was possible?" My job is to create a world for my client to enter into, even if it's only temporary, in which life never shrank, but instead all possibilities of life are available to them. In this world, there is no right/wrong, should/shouldn't, shame, external rules, constricting logic or history, or fear limiting their options.

It is important to not get into a philosophical debate with your client (or your own mind) about whether or not it is actually "true" that there is free choice. When I have my behaviorist hat on, it looks to me like we are all largely products of our learning history. However, that's not a very useful hat to wear when I'm trying to explore values with clients. So, I choose to wear the free choice of infinite possibility hat during those times. What you or your client *believe* about free choice is somewhat irrelevant; what is important is that you help your client enter into a world where free choice does exist, to see what arises. What would they actually choose to value *if* it were the case that they could choose anything? It's a remarkable, sometimes freeing, sometimes overwhelming question to explore.

Likewise, we also aren't really interested in debating whether or not the person can actually have what they would choose. Values aren't about getting to some destination or obtaining something; they are about the journey. Certain goals, actions, or outcomes might not be available to us, but the valued direction is always possible. If you find yourself in a conversation about whether something is or is not possible, it's likely a sign that choice is not present and you need to reorient.

As I talked about in chapter 3 and exemplified in the case example of Charlotte (see http://www.newharbinger.com/43218), some people have had little practice in choosing. Maybe they grew up in a more rigid environment in which there were very clear black-and-white rules to be followed. Or maybe they never had anyone around them who showed much interest in them or asked them questions about what their own thoughts, preferences, or choices would be. For clients who have little practice knowing their own preferences or desires, choosing between too many options can be overwhelming at first and unlikely to result in any learning. In these cases, it's fine to narrow down the choices a bit at the start, for example, by using something like the Values Card Sort exercise in the previous chapter. The idea is just to have the sense that the person is actually experiencing the values exploration process as a process of freely choosing. That's the quality you're going for and you can always work up to expanding the choices available to your client as it seems workable.

Practice: Identifying Vitality, Present Focus, Willing Vulnerability, and Choice

Many of the qualities present in effective values conversations are nonverbal, or at least they can't be conveyed simply through words in a transcript. So, in order for you to practice identifying these qualities, we have created a role-play of a values conversation video for you to work with. To watch the video, go to http://www.newharbinger .com/43218. As you watch it, use the accompanying "Four Qualities of Effective Values Conversations" handout (http://www.newharbinger.com/43218) to code the presence of vitality, present moment, willing vulnerability, and choice in the role-play. Once you've given it a shot, compare what you observed with our responses that can be found at the bottom of the handout.

Deeper Values Exploration

Now you hopefully have a sense of the qualities that can guide the direction of your values conversation. When you see these qualities in the room, you're probably on the right track. Then it's time to go deeper, moving from the more general and ambiguous to the specific and rich.

Exploration Versus Identification

As we start digging deeper into values work with a client, it's important we don't lose what is essential in this work. Humans love to figure things out. We like to name things, categorize them, and put them in boxes. This is a very normal and often useful tendency of our species. But sometimes in our quest to "identify" or put a word to our values, we can lose what is essential and they become nothing more than words.

It is all too easy for the words we use to identify our values to begin to replace our experience of actually living out that valued life. For this reason, once a client has a general idea of what I'm talking about by "values" and the process of choosing, I try to hold off on having the client identify specific values words. Instead, I generally work with the client to paint me a metaphorical (or even literal in some instances) picture of what it looks like when they are living out their values. I want us to get to know values from the inside out. I don't care so much whether we know what it's called. I want us to have a deeper sense of it, what qualities it possesses. You might think of this as the difference between saying the word "Grand Canyon" versus seeing a picture of the Grand Canyon or, even better yet, standing on the edge of the North Rim of the Grand Canyon, actually experiencing it.

To do this, I often try to step outside of just using words in my values exploration. Sometimes I ask clients to draw me a picture or bring in a photograph from their life or even a picture from a magazine that seems to represent some of the qualities they think would be embodied in a meaningful, well-lived life. I've also asked clients to bring in poems or songs because, although these are words, words in songs and poetry often tend to function more like pictures or metaphors. Very often I will also use visualization exercises to help clients explore their values.

Tool: Sweet Spot Exercise

The Sweet Spot is a great visualization exercise that can facilitate deeper values exploration. In it, the therapist leads the client through an eyes-closed exercise in which they are asked to recall a time in the past when they have been in contact with the positive affect that is often, though certainly not always, associated with valued living. The basic idea behind the Sweet Spot exercise is to create a context where you and your client can step into a world in which their values are clearly present and being lived out. We do this by shifting perspective such that both of you are transported to a time in the past. The Sweet Spot can help bring values to life so that you and your client can explore valued living experientially.

This is an exercise I often use toward the beginning of therapy, but typically after my client and I have already collaborated around a treatment plan and established initial values-based therapy goals. As such, I often have a general sense of what area or valued domain(s) the client is most interested in working on by the time we embark on the Sweet Spot exercise. I inevitably find myself returning to the images and emotions that showed up during the exercise (or sometimes even repeating the exercise itself) throughout the course of therapy. Moving toward the specific, detailed, and concrete tends to be more evocative, and thereby serves to bring the client into contact with the intrinsically reinforcing properties of values. Thus, contacting values in this way can serve as a motivator to persist when faced with difficult tasks (such as exposure work, confronting regrets, or forgiveness of self and others) to come later in therapy.

I have found this to be a particularly useful exercise for clients who have been in more contact with their values at one point in their lives, but who may have moved away from those ways of living that were important and meaningful to them. Alternatively, this can also be helpful for individuals who are more closely in contact with their values in one domain but not others. In that case, you can explore the domain in which they are more connected with their values during the exercise, reflecting on what was present in that "sweet spot" and what that might suggest about the other valued domain(s) that are the focus of your treatment plan.

INSTRUCTIONS FOR THE SWEET SPOT EXERCISE

The variation for the Sweet Spot described below can last anywhere from about fifteen minutes to an entire session. At the end of this section there is also a sample script so you can have a sense of what it might look like all put together. This is but one of many different variations of this classic ACT exercise, others of which can be found in other texts (see Stoddard & Afari, 2014; Wilson & DuFrene, 2009; Wilson & Sandoz, 2008). However you decide to use the exercise, remember to keep your nose to the ground for the four qualities we're looking for in these values conversations (vitality, present focus, willing vulnerability, and choice). Let those always guide your exploration.

Step 1: Identify a valued domain. I find it useful to have already identified a valued domain, such as work, friendship, family, or health, that the client would want to focus on before entering the eyes-closed portion of the exercise. You might already know this from your treatment plan, or you could use one of the assessment measures mentioned in chapter 3, such as the VLQ-2 (Wilson & DuFrene, 2009) or the BEVS (Lundgren et al., 2012) to identify a priority domain to target. Or you could simply ask the client what domain they would want to focus on during the exercise.

Step 2: Provide an introduction and get permission. Once you have a sense of what area you're going to be exploring, provide a brief introduction of the exercise to your client. You will likely need to give them some explanation of what is meant by a "sweet spot," since that term is somewhat amorphous. As this exercise is trying to access values through their positively reinforcing qualities, your description of what a "sweet spot" is will likely rely on feeling words. You can describe a sweet spot as a moment in their life that had a sense of completeness to it, or maybe there was something precious or tender or simply "sweet" about it. Depending on the client, I will frequently also give an example from my own life at this point. This self-disclosure serves at least two functions in this context. One, I am giving a real-world example of a "sweet spot," and two, it's an opportunity for me to share some of my values with the client, which can be particularly helpful if the values disclosed are connected to my relationship with my client or our work together. (See chapter 9 for more about therapist self-disclosure of values.)

It can be important to make it clear that a sweet spot does not have to be a big moment. In fact, they are often very simple, even ordinary moments. The exercise doesn't need to focus on an intense emotional experience (what my clients sometimes call a "peak experience"), which tends to be associated with feelings of elation, thrill, excitement, or mastery. In fact, I've often found it most effective when the visualization focuses on more subtle emotional experiences, ones that may involve a sense of belonging or connectedness. These are often times when the person was engaged with someone or something they really care about. They tend to be times of tenderness, contentment, or a sense of meaning or completeness. For more about the distinction between these different types of positive affect experiences, see the troubleshooting section later in this chapter.

Step 3: Do an eyes-closed visualization. In this part of the exercise, you guide your client to inhabit their sweet spot memory. You can begin with some mindfulness or centering instructions to help the client get in contact with their experience in the moment. Then, typically with their eyes closed, you ask them to recall a sweet spot memory that is within the domain you've decided to focus on. You might ask them to provide some indication (such as a nod or a slight raise of their hand) to indicate when they have been able to imagine themselves in the moment of the sweet spot. At that point, your task is to help them explore the scene a bit from the inside. What do they see? What do they feel or hear or smell in this place? Have them notice what they are doing in the scene. And more than just *what* they are doing, help them contact the qualities of their action, *how* they are behaving. You can also ask them to engage in some shifts of perspective, for example, taking the perspective of an observer. As they are watching this scene, how do they feel about the person that they are in the image? How would they describe this person they are watching?

During this stage, the client's task isn't to describe anything to you and often they aren't saying anything at all. But you want to be watching their nonverbals as this can help you have a sense of whether things are on track. If you are unsure whether they are following along, you can simply check in from time to time about what they are experiencing. The main things to remember are to go slow, linger, and help the client not just remember, but actually *recontact* being in that sweet spot.

Step 4: Debrief. This is the stage when you ask the client to bring you into the sweet spot they have just been exploring (you can do this before or after you ask them to open their eyes). A useful way to prompt this is to say something like, "I really want to understand what it's like for you. Help me see what that sweet spot is like from behind your eyes. Paint the picture for me." You can ask questions to help with the reflection or you can leave it largely open-ended, allowing the client to share whatever comes up. Try not to focus on getting the client to name a value or come to some conclusion. Your job is simply to be present and see if you can notice hints of the sweet spot emerging. Be on the lookout for the four values qualities. Pay particular attention to elements of the scene that have more vitality or a sense of choice or where willing vulnerability seems to show up. When you see those places, ask the client to go into more detail, to dig around a bit. This is the stuff of truffles!

WRAP-UP AND HOMEWORK

Often, I've found there isn't much need to verbally summarize this exercise. However, it can be helpful to say something like, "Values can be found in places like the sweet spot we just explored. By becoming more familiar with them, you will start to be able to notice when qualities that were present in that sweet spot are present in other moments of your life. This can serve as an indicator of what directions you might want to orient your life toward." Here are a few out-of-session practices you might suggest to your client to build on the experience:

- Share your sweet spot with a trusted loved one as a way of connecting (if that would be a valued action) and also further exploring the qualities of the sweet spot.

- See if you can notice one thing each day in your everyday life that was reminiscent in some way of the sweet spot. Write those down and bring them to the next session.

- Spend some time drawing or writing about your sweet spot as a way to further explore it.

- Consider what elements of the sweet spot you could strip away and still have it be a "sweet spot." (Here we're trying to get down to the essential qualities beyond the logistical details.)

TROUBLESHOOTING THE SWEET SPOT EXERCISE

While the Sweet Spot exercise is very impactful for many clients, this exercise doesn't hit home for everyone. More than any of the other exercises in this book, I've found the Sweet Spot exercise to be either a "love it" or "hate it" kind of exercise. When it works, it can be incredibly powerful. However, there are other times when it really hasn't worked to serve its intended function of helping the person contact the reinforcing properties of values. Therefore, with this exercise especially, I think it's very important to consider contextual factors before deciding to try it out with a client.

Clients with low levels of positive affect. In particular, this can be a difficult exercise for clients who have more limited access to positive affect, for example, clients we might describe as alexithymic or who are less sensitive to positive reinforcement or reward. For these individuals, even when they can connect with a "sweet spot," they don't tend to experience much, if any, emotional response to the stimulus. This can result in the client feeling shamed by their response, or lack of response, to the exercise. Alternatively, it can reinforce unhelpful stories the client may be attached to, like "There's something wrong with me" or "I knew I was a cold and heartless person." The result is that the exercise doesn't serve the main function we are wanting, which is to help the individual get in contact with the reinforcing properties of values-consistent behavior.

Clients unable to recall positive memories. Relatedly, this may not be the best exercise for clients who have difficulty recalling anything positive, sweet, or tender about their history or for whom being vulnerable was associated with danger, as in the case of clients with intense abuse histories. If, when a client thinks about their life or their history, it is so filled with pain (abuse, shame, regret, and so on) that the exercise immediately triggers these things and not a sweet spot, then this may be too advanced for them, at least in the beginning. It's not that these painful feelings are harmful; it's just that if that's what gets evoked by this exercise, then it probably won't serve its intended function. You may want to wait until later when the therapy relationship feels more secure and when you probably have a good sense for at least one sweet spot stimulus you can use. Or maybe you need to work on creating sweet spots with the individual first. For some clients, it may be that the only sweet spot they can connect with is something that happened in your relationship with them. In any case, give it time.

Reward-focused clients. Other modifications are sometimes needed for clients who are overly focused on consequences related to reward and the intense feelings that come from reward. These are often clients who would identify as "overachievers," "workaholics," or "adrenaline chasers." Without some additional instruction, these clients will often focus their sweet spot on "grand" moments associated with more intense, though often short-lived, positive affect: for example, summitting a mountain, winning the big election, or publishing their first novel. Clients sometimes refer to these as "peak experiences." The problem with focusing the sweet spot on these "peak experiences" is that it tends to feed these clients' narrowness of focus, a focus that is often fueled by experiential avoidance and fusion. In particular, this narrowness of focus tends to get in the way of their ability to experience the reinforcing consequences of what are often more subtle or lower intensity social experiences involving bonding, connection, or intimacy.

For rigidly reward-focused clients, it may be helpful to do a little educating about the different types of reinforcers before beginning the Sweet Spot exercise. For example, it can be helpful with these clients to make a distinction between what I refer to as reward-based reinforcers, which have to do with achievement, mastery, winning, or accomplishment, versus more social or relational reinforcers. The former set are often more intense and are associated with higher arousal, whereas the second set are more "laid-back" and are associated with lower arousal. Examples of social reinforcers might be having your kids crawl in bed with you early on a Sunday morning, or sitting by the side of the lake at the end of a great hike with your best friend appreciating the adventures you've shared together over the years. These types of reinforcers relate to neurophysiological systems known to regulate experiences of safeness and contentment (Gilbert, 2010) and social engagement (Porges, 2003), or as one of my dog-loving clients described it, they are the "roll over and get your belly scratched" kind of reinforcer. They tend to be associated with qualities of tenderness, belonging, contentment, and a sense of safeness or completeness, as opposed to the excitement or adrenaline rush more often found with reward-based reinforcers. So, if you're working with someone who tends to spend a lot of time pursuing more intense, reward-based reinforcers but doesn't have much access to or experience with these other types of reinforcers, you may first want to see whether you can identify realms in their life when they are more at ease or, in the words of my client, have the experience of "getting their belly scratched" to see whether there is a sweet spot to explore there.

CLINICAL EXAMPLE: JACKIE

Jackie first presented in therapy as a guarded and angry eighteen-year-old who had just been released from the hospital following her second suicide attempt. Our first few sessions were a little rough, with both of us trying to feel each other out. But I quickly realized that, in addition to all the black eyeliner and "don't #$%@ with me" mannerisms that seemed to function to guard herself from others, Jackie had one of the biggest hearts of anyone I've ever had the privilege of working with. This was a young woman who felt and cared intensely, but who had also felt repeatedly disappointed in and rejected by the people in her life.

The following vignette comes from about our fifth or sixth session. We had already made significant progress in building a strong therapeutic relationship. In our collaborative treatment planning, we had decided to focus primarily on the domain of her relationships, both with peers and with her family. I used the Sweet Spot exercise to help us explore what valued living in that domain might look like for her.

Therapist: (Step 1: Identify a domain) So Jackie, we've talked about how you'd like our work together to be, at least in part, in the service of helping you have more meaningful, satisfying relationships and helping you be more of the person you'd want to be in your relationships. *(Jackie had a lot of shame about how she had behaved in past relationships and also how she had, as she saw it, "allowed herself" to be treated in many of those relationships.)* I want us to both get a better sense of what that might look like for you. So I thought we could do an eyes-closed exercise to get a better picture of what it's like when you're at your best in relationships and what it looks like when your relationships are more satisfying and meaningful for you.

Client: Sure, that's fine.

Therapist: (Step 2: Introduction) Great, so I'm going to lead you through an exercise where I'll ask you to identify a sweet spot you can recall in one of your relationships.

Client: What the hell is a sweet spot?

Therapist: I know, kind of a hokey word, but that's what those times feel like to me. Maybe you can come up with a different word. But for me, a "sweet spot" is one of those precious moments in your life when, if you were to pause to look at it, you'd feel touched in some way. It's a little hard for me to describe because it's kind of more of a felt thing. It's just one of those moments when you might have a heartfelt sense of "Ah, this is it." You might feel a sense of tenderness or contentment or simply completeness. And it doesn't have to be anything big. Often sweet spots are very simple, a tender moment that seems to encompass so much more than words can describe. Do you have a sense of what I'm talking about?

Client: I'm not really sure. Maybe.

Therapist: Would you want me to give you an example from my own life?

Client: Yeah, that would be nice. (*In our previous interactions, Jackie seemed to appreciate and respond well to my willingness to share and be vulnerable, something that she hadn't experienced in prior therapies. Therefore, I felt offering such self-disclosure might be useful in this case.*)

Therapist: Sure thing. As you know, some of the most important relationships I have had are those with the dogs I have shared my life with. (*The care for non-human animals was something we had in common and had previously connected around. I also felt my values around being committed and loyal in those relationships with my dogs would be applicable to our therapeutic relationship. So that is why I chose to share this sweet spot in particular with her.*) Here's one of my sweet spots related to that. In this sweet spot image, it is very early on a cold and foggy morning. It is still dark outside and my dog Grace and I are at the corner of 15th and Highland about forty-five minutes into our morning exercise walk. (*I'm being very specific and detailed because that specificity tends to be more evocative.*) I look down at her and she's looking up at me, wagging her tail. I pause on the corner to give her a little treat and I stroke her on her back. And in that moment, I see myself caring well for her, being loyal and committed to caring for this creature that is relying on me. That moment needs nothing. I don't need to be any different in that moment. That moment represents me at my best in terms of being committed, loyal, and caring well for this pup I love. (*Another advantage of talking about your own sweet spot is that it can start to elicit some of the qualities of an effective values conversation and set the stage for the client's sweet spot.*)

Client: Okay, so you're right. That is sweet.

Therapist: Thanks. I think so too. But your sweet spot doesn't have to be like mine. There is no right or wrong here. It doesn't have to be anything big either.

It's just important that you recall something specific, a specific instance or image. And all I want us to do is explore what that sweet spot is like, as if we were looking at a painting of it and trying to fully take it all in.

Client: So how do I do this?

Therapist: I'm going to guide you through some steps that will help you hopefully bring to mind an image of a scene that might be a sweet spot for you in your relationships. You don't need to say anything. I'll just help you linger there a bit and see what you can notice. Whatever comes up is just right. Then, after a while, I'll ask you what, if anything, you would choose to share with me from what you saw and experienced. How does that sound?

Client: Sounds good.

Now I moved into step 3 of the sweet spot exercise, the eyes-closed exercise.

Therapist: All right, just allow yourself to sit comfortably, maybe with your feet on the ground. Gently let your eyes close... *(I led her through a few minutes of mindfulness practice to help her center herself in the present moment. Throughout the remaining part of the exercise, I paused frequently to let her reflect on her experience.)* Now I'd like you to imagine that in front of you there is a file cabinet. There are lots of drawers in this file cabinet. Each drawer is labeled with one of the important relationships in your life. *(In this context with Jackie it was helpful to give her some guidance around narrowing down her choices a bit.)* One says "Mom," another says "Susan" *(her sister)*. The one below says "Sam" *(her former best friend)*, and one says "Blu" *(her beloved dog)*. Just notice what other drawers are labeled *(pause)*. Now notice what it feels like to stand in front of this file cabinet and choose which drawer you will open in a moment. *(Here I'm helping her track the process of choosing.)* Do you feel drawn to open one drawer, a resistance to opening another? Just notice what shows up for you.

Now I'd like you to imagine that you open that drawer you chose. Feel the weight of the drawer in your hand. Hear it open. Notice what your heart is doing right now, what sensations are going through your body, what thoughts your mind is giving you...

And then you reach in to that drawer and in the drawer is a picture, a picture of a sweet spot in that relationship. Whenever you can start to see the picture, just nod your head so I'll know... *(Client nods.)*

Great. Now take that picture out of the file cabinet. Feel it in your hands. Notice the look on your face in that picture. Let yourself notice the details surrounding you.

Now, I want you to see if it's possible for you to enter into that picture. Go from looking at the picture to being transported into the scene. You're now inhabiting that scene. What do you see? Notice the sensations that you feel on your own skin in that place. If you're outdoors, perhaps you feel a slight breeze. If you are with a person or with Blu, see if you can notice any warmth from standing near them or maybe their scent or the smell of this place you are in. Let it be as if every cell in your body can feel what it is like to be in that place. Just take a moment to let yourself be absorbed in it, to bask in the presence of this scene.

And now, focus on how *you* are in that moment. Notice the quality of your actions. As you are standing in that place, notice what is important to you right at that moment, that moment that doesn't need anything else to be complete, where you don't need to be anyone else, anywhere else. *(You could spend more time guiding the client to visualize the scene depending upon what you thought was needed.)*

Now, Jackie, I'm going to ask you to bring your awareness back to your body right now in this moment. Keeping your eyes closed, notice what you are experiencing now after having spent some time in this sweet spot. Notice what you are feeling, if you have any longings or urges. Consider whether those feelings tell you anything about what truly matters to you. Did being in that sweet spot tell you anything about what really is meaningful for you in your relationships, what you want to be about in your relationships?

After this I went on to ask Jackie to open her eyes and share with me what she noticed, asking about details of the scene so I could figuratively enter it as well. We also discussed what she had felt in reaction to the scene and any thoughts that came up for her in response. Then, as a way to continue the work beyond the session, I asked Jackie, an artist, to draw a picture of her sweet spot. The next session she brought in a painting she had made that represented her experience of the sweet spot. She brought that painting to almost every session we had thereafter and we used it throughout the rest of therapy together as a guide and reminder of what our work was in the service of.

Pitfalls in Beginning Values Exploration

As you and your client begin the values exploration process together, here are a few common pitfalls that might pull you off course.

Moving Too Quickly from Exploring to Naming

Many therapists I work with have the urge to move too quickly into having the client come up with descriptive terms or words for their values (for example, love, compassion, adventure) and in doing so, lose the essential quality of valuing. This is important because values provide the positive motivation for our clients to persist or change as needed and do the hard work of therapy (and life). Values aren't a very powerful reinforcer if all you know about them is their name. You need to have been in contact with them, to know what it feels like to live them, in order to be able to utilize their full power. So, if you walk out of your first or even your tenth values exploration session with the client not being able to name their values, you might just be on exactly the right track!

Expecting Only "Positive" Feelings

Even though we've talked a lot in this chapter about how valued living, and especially things like "sweet spots," are often associated with positive affect, values aren't feelings any more than they are words. Often, we get to experience pleasant feelings such as joy, contentment, or pride when we are living out our values. Often, we do not. For example, in the sweet spot example I shared with Jackie, in those moments at 5:30 in the morning when I'm out exercising with Grace, I'm rarely feeling much of anything positive. In the split second when I pause to look down at Grace and notice the valued action I'm engaged in, I do often feel a sense of pride or contentment. But I'm also usually feeling irritated, tired, cold, and uncomfortable. I exercise with her not because doing so is enjoyable for me (trust me on this one!). Instead, I do it because I would choose to live a life where I care well for the "critters in my pack" (both human and nonhuman). The values set the direction. The actual steps involved in the journey are invariably a mixed bag emotionally, as is any extended journey. So be cautious that you don't imply to your client that valued living only involves positive feelings and that if they aren't feeling something "positive" then it must not be an authentic value.

Following the Rules and Not the Qualities

You can do the Sweet Spot exercise (or for that matter any of the exercises in this book) exactly as described and be completely off base. Focusing too much on doing the exercise according to the rules can make you rigid and unresponsive to your client. Yes, it's fine to follow a script, especially at first, but also make sure you don't lose sight of the qualities of effective values conversations. Those qualities should be your guide over any script or set of steps. The script is a guide, but it's not a map to the truffle. If you're trying out the Sweet Spot exercise from this chapter and it flops, start by asking yourself which, if any, of the four values qualities were present and which were absent from your conversation. That will give you a place to focus as you continue your values exploration with that client.

Takeaways

This chapter covers much of what I think is the hardest stuff to master when it comes to doing values work. So, be kind to yourself and be patient; this isn't easy stuff. Below are a few things to keep in mind as you make your way out into this realm of values exploration.

- Pay more attention to the "how" (the qualities) than the "what" (the content) of your values conversations. Pay particular attention to nonverbal cues. Use your body and tone/pacing of voice to evoke and heighten desired qualities.

- Get specific and bring it into the now. You want to bring the values into the room so you and your client can explore what that world looks like.

- Let go of trying to identify values words. Rather than focusing on coming up with words for values, you're trying to paint a whole picture of what living a valued life would be for this person specifically.

- If the client does come up with values words, be curious about what kind of life the words point to. Valued action is what creates a life well lived. For example, what is "compassion" as a lived experience? What does it feel like? Look like? What are they doing when they are living compassionately? What are they not doing?

Next Steps

- Choose one of the four values qualities discussed in this chapter (vitality, present moment, willing vulnerability, and choice) to focus on in one of your therapy sessions this week. See if you can facilitate the conversation in such a way as to evoke that quality in your conversation. What impact do you think that had on the conversation?

- Practice leading a colleague or friend through the Sweet Spot exercise. Get feedback at the end on their experience of it. What worked for them, and what didn't? Consider how this might influence how you would do it with a client.

- Pick a session with a client that didn't seem to go as well as you had hoped this week. Spend some time considering what you might have done to evoke more willing vulnerability, vitality, a sense of choice, or a focus on the present moment to shift the conversation.

- **Inside-out learning:** Pick a valued domain of your life (such as work, family relationships, or health) you'd like to focus on and then lead yourself through the eyes-closed portion of the Sweet Spot exercise. After you've gone through the visualization, spend some time reflecting or writing about what showed up for you during the exercise. How would you describe the quality of your actions as you observed yourself in the scene? Do you notice having any urges or longings after doing the exercise? Are there any actions you might want to take that emerged from this exercise (even really small ones)? If so, what would be a next step?

CHAPTER 5

Finding Values in Pain

If there is a meaning in life at all, then there must be a meaning in suffering.
—Viktor Frankl

As values-guided therapists, we often help our clients contact values through their positively reinforcing qualities, which are frequently accompanied by feelings like joy, connection, pride, or fondness. Such was the focus of the previous chapter. However, values can also be found in the painful moments of life. In fact, it is often times of pain that provide the most powerful doorways to contacting what really matters. Sadness and longing can help us contact values around connection, belonging, or contribution. Anger can help us connect with values related to making a difference in the world or standing up for what we feel is right. Even something as painful as shame can serve to remind us of values we have related to living in harmony with others or our planet. All the qualities of effective values conversations, including a sense of choice, willing vulnerability, vitality, and a focus on the present moment, can be found in pain as much as they can in times of joy or tenderness. Attending to our suffering in open and mindful ways can teach us much about who we are and who we wish to be in this world.

Indeed, implying that positive affect always accompanies valuing can foster avoidance of the sadness, grief, disappointment, anxiety, anger, or other painful emotions that may lie on the road toward valued living. Chasing positive affect may take you in exactly the wrong direction when painful experiences are signposts to where values lie. Therefore, developing ways to understand and work with emotional pain is essential if your therapy is to be anchored by values. In this chapter, we'll explore how emotional pain and values are connected; when you might want to use pain, rather than positive affect, to explore values; and how to foster the qualities that make for effective values conversation even in times when emotional pain is what is most present.

When Pain Guides Us to What Matters Most

Choice, willing vulnerability, vitality, and a focus on the present moment lead us to values regardless of the terrain we are exploring. While these qualities are our guides to exploring values in both the painful and the sweeter times of life, my experience has been that exploring values using pain as the entry point tends to be somewhat less structured than when we enter via positive affect. Opportunities to explore values often emerge organically when painful affect arises as a client talks about troubling experiences in the presence of a careful listener. Knowing that these painful experiences can be doorways to new possibilities, the values-guided therapist can take advantage of spontaneously arising pain by exploring it while keeping an eye out for the four qualities that we use to guide that work. Thus, as you are exploring values with your clients, make sure that you remain flexible and are able to shift course, so that you can move toward and open up to emotional pain when it does emerge.

Clients for Whom Pain May Be the Best Route to Values

Learning to find the values in pain is essential when working with any client. However, for some clients, emotional pain may be the *most* accessible entry point to values exploration. For those clients, you may want to intentionally use pain as the primary jumping-off point for your values exploration as opposed to beginning by exploring the positive affect route covered in chapter 4. In particular, you might consider emotional pain as the preferred entry point for values exploration for clients who:

- Experience relatively low levels of positive affect

- Are less reward sensitive or are more sensitive to aversive contingencies than they are to appetitive contingencies

- Are relatively unexpressive, flat, or emotionally disconnected

- Have difficulty feeling much, if any, sense of ease, safety, belonging, or contentment, especially with others

When working with these clients, exercises like the Sweet Spot (chapter 4) or other stimuli intended to evoke positively valanced emotions can be tricky. That's not to say it isn't possible, and even important at times, to help these clients contact the positively reinforcing properties of values. It's just that their contact with and expressions of positive affect are less frequent and typically more subtle. Utilizing more nuanced positive affect can be more challenging. Because life for these folks is usually a pretty mixed emotional bag, with unpleasant and difficult emotional states being more persistently present, it often makes more sense to use these already present and more intense experiences of emotional pain as a doorway to values exploration.

Regardless of who you are working with, though, emotional pain will almost certainly be a part of any values work. If values are the core of a well-lived life, then it is also in pain that values must be found. In order to do this, however, we may first need to reexamine how we approach pain, moving from viewing it as something to be eliminated or, at best, a "necessary evil," to seeing it as having something valuable to offer.

Pain as Teacher

All of our emotions, including the painful ones, provide us with essential information. Emotions have associated "needs" or wants and motivate us to act toward goals. Pain is the driving force behind many of the important changes we make in our lives. Whether it is physical pain that motivates a person to avoid something that may cause death or injury, or emotional pain, such as shame, that can motivate an individual to change their behavior or make amends in order to avoid ostracism, pain motivates us to action (Nesse, 1991). Without pain and distress, many of our clients simply would not be motivated to make the difficult changes therapy asks of them.

In addition, emotions communicate. The communicative function of emotion is often thought to be an *interpersonal* one. If I smile or frown at you, that communicates something to you about how I feel toward you, and also how I am likely to interact with you. But emotions also have an *intrapersonal* communication function; they can tell us something important about ourselves. Painful emotions like loss, grief, regret, sadness, and anxiety are like a built-in GPS guiding us to what matters. It can be tempting to try to ignore, change, explain, justify, regulate, or deny these painful emotions, but in doing so we close ourselves off to important learning opportunities. By exploring our clients' pain with them and helping them reflect on questions like "What does this pain tell me about what really matters to me?" or "What does this pain tell me about what I need to learn?" we help our clients turn their emotions from problems to be managed into potentially valuable teachers.

Tracking the Scent of Values in a Landscape of Pain

In the last chapter we talked about how, as values-guided therapists, we need to know the "scent" of values. The qualities of choice, vitality, willing vulnerability, and present-moment focus guide our values exploration, whether that exploration is of the sweeter moments of life or the emotionally painful experiences.

Fostering Awareness of Choice Inside Pain

Humans are in a bit of a bind when it comes to pain. Most of us, including the people we serve, have been conditioned to equate pain with pathology. We are taught that we can and *should* work to eradicate physical and emotional pain from our lives. We are constantly bombarded with messages from ads, self-help books, or "experts" promoting new ways to rid ourselves of anything that causes us distress or discomfort. The pain-killing industry (both physical and psychological pain) is a multibillion-dollar operation and continues to expand at alarming rates (Bastian, 2018).

And yet, as the old Spanish proverb goes, "Where there is love, there is pain." Anyone who has ever loved, anyone who has ever cared deeply about someone or something, knows that it's not possible to invest one's heart without also getting hurt. Values are linked to our heart's deepest longings, and so it stands to reason that where there are values, you'll also find pain. Thus, like two sides of the same coin, values and pain are inextricably linked.

CHOICE REQUIRES KNOWING THE COST

If pain and values are two sides of the same coin, then if we choose to orient around getting away from pain, we may also be turning away from our values. But often our clients aren't aware of the price they are paying. Being free to choose means knowing the cost of the available options from which one is choosing. A key part of values work is helping our clients become more fully aware of what they are choosing to value and, equally important, what they are *not* choosing to value.

One question I frequently ask my clients to help them contact the often-hidden costs of turning away from pain is, "What would you have to not care about in order for this to not hurt so much?" Sometimes the connection between pain and values is obvious when you ask this question. For example, the person who is grieving the death of a loved one can often see that in order to not feel that pain of loss, they would have to not care about their loved one. Having that sense of choice highlighted can bring honor to the pain and they can even willingly embrace it as an act of love.

However, uncovering the true cost of valuing decreased pain may be less obvious in other cases. For example, if a client is struggling with social anxiety, they may feel like not having the pain of anxiety would simply mean they wouldn't care anymore about "being perfect" or "messing up," responses which are probably still about avoidance. In this case, you may need to continue digging by asking questions like "What activities would you have to give up in order for your anxiety to go away?" or "What relationships would you need to let go of if you didn't want to feel anxiety anymore?" to unearth potential values that may be connected with the pain they are attempting to avoid. Through digging deeper in this way, the person may come to see the pain of anxiety as being inextricably tied to values around connection or belonging, for example. To get rid of their anxiety, they also would have to abandon these values. By bringing these costs into the light, we bring a sense of choice to the pain. Through that we help them contact what they would choose to make most important in the midst of their pain, thus opening up possibilities for new ways of thinking and behaving in these difficult situations.

TOOL: TWO SIDES OF A COIN/PHOTO

One way to explore the relationship between pain and values is through creating a physical "coin" (usually a note card or piece of paper). In this exercise, the client selects a value they have identified as being important to them and writes that on one side of the "coin." Then, they are asked to reflect on what painful thoughts, feelings, and other experiences often arise as part of living out that value. Those painful experiences are written on the opposite side of the coin card. The therapist then leads the client to interact with the "coin" (by looking at, reflecting on, or talking out loud about it) while also being coached to notice painful thoughts, feelings, sensations, or memories that emerge. Through the exercise, clients often develop a greater ability to embrace the pain that comes up in relation to that value and as a result, a sense of choice opens up. An outline for how to do this coin exercise can be found at http://www.newharbinger.com/43218.

Personal photos or images can make the coin exercise more personally apt and evocative. In order to do this, the client is asked to bring in a photo of something or someone they care about, but around which they also have some pain or struggle. Alternatively, if you are working with someone who reports having lost touch with anything they care about, you can ask them to bring in a photo or an image of something they used to care about at one point, but with which they feel they are now disconnected from that caring. The photo can be a picture of their children, their partner or other loved one, themselves as a child, or a scene that represents some valued domain such as nature or spirituality. In this version, the photo is used in place of the coin, but the exercise essentially proceeds the same way. You can find a clinical vignette that demonstrates how a photo can be used in this way at http://www.newharbinger.com/43218.

Finding Values in Pain Through Willing Vulnerability

Being alive means that we will suffer. The Buddhists sure got that one right! And the more we care about something, the more we open ourselves up to pain. Caring creates vulnerability. The author C. S. Lewis writes beautifully about this:

> There is no safe investment. To love at all is to be vulnerable. Love anything, and your heart will certainly be wrung and possibly be broken. If you want to make sure of keeping it intact, you must give your heart to no one, not even to an animal. Wrap it carefully round with hobbies and little luxuries; avoid all entanglements; lock it up safe in the casket or coffin of your selfishness. But in that casket—safe, dark, motionless, airless—it will change. It will not be broken; it will become unbreakable, impenetrable, irredeemable. (Lewis, 1960, p. 169)

People often shut themselves off from caring to avoid being vulnerable. This is an understandable and normal response to painful events and trauma. However, that perceived self-protection often comes at a high cost. As the result of this armoring and closing of the heart, life becomes more meaningless, less full, and options appear to constrict. Many of our clients come to us in this state. Therapy can reverse this process through allowing a space for clients to be vulnerable, willingly opening up to the emotional pain they have tried to protect themselves from, and thereby reconnect (or sometimes connect for the first time) to the values that bring meaning, purpose, and richness to their life.

VALUES BRING HONOR TO PAIN

The last few years of our sweet old dog Dalai's life were filled with intense sadness and fear for me. I loved this little creature so much and yet being with her as her body was failing was a constant reminder that my time with her was getting ever more finite. The pain felt so threatening at times, with an intensity that seemed like it could consume me, that I would frequently have the urge to do anything I could to get away from it, even if that meant getting away from Dalai. Loved ones who saw me suffering would say well-intentioned things like, "You just have to enjoy the time you have with her" or "She's not gone now so you should just focus on being happy about that." Unfortunately, those strategies only ended up highlighting the vast discrepancy between what I was "supposed" to feel (happy that she's here) and what I did feel (fear, sadness, anxiety, and even resentment at times), which brought on even more painful thoughts and feelings. What eventually transformed my pain was when I began to see it as a sign about what was most meaningful in my life—being dedicated, steadfast, and committed to caring well for those in my life, including this dying dog. I came to see my willingness to sit with and experience my pain, rather than turn away from it and inevitably her, as some of the final loving acts I could offer the sweet pup who had given me so much. Turning toward this suffering meant I felt intensely vulnerable, totally uninsulated from the pain of the impending loss. However, embracing those feelings helped me remember who I wanted to be and provided a sense of purpose and direction for the time we had together, rather than just waiting for the painful end that would inevitably come regardless of how I engaged in the process. Values brought honor to my pain.

Fostering willing vulnerability in order to connect with values requires that we help our clients slow down, explore, and linger with painful feelings they normally avoid. Rather than trying to brace against the waves of pain crashing down, we teach our clients how to dive into those waves. Pain is then transformed from something to be avoided, diminished, or white-knuckled through into something that has honor and value precisely because it is linked to something we care about. One way I do this with clients is by exploring what I call an "unsweet spot."

TOOL: EXPLORING AN UNSWEET SPOT

The Sweet Spot exercise described in chapter 4 relies mainly on exploring "sweet" or tender memories. While sometimes painful feelings can also emerge during the exercise, including feelings of regret or loss, the main focus is on exploring values via contacting a time in the person's life that is generally associated with feelings of tenderness, connection, joy, wholeness, or contentment. Being willing to be vulnerable and openly exploring this relatively "sweet" terrain is one thing. But if pain tells us something about what matters, then it is important to have that same posture of openness and willing vulnerability when exploring more painful experiences, like times when we have felt longing, regret, isolation, or fear. Thus, I will often use some of the same basic strategies employed in the Sweet Spot exercise to explore what I call "unsweet spot" memories, which are more predominantly painful.

Instructions for Unsweet Spot exercise. For this exercise, you can follow the same instructions found in chapter 4 for the Sweet Spot exercise with only a few changes. As in the Sweet Spot exercise, first choose a valued domain that you and the client are going to explore. Then, lead your client through the same kind of visualization described in chapter 4. However, instead of a sweet spot, ask them to recall a specific time when something painful occurred in relation to the domain they are focusing on, such as a loss, a defeat, a time of hopelessness, or an emotional injury. Hopefully, you'll already have a sense of the experiences that are most relevant for the client and you can ask specifically about a time that involved that feeling. For example, you might say something like:

Therapist: I'd like you to recall one specific time when that feeling of isolation/ emptiness/fear/sadness/shame was present for you in this domain or relationship. It doesn't have to be the most intense time you've experienced that feeling, but just one specific time that you have some vivid memory of.

From there, explore the scene as you would with a sweet spot memory, looking for what the person is doing or not doing, what they see and feel in that moment. However, because the pain can be such a dominant presence in these unsweet spot memories, you'll likely need to explicitly guide them to look for signs of values that may also be present. You can do this by asking questions like:

- As you are there in that scene, do you notice anything that matters to you?

- What do you notice yourself longing for in the midst of this pain?

Facilitating shifts in perspective also helps. For example, the Sweet Spot exercise instructions include ways to help your client view the scene from an "observer self" perspective. From that same observer self perspective, you can ask your client to observe things in the unsweet spot, such as:

- As you are watching the you that is there in this painful moment, what do you want for her/him/them?

- In your ideal world, if you could have that you that is there in that painful situation do or say anything, what might that be?

These questions are all designed to help the client notice the potential values that might otherwise be obscured by the pain.

By supporting our clients in openly exploring a painful memory or image, we bring a sense of willing vulnerability to the pain. By being willing to make themselves vulnerable to the pain in this unsweet spot memory, clients allow for the possibility of exploring and contacting the values buried within its painful recesses.

Finding Vitality in Pain

As stated earlier, values can bring honor to pain. But the connection between pain and values isn't a one-way relationship. Pain isn't just some kind of unwanted but ever-present tagalong on our values journey. Pain brings something to the table as well. Pain is essential. Research shows that distress and pain can serve many adaptive functions, including increasing cooperation in groups (Bastian, Jetten, & Ferris, 2014), enhanced self-efficacy and compassion (Joseph, Linley, & Harris, 2004), and facilitating empathic responding from others (Hadjistavropoulos et al., 2011). As social psychologist Brock Bastian states, "Pain and suffering are neither antithetical to happiness nor simply incidental to it. They are *necessary* for happiness" (Bastian, 2018, p. ix). You cannot have light if there is no such thing as darkness.

In his poem "On Pain," Kahlil Gibran (1995) writes:

Your pain is the breaking of the shell that encloses your understanding.

Even as the stone of the fruit must break, that its heart may stand in the sun, so must you know pain.

THERE IS MEANING AND PURPOSE IN THE STRUGGLE

There is evidence that pain can help give actions and events a sense of purpose and meaning (Bastian, Jetten, Hornsey, & Leknes, 2014; Liu, Liu, & Elliott, 2010). People don't climb Everest purely for the view. It just wouldn't be the same if a helicopter deposited you on the summit to snap a selfie at the top of the world. Part of what people find so meaningful about that experience is the pain and struggle that is required of the journey. Consider some of the events that people cite as very meaningful, such as giving birth, getting that hard-earned degree, or accompanying a loved one as they die. Pain and struggle are an intrinsic part of each of these events.

USING THE PAIN OF PRESENCE VS. PAIN OF ABSENCE TO GUIDE VALUES EXPLORATION

Whatever path we take in life, pain will be part of the journey. However, not all types of pain are the same—there is the pain of presence and the pain of absence (Hayes, 2005). The pain of presence is the kind of pain that shows up as you live a life of meaning and purpose. This includes the feelings of loss or sadness when a loved one leaves you by death or otherwise, the inevitable failure that is part of trying just about any new activity, or the fear you feel when you stretch outside your comfort zone in order to grow. In contrast, the pain of absence is the pain you feel when you are spending too much of your time caught up in experiential avoidance (EA), living outside your values. Often this includes a sense of emptiness, meaninglessness, regret, or directionlessness.

The pain of presence has a sense of life or vitality to it, some energy that can be noted. The pain of absence, in contrast, will often have more of a dead, lifeless, absent, or lost quality. If clients can learn to discriminate between these two types of pain, then the pain of presence can be transformed from something to be avoided into a beacon that can guide them toward a life of purpose and meaning. Conversely, clients can learn from the pain of absence about what is missing in their lives or what they may need to change.

Below is an example of how you might talk with a client about the concept of the pain of presence versus the pain of absence.

CLINICAL EXAMPLE

Therapist: What if the way life works is that you don't get to choose whether or not you will have pain, but do get to choose the *type* of pain you will have? In this way of viewing things, there are two types of pain. The first type is called the pain of presence. That's the pain that you feel when you are living well, following your values. (*What follows are some general examples, but ideally you'd use examples from the client's own life.*) It's the sense of disappointment you have when something doesn't work out or the hurt you feel when someone you cared about betrays you. It's the loss you feel when you have really opened your heart to a friend, and they move away. It's the inevitable feelings of failure you experience when you try something that stretches you in new ways. The pain of presence is what happens when you choose to live your values. It's an inevitable part of living a life of meaning and purpose.

But there is another type of pain, the pain of absence. The pain of absence usually occurs when you are living a life oriented toward not feeling pain. Life lived in the service of not feeling pain is a life not guided by your values. But that life too brings pain with it. (*Again, ideally you'd choose examples from the client's life.*) The pain of absence is the sense of meaninglessness you feel when your life involves being on the hamster wheel of finding the next fix. It's the sense of disconnection from your family when you've closed your heart to them. It's the hopelessness found in giving up on ever really connecting with someone. What if it's true that your only real choice in life is between the pain of absence or the pain of presence, not *whether* you will experience pain? If you are open to it, it may be helpful for us to explore which pain you've been choosing.

Once the client has a sense for these two types of pain, you can then help them explore pain that has a vital quality (the pain of presence) with an eye toward what that pain has to tell them about what might be important or meaningful for them in that activity, relationship, or way of being. If the pain has a more lifeless quality (the pain of absence), then you and your client can explore that pain to see what is missing, what they are longing for, or what that pain says about what they might want to make important in their life.

Making Pain Present to Find Values in the Moment

Most of our clients come to us in pain. Sometimes that pain is obvious. Maybe there was a death, a trauma, or something else that shook their sense of identity and security in the world. Emotional pain is usually front and center when we are sitting with folks facing these life events. Pain can also emerge organically from simply talking about values. I sometimes joke with my clients that I have a magic crying couch in my office—all you have to do is sit down on it and the tears start flowing. Because pain and values are so intertwined, pain frequently just emerges naturally in the values conversations I have with clients.

However, sometimes clients have been so effective in their EA that they aren't feeling much pain at all. The problem is, EA is a pretty blunt instrument. Successfully numbing some emotions tends to numb most other feelings as well (Durso, Luttrell, & Way, 2015). You can see this phenomenon clinically in individuals who are more emotionally flat or alexithymic. These individuals may have lost contact with the cost of their EA, and thus may have also lost contact with the feelings that might help them know what would be most meaningful and rewarding. They don't feel much pain, but they also don't feel much of any of the other emotions associated with living a full, rich, and vital life, like joy, meaning, or connection.

For others, life has shaped them to keep the expression of their emotions under tight wrap. These more affectively overcontrolled clients may actually be experiencing the pain that could be useful to explore in therapy, but they have significant difficulty expressing it. As I said before, emotions serve both motivating and communicative functions. Thus, if a client is not able to express emotions, including painful ones, a huge avenue for communication between client and therapist (as well as with anyone else in their life or even just within the client themself) has been shut down. Helping these clients access and express the full range of their emotions opens up important pathways for both interpersonal and intrapersonal communication.

If a client is unable to access their pain, then one of the first things a values-guided therapist may need to do is to make pain present in the room. Most experiential therapies, including ACT (Hayes, Strosahl, & Wilson, 2012), functional analytic psychotherapy (FAP; Kohlenberg & Tsai, 1991), and emotion focused therapy (EFT; Greenberg, 2015), place a strong emphasis on evoking and utilizing emotions present in the therapy room. While even a cursory discussion of the myriad ways these and other therapies evoke emotion in the therapy room is beyond the scope of this book, what follows is one values-focused tool you can use to allow emotional pain to emerge such that it can be utilized in the present moment.

TOOL: FEARED EULOGY

The Feared Eulogy is a tool that can bring the painful consequences of living a life disconnected from one's values into the present moment. This is a variation of the more standard eulogy or 80th birthday party exercises (Hayes, Strosahl, & Wilson, 2012), a script for which can be found at http://www.newharbinger.com/43218. This Feared Eulogy variation focuses on what would happen if the client were to die today, and is intended to help people look at their life through the eyes of other people who know them, thus facilitating perspective taking on their actions and what they have been valuing.

The Feared Eulogy exercise often embodies the present-moment quality that we are looking for in our values work by bringing an imagined future based on the trajectory of the client's current valuing into the present moment. Turning toward what we really care about necessarily means encountering the painful emotions (such as regret, shame, guilt, loss, or sadness) that arise when we consider the gap between what we would choose to care about and what we have been caring about by our actions or inactions. Helping our clients contact the painful emotions associated with what they have been valuing offers an opening for them to more fully explore alternatives for what they would want to orient their lives around before it is too late.

Because the main aim of the exercise is to highlight the gap between what a person is currently valuing by their actions and what they would most want to value, this exercise can be especially useful for clients who may be more disconnected, unemotional, or out of contact with the costs of their actions. I especially like to use it when working with clients around relationship values and how they would want to be to the important people in their life.

Instructions for Feared Eulogy exercise. What follows are instructions for how to do the exercise in session with an individual. However, you can also give this exercise as homework for the client to do outside of session. There is a handout that includes both the Standard Eulogy and the Feared Eulogy versions of this exercise that you can give clients to do as homework at http://www.newharbinger.com/43218.

Step 1: Introduce the exercise and gain consent. This can be an intense experience for some clients, so gaining consent and setting the stage for a potentially powerful experience is particularly important. Here's an example of what you might say:

Therapist: It is common for people to have the experience of getting a second chance after a big crisis occurs, whether that's after the death of a loved one, a life-threatening accident, a major loss, or a serious illness. These kinds of events can lead us to think about what is really important in life. Painful experiences in life can sometimes be our best teachers. I'd like to suggest an exercise in which you will imagine attending your own funeral as a way to reflect on what your time on this planet has been about. Are you interested in doing this exercise as a way of exploring what's most important to you? *(Continue if permission is gained.)*

Step 2: Help the person get present and imagine the scene.

Therapist: People have all sorts of different experiences with this exercise. It can be quite emotional for some people, but not for others. Some people find something interesting or surprising comes up in the exercise and others sometimes feel like it simply helps them get in touch with something that they've known all along. Whatever you experience is fine. Let's just see what happens for you.

If you're willing, you can gently close your eyes or if you prefer, you can just rest your gaze at a spot on the floor. *(Lead them through a brief task to help them get centered, such as noticing the breath or their five senses.)* I'd like you to imagine that through some twist of fate you die tonight in your sleep. The people in your life organize a funeral. Somehow, though, you are able to attend your own funeral in spirit. You can be there silently and undetected to observe how it goes. Just take a moment to get a sense of any reactions you are having as you imagine having reached the end of your life, with no more time to do the things you've wanted to do, no more time to fix the mistakes you've made, to correct the regrets. Notice whatever comes up *(extended pause)*.

So here you are, watching and listening to the people who are gathered at your funeral to remember you and this life you lived. Your friends, your children, your partner, colleagues, and parents *(list specific people who might be there for the client based on what you know of their history)* are all there. See if you can picture in your mind's eye what it's like being there in that room. Notice what smells are in the room, all the different sounds, notice what the lighting looks like *(pause)*.

Now, as they do during funerals, some people stand up to give a eulogy. Take a moment to imagine who you would want the first person to be to stand up to speak for what your life has been about. Imagine a specific person. This could be anyone you want, even a person who has already died or maybe a person you haven't met yet. Just imagine who you might want to get up to speak about your life. *(You could also suggest a particular person based on what you know of the client. Then pause to give them some time to picture that person.)*

Step 3: Have them imagine what a particular person would think and say.

Therapist: Now imagine that this person you pictured stands up to speak. But there's something different about this funeral. During this funeral, everyone is completely honest. People aren't just saying a bunch of nice things simply out of respect. They are really trying to accurately remember you and what you have made most important in your life as it now stands. So, here is this person who is going to be reflecting on the life you have actually lived up until this point and, to the best of their ability, they are going to accurately and honestly describe what your actions and deeds have been in the service of. Take a moment and see if you can hear what they say about what you have shown was important to you by your actions up until now. *(Pause for thirty seconds or so to give the person time to imagine it. If you feel it would work better, you can also ask the client to open their eyes and write what they believe the person would say.)*

Now take some time to consider, if this person were being totally honest, what they would say about how you have been in your relationship with them and what kind of an impact you've had on them, if any. Let them be honest and speak openly about how you have been in your relationship with them. Maybe they even include ways you have let them down or hurt them if that's true. See if you can actually hear those words coming out of their mouth. I'll give you a bit to imagine that. *(Pause and allow time for the client to imagine what they would want that person to say.)*

Notice what it feels like to have those things said about the life you have lived up until now and how you have affected this person. Notice any feelings or sensations in your body. Notice any thoughts that are showing up.

Step 4: Imagine additional people giving eulogies.

Therapist: Now imagine that another person stands up. Maybe it's *(name some possible people that it might be important to explore the client's relationship with based on what you know of the client)*. Picture this next person standing up and walking to the stage in order to speak about the life you have lived, what you have made important by your actions, and what you have stood for in this world and in your relationship with them. Again, this person is being totally honest in their assessment of what, from their perspective, you have made most important and spent most of your life's energy on up until this point.

(Repeat step 3 and do this for a total of about three people before moving on to step 5.)

Step 5: Debrief. Take some time to help the client gently transition back to the room and debrief the exercise. During the debrief, help them explore what they noticed and experienced during the exercise. Be sure to look for the four qualities (choice, willing vulnerability, vitality, and present moment) in the debrief as well, building on them when they are present and trying to evoke them when they are not. Questions you might ask include:

- Did one of the eulogies stand out to you? If so, which one and why? What did that person say about you or your relationship with them?

- What were some of the words people used to describe you and the life you have lived and how you were with them? How do you feel as you reflect on the words that people used to describe how you have lived?

- Did you notice any difference between what you are currently spending your time "importanting" *(using this made-up word can be a helpful way to highlight the verb-quality of valuing)* or struggling with, and what you would ideally want people to say about the life you have lived and what has been important to you?

This exercise can bring up a lot of feelings, including painful ones. Clients may feel intense regret or shame. But it is often contacting pain in the present moment that allows the person to reconnect with what matters most to them and shift their life accordingly. Here's an example of how you might want to wrap up the exercise to utilize the pain that may have emerged and to help the person take a step toward their values.

Therapist: One important step you have taken by doing this exercise is exploring the discrepancy between the life you want to live and life as it is today. That's not an easy thing to do. But that gap also creates room for changes to occur. It creates a space where both pain and values can be a part of your life. These painful thoughts and feelings can give you a sense of direction and help you take steps toward what you would choose to value going forward. You might feel confused right now and wonder what this means. You might be having thoughts and feelings like you can't do it or you don't know how to change. That's okay and normal at this point. This isn't something you can understand with your mind, but rather something you have to experience in the present moment, through living your life and making choices. We'll continue to explore this in the sessions ahead. Just by being willing to do this exercise, you took a step toward your values and toward creating the life that you would most want to live.

Follow-up homework. This isn't a one-and-done kind of exercise. I will frequently return to this exercise throughout therapy. It is also important to have your clients follow up on whatever has emerged from the exercise. Here are some ideas for next steps clients can take on their own after doing the exercise with you:

- List several words people used in their eulogy to describe you and the life you have lived. What thoughts and feelings come up for you as you look at this list of words? Next to this list, write down some of the words that you think would describe what a well-lived life would be for you.

- Spend some time writing about what kind of a relationship you would want with each of the people who spoke at your funeral. Who would you want to be to them, and what kind of person would you want them to know you to be? What might you need to start doing right now, in the present, to begin creating the relationship you would want with them? Write down any ideas that come up, whether they seem realistic or not.

- Spend some time reflecting on what you would need to do differently, start doing, or stop doing in order to make the changes you'd like to make based on what came up in this eulogy. What do you think has been getting in the way of making that change? What do you think might be future barriers to living that life?

- Write out a detailed eulogy you would want to have read at your funeral, one that reflected your ideal, well-lived life. Be as detailed as possible about what you would want said about the life you'd most want to have lived. What did you make important in your life? What kind of an impact did you have? What and who mattered to you? What or who didn't really matter to you? How did you act toward the people in your life that were important to you?

Troubleshooting the Feared Eulogy exercise. In order for this exercise to be effective, your client needs to be able to engage in some perspective shifts and really step into an imagined future. The perspective shift of bringing the future into the now is essential to the present-moment quality of the exercise. Imagining one's own mortality and death can be difficult for younger people to do, especially if they are currently in the "I'm invincible" stage of life. Similarly, people with acute or unresolved grief or trauma may be so distracted by thoughts around death that they may be unable to engage in the exercise as written above. Others may be too overwhelmed by the emotions to participate. If you suspect this may be the case, but also think it would be helpful to use an exercise like this, you might try a variation where you ask them to imagine a school graduation, the end of their current job, or some sort of transition like moving away from home or going on a long trip. The idea is to have them transport themselves into being at some important future event that is a moment of loss or transition and imagine what others would be thinking or feeling as they reflect on the client.

It's not uncommon for some clients to get stuck on the thought that "people wouldn't really say something that hurtful at my eulogy" and thus have difficulty imagining people saying more painful things at their funeral. In this case, you could instead ask them to imagine what people might really be thinking even if they never said it out loud. Or, you could have them imagine what the person would write in a personal diary that they thought would never be read. Alternatively, they could imagine a time when they were not their best (such as after a fight with their spouse, when they were unkind to a friend, or when they didn't make time for their kids). Then have a conversation about what their loved one might have been thinking or feeling about them at those times. If you suspect your client might have a hard time with the Feared Eulogy, then you might even do these things prior to the exercise to help orient them. Of course, none of us has fully all good or all bad evaluations of our loved ones. But in the Feared Eulogy, we want to tap into some of the more painful stuff that we often avoid thinking about. Helping the client remember times when their loved ones may not have been having all positive evaluations of them can help them get in contact with some of this painful stuff.

Pitfalls When Exploring Values Through Pain

Taking this path of exploring values through pain isn't easy; the road less traveled isn't usually a smooth or easy one. So here are a few potential pitfalls to be on the lookout for as you are on the road to exploring values through pain.

Sugarcoating or Problem Solving Away Pain

Be careful that you don't jump too quickly to trying to find the "bright side" of the pain/values coin. Moving too quickly from pain to the values that may be connected to that pain can feel invalidating and inauthentic for clients who are fully immersed in the pain. Allow them to linger, open up to, and explore their pain. The values will naturally emerge through that exploration.

Moving too quickly to pointing out the values in the pain can also be a form of EA on the part of the therapist. It can be a way to try to sugarcoat or problem solve away the pain. So make sure that you are focusing on connecting pain and values, rather than negating pain with values.

More Isn't Necessarily Better

In order for learning to occur, a person must be able to remain present and open. If someone becomes too disorganized by extreme emotion or begins to shut down in response to overwhelming threat, they will likely not learn anything new. These responses, which can include things like dissociation or more intense emotion dysregulation, aren't inherently dangerous (although the strategies clients use to cope with these distressing experiences can be damaging, such as self-harm behaviors), but they can interfere with new learning. Thus, for clients where shutting down, flatness, or numbness are related to trauma, evoking pain in the service of values clarification may need to be titrated. For example, you may need to work on helping them ground themselves during these times, identifying ways to remain open and willing even in the face of distress. You might need to modify exercises to make them less evocative. It can also be useful to help your client contact more of the social/relational reinforcers we discuss in chapter 4 as a way to soothe themselves. For example, if you are experienced as a source of safety or connection for the client, you may choose to sit next to the client during the exercise, or even put your hand on their shoulder during particularly pain-evoking exercises.

Emotions Associated with Values Aren't Always in Technicolor

Not everyone's experience of contacting values involves intense emotions, whether that is euphoria or intense gratitude or, conversely, agony and intense shame. Sometimes the "positive" feelings associated with values are experienced as fondness rather than love, contentment rather than joy or excitement. Similarly, the pain that may lead to values doesn't need to be profound grief or intense isolation, but rather may be a vaguer sense of disconnection or malaise. You don't always need intense emotions in order to explore values; sometimes values lie in the more subtle and nuanced ones.

Therapists Avoid Pain Too

It's difficult to see our clients in pain and even more difficult to knowingly lead them into it. As therapists, we too can get caught up in our own EA strategies, seeing our clients as fragile or incapable. In these times it is helpful for us to get back in contact with our own values, to remember what we're playing for, as that can serve as our motivation to do what is difficult, including seeing someone we care about suffer without rescuing them.

Takeaways

- Where there is emotional pain, so too are values. With some clients, emotional pain may be the most effective pathway to exploring values.

- Painful emotions are like a built-in GPS guiding us to what matters. By helping our clients explore their pain, we help turn these emotions from things to be managed into valuable teachers.

- Help your client contact the choice in pain by seeing the interconnection between pain and values.

- Rather than simply learning to withstand or tolerate pain, we transform it into something that is honorable by opening up to it with willing vulnerability.

- There is life and vitality in pain. Pain is essential and can add to our sense of meaning and purpose.

- Don't take emotional numbness as a sign of a lack of values. It's probably a sign of "successful" experiential avoidance. You may need to make the pain present in order to help the client reconnect with what would create meaning in their life.

Next Steps

- Practice using the coin metaphor (with or without the photo element) in session with a client, highlighting the choice present in the interconnection between pain and values.

- Practice doing the Feared Eulogy exercise with a colleague or friend. Ask for feedback to shape how you might deliver this with a client.

- **Inside-out learning:** Write about an important failure you had at work. It could be something that feels big, like a client who fired you or an instance when you got in trouble with your boss, or it could be something more subtle, like a session where you know you didn't give it your best. Whatever it is, choose something that has really stuck with you, something that makes you wince at least a little when you think about it. What emotions do you feel when you think about this event? What thoughts do you have? Do you notice any urges? Consider what this might say about what you value or what is most important to you.

   Now consider another failure, again big or small, but this time it's not one of those things that has stuck with you. Even though this was also "failure," when you contact this event it doesn't cause you much, if any, significant pain. Does this tell you anything about what might not be of importance to you?

CHAPTER 6

Exploring Through Doing

We do not need, and indeed never will have, all the answers before we act...
It is often through taking action that we can discover some of them.
—Charlotte Bunch

Sometimes the best learning comes through doing. You can read all the books in the world about playing the piano, spend hours listening to the greatest masterpieces, even buy yourself a beautiful Steinway, but if you don't start putting your fingers on the keys, you'll never be a piano player. In fact, you can't even really know for sure whether you would want to be a piano player until you actually start playing the piano. Values are kind of like that. Helping our clients get to a place where they think they know what they *would* want to value doesn't mean much if they don't actually test it out by valuing those things with their actions. In this chapter, I'm going to cover how to help your clients learn more about what kind of life would be most meaningful for them by testing out different versions of that valued life. I call this "values prototyping."

Regardless of your approach to therapy, it's likely that an ultimate aim is to help your clients make behavioral changes that result in better living. There are countless resources that can offer guidance on how best to help your clients set and maintain behavior goals. If you are interested in learning more about how to support your clients in taking consistent action on their values from an ACT perspective, I suggest reading *Committed Action in Practice: A Clinician's Guide to Assessing, Planning, and Supporting Change in Your Client* (Moran, Bach, & Batten, 2018). However, in this chapter, rather than focusing on identifying workable ways to act upon and live out already identified values, here we are using action as a way to further explore values prior to committing to them. In values prototyping, clients take action to test out various versions of valued living, gaining experiential knowledge as they experiment with what a life in the service of certain values might be like. Prototyping different versions of valued living allows clients to reflect on the question "What feedback does engaging in this valuing give me in terms of what might be most important to me?"

Learning Through Valuing

I began this book by saying that values aren't really things at all; valuing is behavior. It is through that act of valuing that our clients best learn what kind of life would be most meaningful and vital to them. But before we can help our clients try out different values prototypes, we first need to help them notice what they have been valuing and the consequences of that valuing, because there is a lot to be learned from that as well.

Valuing Is Constantly Happening

We are all currently valuing something by our behavior. The problem is, our actions may not be valuing what we would most want to value if we were free to choose. Dr. Jane Goodall, one of my personal values heroes, is quoted as saying, "You cannot get through a single day without having an impact on the world around you. What you do makes a difference, and you have to decide what kind of difference you want to make" (Goodall, n.d.). Each of our lives is going to have an impact simply by the fact of us living it. That impact isn't based on what we *say* we value; it will be the footsteps our actions leave behind that tell the story of what our life has meant. Thus, we need to know how to help our clients pause to notice the direction of those footsteps and where their valued actions are taking them. In order to do that, we have to help our clients become better values trackers.

Tracking Valuing

We go through much of life on autopilot. At any given moment, most of us aren't really aware of what we are valuing through our choices of how we spend our time and other resources. Autopilot is useful if you're on the right course and if there aren't any serious obstacles around that you might need to navigate. But most of the time, when our clients come to us for therapy, it means they have gotten off course somewhere along the line and/or they are facing some significant obstacles in their path. During these times, it's important to help them disengage the autopilot.

Helping our clients learn to track what they are valuing helps put them in contact with the consequences of that behavior. It turns off the autopilot, which allows them to set a new course if need be. Just like tracking monetary spending, tracking time/ energy/resource spending can be an eye-opener. Sometimes it can be painful for a client to realize what they have and have not been valuing. However, this pain also brings with it an awareness that allows for the freedom to choose something new.

There are various ways you can help your client start tracking what they are valuing in an ongoing way. You can start by asking questions in session, such as:

- What did you spend your time doing today? *(This may seem like an obvious question, but you may be surprised to discover how little you know about how your client actually spends the various hours of their day.)*

- What was that behavior in the service of? What was the function of the behavior, both in the immediate and in the longer term?

- Was the behavior aimed at moving *toward* something that was important to you or was it aimed at getting *away* from something you did not want (such as an unpleasant thought, feeling, sensation, or memory)?

Also, any time your client is talking about some activity they engaged in can be an opportunity to help them learn to track the valuing in that action by asking things like:

- What do you think you were "importanting" by choosing to engage in that activity?

- As you were engaged in that activity, *how* you were behaving? What kinds of descriptors or adverbs would you use to describe how you were behaving during the activity?

In addition to these in-session inquiries, it can often be helpful to have your client track their valuing as it is occurring outside of the session. This real-time valuing tracking can also provide important information about the consequences of their valuing behavior. Using a structured tracking form can provide more specific and accurate data compared to simply asking your clients to recall events and consequences from memory.

TOOL: DAILY VALUING TRACKING FORM

In order to help our clients reflect on their patterns of valued action, we created a modified version of Pielech and colleagues' Values Tracker tool (Pielech et al., 2016). You can find a copy of our form, which we call the Daily Valuing Tracking Form, at http://www.newharbinger.com/43218. Clients can use this form to provide the following daily ratings:

- How effective were you in taking actions that contributed to a better, more vital quality of living today?

- How effective were you in making progress in the areas of your life that matter to you today?

In addition, the form asks clients to identify a specific example of a values-based action they engaged in each day that relates to the two statements above. Thus, clients not only track how "successful" they felt they had been at engaging in valued action, but they also gather information about what specific valuing behavior they engaged in that contributed to that success.

By reviewing the data collected on the Daily Valuing Tracking Form, you and your client can explore some of the larger patterns of valuing that seem to be emerging. Based on that, they can begin to consider any changes they might want to test out in terms of their valuing. Questions to facilitate these conversations can include:

- What kinds of behaviors were you engaged in on those days that you rated as being more effective in terms of helping you live a better-quality life or progressing in areas that matter to you? Did you notice any patterns in terms of what you were *not* engaged in on those days?

- Given your observations about what you have been valuing, is there anything you'd ideally like to change in how you are spending your time and energy?

- What might be getting in the way of you spending more of your time valuing the things that would be most important to you? What would need to change in order for you to spend more of your time engaged in those ways of living that would make for a more meaningful and well-lived life?

Not Just *What* but *How*

Helping clients notice what they are valuing by tracking the specific behaviors they are engaged in is a great starting place. However, it's also important to help them track not just *what* they are doing, but also *how* they are doing it: in other words, the quality of their actions. Tracking the quality of their actions is key to understanding the function of their behavior.

Looking at the quality of the behavior can help us distinguish whether or not the client is staying on track with the value while engaging in the action. Let's say, for example, your client chooses to value lovingly supporting their family. They identify that going to their kid's baseball game is something they do that is consistent with this intention. Now, going to their kid's baseball games *may* be a way for someone to lovingly support their children, but not necessarily. What they do while they are there and the quality they bring to the action is essential. They may be sitting in the stands but be rigidly focused on how others are perceiving them. Or they may be so absorbed in their phone, posting on Facebook about what a "supportive" parent they are being, that they totally miss what their daughter is doing on the field. Or maybe, rather than actually lovingly supporting their son when he has struck out for the third time in a row, they become yet another voice in the stands who is shouting at the kid to "get it together!" As you can see, it isn't just the fact that your client went to their child's baseball game, but the qualities of their behavior while they were engaged in that activity that can provide important information to both of you about what that behavior was truly in the service of. Keeping with this example, a therapist might ask questions like the following to help the client track the qualities of their valuing behavior:

- How would you describe your actions as you were there at the game?

- If someone watched you at the game, how would they know that you being there was in the service of lovingly supporting your kid as opposed to being about something else? What would they see you doing or not doing that would make that value clear?

- If you were going to be at the game but not do it in a loving and supportive way, what would you be doing or not doing?

Questions like these can help your client reflect not just on what they are doing, but also whether their actions reflect the intentions behind what they would choose to value.

One thing to keep in mind is that clients will often report how they *felt* as they engaged in a valued action rather than the quality of their action. While I will frequently ask my clients about any feelings, thoughts, or sensations that showed up as part of the valuing tracking process, it's important not to conflate quality of action with feelings. You want to be sure you don't implicitly give your clients the message that they should be trying to pursue having a particular feeling as a result of engaging in a valued action and that if they aren't feeling something positive it must not be a valued action. Engaging in valued action frequently results in positive feelings, but certainly not always. Most of the time it's a mixed bag. It's also important not to imply that the client can only act on their values when they feel like it. In the example above, part of this client lovingly supporting their family means acting on this value even when emotions pull them in another direction. What is important is how they are behaving—are they being the kind of person who they would most want to be regardless of how they feel in the moment? Feelings can provide data, but they aren't a criterion for valued action.

Reinforcing Intentional Valuing

As our clients are considering ways to chart a new values course, it's helpful for us to be clear about our role as their guide. As I see it, our job is not to tell them what or how to value, but to reinforce the very act of intentional valuing. I was talking about the idea of the therapist reinforcing the act of valuing itself with my colleague Barbara Kohlenberg. She likened this to how a parent might respond to their child dreaming out loud about what they want to be when they grow up. If your child tells you, "I want to be an astronaut and a professional cowgirl and a garbage collector," hopefully you don't say, "You can't possibly be all of those things! Do you really think it's wise to pursue being an astronaut given all the NASA funding cuts? How are you going to get health insurance or contribute to a retirement fund as a cowgirl?" No, hopefully, as a parent you say something like, "That's awesome! Go for it!" And you then do things to help them explore those dreams. You take them to the science museum. You watch old Westerns with them. You introduce them to the garbage collector the next trash day. You do those things not because you are actually trying to groom them to be an astronaut or a cowgirl or a garbage collector. You do it because you are reinforcing your child's act of valuing (dreaming about what they want to be when they grow up is kind of like a child's version of "This is what I want to make important"). By saying "That's awesome! Go for it!" and then helping them take steps to explore their dreams, you are responding to a class of behavior that is about dreaming and creating a life. You are helping them open up to and explore all the possibilities that life holds. That's exactly what we want to do for our clients as well.

When our clients are actively and intentionally valuing, they are caring about and nurturing *something*. It's not *what* they care about, nurture, or value that we need to attend to; it's the act of intentional valuing that we want to reinforce. Thus, our job isn't to get them to value the right things, but instead to reinforce the act of intentionally caring about and nurturing something with their lives.

Charting a New Values Course

Once someone has started tracking the trajectory of where their current pattern of valuing is taking them, they may decide they want to start charting a new course. This, however, is often where many clients get stuck, not knowing how to proceed. Making life changes, especially more fundamental ones, can feel daunting. Deciding that they want their life to be in the service of something different than what they have been valuing can feel like a huge life change. And it is. But looking up at the peak of the mountain that lies in front of you is not always the most helpful perspective to take when you're just about to start the uphill trek; sometimes you need to just look at the next step in front of you.

Use Your Turtle Power!

I was reminded of just how daunting starting a new journey can be when I recently went on a two-week trek through a remote region of Nepal. Now, if you were to see me, you would almost certainly not think, "Oh, there's a Himalayan mountain climber!" I am a slow, very reluctant adventurer at best; for all you Lord of the Rings fans out there, I am way more Samwise than I am Legolas. So, despite spending six months training hard for the trek, on that first day when I was surrounded by incomprehensibly stunning but daunting peaks, I wanted nothing more than to hitch the first ride I could back to Kathmandu, reengage my autopilot, and get back to something closer to my comfort zone, which would likely involve a comfortable hotel room and a nice glass of wine. I was certain there was no possible way I could climb those mountains that were staring me in the face. I couldn't even comprehend how to start. I remember having the thought, "I am not the 'kind of person' who does this sort of thing!" (How many times have we heard our clients utter those same words, limiting the life they could live?) Turns out I was wrong; I am that "kind of person." When I thought of it as climbing up massive Himalayan peaks, it seemed too overwhelming to try to tackle. But I came to discover that by taking just one small, slow step and then another and then another, eventually (sometimes *very* eventually), I would reach the prayer flags at the summit. My fellow adventurers on the trek nicknamed my slow, methodical next-step strategy "turtle power." But it's precisely that turtle power that helped me accomplish something I never thought I could do. I didn't need to know how to climb the whole mountain; I just needed to take the next smallest step over and over and over again.

Trekking in the Himalayas is nothing compared to the monumental challenge many of our clients willingly take on when they choose to turn off their autopilot and shift the course of their lives. But no matter how formidable a challenge, beginning that journey requires exactly the same thing: one small turtle power step. Like my wise and gentle guides did for me in Nepal, we can help our clients find their own sustainable pace, set workable goals, and, above all else, support them in simply putting one foot in front of the other on their values journey.

Starting small makes experimenting with new behavior and learning from those experiments easier. But even very small shifts in a trajectory result in vastly different ending points over the course of years or decades. So, start small and go day by day, focusing on one action by valued action at a time. Over the course of a lifetime, those little molehills of valued action will become a mountain of a well-lived life.

Paraphrasing Aristotle, philosopher Will Durant wrote, "We are what we repeatedly do. Excellence then, is not an act, but a habit" (Durant, 1961, p. 98). A well-lived life isn't achieved through a few big valued acts. Instead, a valued life results from chaining together smaller values-based actions over and over and over again until they create a larger pattern of a whole well-lived life. So, even as you are guiding your clients in taking one small valued step at a time, it is also important to help them see the bigger picture of the valued life they're working to create. It is our job as guides to help our clients pause and notice the magnificent landscape they are creating for themselves one turtle power step at a time. One way to help structure this process of taking small steps that build upon each other to create a whole valued life is through the process of values prototyping.

Values Prototyping

The concept of prototyping is usually used by those in the design or manufacturing world. However, Bill Burnett and Dave Evans, who teach in the Design Program at Stanford University, have developed a program and subsequent book, *Designing Your Life* (2016), in which they take the same design principles used to create new products, including the idea of prototyping, and apply them to help people create their lives. Their mantra, "building is thinking," reflects the central concept that prototyping is a way to learn through doing. Prototyping helps people further explore and gather data about something they are interested in creating. According to Burnett and Evans:

> When we use the term "prototyping" in design thinking, we do not mean making something to check whether your solution is right. We don't mean creating a representation of a completed design… [Prototyping] is all about asking good questions, outing our hidden biases and assumptions, iterating rapidly, and creating momentum for a path we'd like to try out. (2016, p. 112)

This same prototyping idea can be applied to exploring values. Values prototyping is not a thought experiment; it's about learning through action. Taking action affords our clients new experiences from which they can learn more about themselves and the paths that they may want to commit to in the longer term. Taking action also allows for serendipity. They may meet new people, discover new things, or encounter new opportunities. In addition, through active experimentation with different versions of valued action, they get to actually *feel* what it is like to live out the valued direction, not just imagine it. Taking action is essential for all these forms of learning. Values prototyping is a way for our clients to take valued action with the aim of learning more about what they would choose to value.

Sometimes we can spend so much time trying to "figure it out" or "get it right" that we stall out before we ever get started. Through years of teaching, I've seen many students struggle with this when it comes to writing research papers. They spend so much time researching every angle on the topic that they leave little time for the writing process itself. Unfortunately, it's through the writing process that they would likely be best able to refine and clarify their thinking. Less time researching and more time writing would result in a much better paper. The same thing happens to many of our clients. Through the initial phases of values exploration, clients may have developed some sense of what values they might be interested in exploring further, but how to actually live out that life often eludes them. Clients (and sometimes therapists) often then think that more "research" or thinking is what is needed to clarify their values. However, I would argue that often, a more effective strategy at that point is to learn by doing. That's where values prototyping comes in. By experimenting with various ways of living out a value or testing different hypotheses about how best to live out their values in a particular valued domain, clients can start to learn more about what would be truly important and meaningful to them. Through values prototyping, "figuring it out" comes through testing it out rather than just thinking it out.

Elements of an Effective Values Prototype

When it comes to selecting effective protypes, there are two essential features to consider. You want to make sure that the prototypes you design are 1. active and

2. focused on qualities of action and not just the form of a certain behavior. Other concepts for how to select effective goals can also be useful here, but we will not focus on these (to learn more about effective goal setting, see Luoma et al., 2017, chapter 7, or Moran et al., 2018).

PROTOTYPES ARE ACTIVE

Values are about living a vital, vibrant, meaning-filled life. Therefore, we want to design prototypes that will help move clients toward that vital life. I often talk with clients about the concept of "dead person goals" (Lindsley, 1968). A dead person goal is any goal that a dead person can accomplish better than a living person can. For example, if the client's goal is to not fight with their sister, any dead person is always going to fight less with their sister than any living person will. Not fighting with your sister is a dead person goal. Dead person goals create lifelessness as opposed to a life of vitality. But expressing love and appreciation to your sister is something that a dead person can't do; it's an active goal that has potential. The more we focus on dead person goals in our life, even if we are "successful," the more we're working on becoming more like, well, a dead person. Dead person goals are linked to avoiding or escaping things we don't like, whereas values prototyping aims to gather more information about the kind of life we *do* want and what we would want our life to stand for. An example of shifting from a passive prototype to an active one might look like shifting from "I am going to experiment with not arguing with my sister when we talk on Sunday" to "I am going to test out what happens when I notice at least one thing I appreciate about my sister during my conversation with her on Sunday, and I'm going to share that with her."

PROTOTYPES ATTEND TO THE QUALITY OF ACTION

As we've said, valuing isn't just about what we are doing, but also how we are doing it. It's important that prototyping attends to the qualities our clients are bringing to those actions they are experimenting with. Therefore, for any prototype a client tests out, it is important to have them track the qualities they brought to the experiment (step 2 of the prototyping process, outlined below). In addition, you can also specifically design prototypes that focus directly on the quality-of-action part of valuing. In order to do this, your client can take an action they are already doing, but then prototype what it is like to do that same action in a way that intentionally reflects whatever value they are wanting to test out. For example, let's say your client wants to prototype a value of being curious in their interactions with others. If your client picks up their kids from school every day, they might identify one or more actions they could take while picking up their kids that might foster curiosity. For example, maybe on Monday they will experiment with pausing while they ask their kids, "How was school today?" focusing on what happens when they really listen instead of just asking offhandedly as they are driving out of the parking lot. Maybe Tuesday's experiment would be listening for one thing that surprised them or was somehow new in what their kids were talking about and then asking their kids some follow-up question about that. The action of picking up their kids isn't new, and maybe even asking them "How was your day?" is something they habitually do, but they are prototyping different ways to bring the quality of curiosity into those behaviors.

Tool: Values Prototyping

Values prototyping is best used after you've done some of the work outlined in the previous three chapters with your clients. Maybe you've done a Values Card Sort with them (chapter 3), used the Sweet Spot (chapter 4) or the Feared Eulogy exercise (chapter 5), or used other values exploration tools. Thus, at this point you likely already have a general sense of the contexts (or valued domains) where your client might start prototyping. It's often helpful to zoom in on one domain as you start prototyping. While ultimately we are interested in helping our clients create whole lives of meaning and purpose, because values tend to be fairly consistent across valued domains (a person who wants to patiently support their family usually would ideally want to have some of those same qualities transfer to their friendship relationships or even members of their broader community as well), changes in one domain can often inform later changes in other domains.

In addition, as you start, try to help your clients not take this process too seriously. The whole idea here is to take some of the weight off what can otherwise be a weighty issue. It's not the entire Himalayas your client is trying to climb, it's just one turtle power step to take. This can be especially important for clients who tend to be more perfectionistic, overcontrolled, prone to procrastination, or in some other way rigid about trying to "get it right" such that they risk getting caught up in their minds at the cost of delayed, limited, or no action. They are not committing to a whole life filled with whatever value they are exploring, they are just testing it out. If they end up taking a values step that they, in the end, discover is not something they actually would choose to value, well, that's great information. The point is to get them out there valuing so they can learn through the process.

There are three basic steps to values prototyping: 1. Design a prototype to test, 2. Implement and collect data, and 3. Review, revise, repeat.

STEP 1: DESIGN A PROTOTYPE TO TEST

At this stage, the task is to design a prototype that will help your client gather more information by testing out one aspect of a valued life. In creating a values prototype, clients take some of the initial values concepts they identified in your earlier values work together and translate them into actual behaviors. The prototype allows a specific, practical, and active way to explore a possible interesting future, even if only for a few minutes, an hour, or a day. Testing out new behaviors allows the client to feel what it would be like to live that particular form of their value, even if only for a short while. For example, if your client wants to focus on playfulness, the two of you could work to design a prototype that would help provide some more information about living a life that moves them toward playfulness.

There are countless ways to design a prototype, and the process is only limited to the client and therapist's creativity. Below, we outline three specific strategies for designing a prototype: 1. Building prototypes around questions, 2. Creating prototypes that utilize perspective-taking interviews, and 3. Identifying an "ideal day" that serves as the basis for a prototype. Regardless of the method, the key is to come up with something specific the client can test out in order to learn something about what they would choose to value in their lives.

Building prototypes around questions. The purpose of a prototype is fundamentally to encounter new experiences that can help answer important questions. Good prototypes isolate some aspect of what the person thinks they may want to choose to value and allow them to experiment with it to see what, if anything, they find meaningful or interesting about it. Asking questions is one key strategy for generating new ideas that might lead to a prototype. Here are some questions you might explore with your client (either in session together or through out-of-session writing assignments) in order to identify what concrete behaviors to include in the prototype:

- What might help me foster _____ (e.g., playful engagement) in my life?

- What specific aspects or forms of _____ (e.g., curiosity) do I think might be most meaningful or important to me?

- What impact does it have on my interactions with others when I am more _____ (e.g., lovingly supportive)?

- What is the next smallest step I could take to embody the qualities of _____ (e.g., joyfulness) this week?

- What behaviors would I exhibit if I were embodying _____ (e.g., compassionate living)? What behaviors are not _____ (e.g., compassionate) and thus I would refrain from them?

- Is there something I have done in the past that was in the service of _____ (e.g., caring well for our planet)? What could I do now that is similar so I can see what it's like living out that value as the person I am today?

- What characters do I know from books or films that embody _____ (e.g., justice)? What could I do that would emulate these characters in some way?

Prototypes designed around questions like these can range from activities that can be accomplished in minutes or hours, to more general prototypes involving ongoing activities that may take weeks to accomplish. For example, a client might focus on the question of "What is the next smallest step I can take this week to embody the qualities of living adventurously?" by designing a prototype where they test out asking their partner to go on a hike they have never been on before. Alternatively, a more ongoing prototype to address the question of "What might help me foster gratitude in my life?" might be experimenting with keeping a daily gratitude journal for a month and tracking the consequences. For more about designing a prototype around questions, you can find a detailed clinical vignette of my client Sasha that illustrates this process at http://www.newharbinger.com/43218.

Creating prototypes that utilize perspective-taking interviews. One way to explore a possible value is to talk to people who are already living it. This is a particularly helpful prototyping strategy for clients who are having difficulty generating a sense of what it might look like to live out a particular value. In this strategy, you help your client identify people they know, have known, or could conceivably meet who are living out the quality, value, or valued goal that they want to explore. This may be someone they know well, like a friend or family member, a person they only know peripherally, such as a work acquaintance or a friend of a friend, or someone they have heard of that they might be able to speak with. If your client can't think of anyone they could conceivably interview, then a preliminary step might be to talk to people they do know. Your client can tell those people what value(s) the client is looking to explore and ask people who they think embody that quality or who have engaged in a similar valued action.

Once they have identified a person or several people who have agreed to be interviewed, the client interviews that person or people with the goal of really understanding what it is like to be that person living that value or acting toward that valued goal. You should work with your client to identify questions that they can ask in the interview that will elicit the interviewee's story of how they came to embody that quality, what specifically they do that relates to the value in question, and what it's like to live out that value. For example, let's say your client is interviewing a person about a value of living with generosity. Questions they might ask that person could include:

- What do you do on a typical day to live generously?

- How would you describe what living with generosity means?

- How have you put generous living into practice?

- How did you get started on this path of generous living? What keeps you going on that path?

Keep in mind that the interviewing process is not solely a means to gather information, but it is also a perspective-taking exercise. Thus, the interview needs to help your client take on the perspective of the other person such that they can imagine what it would be like to live out a particular value in the way that this person is choosing to do.

In addition to the questions they will be asking of the person they are interviewing, you should also identify questions for your client to reflect on after the interview. For example:

- What aspects of this person's story was I attracted to?

- What parts of their story did I feel some discomfort around?

- Could I imagine myself doing anything like that person does? What might the impact of that be for myself and those around me?

- What aspects of how this person is living inspire me?

- Does their experience give me any ideas of things I could potentially prototype?

- What do my reactions to their story tell me about what I might value?

Prototypes that are based on this type of interview allow clients to step into the shoes of someone else who may be already valuing whatever it is the client is considering making more central in their life. They learn by taking on the perspective of that person.

Identifying an "ideal day" to prototype. Sometimes it is helpful to identify an "ideal day" related to a value your client is interested in exploring that they can then deconstruct and build prototypes around. This could be an idealized version of an actual day the client has lived when they felt they embodied the value they are exploring. Alternatively, they could create a fictional ideal day based on what they imagine they would be doing if they were fully embodying the value at hand. Whether it is based on a memory or something that hasn't actually happened, have the client image themselves living an idealized version of the day and write about the day in detail from the moment they get up in the morning until the moment they go to bed. Have them include what they would be doing, thinking, and feeling at various points during the day. Once they've written out the day, the two of you can deconstruct the various parts of that day to see what elements they might want to test out through a prototype in order to experience what it is like to bring those values into their life.

Plan for potential barriers. As you and your client are going through the process of designing a values prototype, keep in mind that the point isn't the successful completion of the specific goal or task. The point is to structure experiments that will get clients moving in a potentially valued direction so that they can learn more about what is important to them, and what longer-term avenues and patterns they may want to commit to. Barriers inevitably show up along a valued path. These "barriers" are an important part of the learning process and you will want to plan for them in the design phase.

Here are some questions your client can reflect on that can help identify possible barriers and give you both information about what might make a prototype more workable or other things you might need to attend to in order to address the barriers:

- Do I have the resources, both psychological and physical, that I need to take action on this prototype? If not, what steps can I take to acquire those resources?

- Do I like this idea? How do I feel toward engaging in this action?

- How confident am I that I can actually implement this prototype?

- Is this prototype specific enough so that I know how to take action on it?

- Is this prototype actionable? Is it something I can do with my hands and my feet versus a feeling or thought that I have little control over?

- What difficult thoughts or feelings do I think are likely to show up once I start implementing this prototype?

This last question about the potential internal barriers that might show up is essential, as it is often our minds that generate the most pervasive and tricky barriers. Internal barriers can include thoughts like "I'm not this kind of person" or "I don't feel like it," or feelings of panic, lethargy, or self-doubt. Knowing what types of internal barriers might show up also provides useful information about where our clients might need to develop more psychological flexibility in order to create and sustain a values-based life (see chapter 2 for more on psychological flexibility). For example, if a barrier related to their conceptualized self, such as "I'm not the kind of person who can...," shows up, that may tell you as the therapist that some self-as-context/perspective-taking work would be useful. Or if the barrier is "This isn't going to work," then strengthening defusion repertoires may be in order. Or if sensations of anxiety or physical pain are the internal barrier, it's possible that incorporating some willingness/acceptance into your prototyping would be useful.

STEP 2: IMPLEMENT AND COLLECT DATA

Here's where clients get out and start putting their prototypes to the test. They have a specific, active plan they are ready to test out. They are also aware that barriers are likely to show up along the way and they are ready for them. Because the purpose of prototyping is to gather information, we need to attend to how we collect that data. Clients need to be able to contact and track both the immediate and the longer-term consequences of their valuing. Questions for them to reflect on might include:

- Did my actions make a positive difference in an area of life that matters to me? If so, what kind of a difference did they make?

- What got in the way, if anything, of me fully implementing my values prototype as I would have wanted?

- What would it be like if I continued this pattern of behavior over the course of a month, a year, a lifetime?

- If I were looking back on a life in which I had consistently lived out this value to the fullest, how would I feel about having lived that life? What thoughts or feelings might I have if I were to look back at the end of having lived that life?

- If I decided to not continue valuing in this way, looking back a year from now, what thoughts or feelings might I have about not having lived out this value? What might I think or feel at the end of my life as I look back on a life of not having lived out this value?

- Did I experience anything unexpected while implementing or reflecting on this prototype? What might that say about me or my values?

This last question may be among the most important as it's often the unanticipated outcomes that are the greatest teachers. Reactions or experiences that did not fit with expectations may be troubling for clients, but they are also very useful as they indicate that the person has encountered feedback about themselves or their environment that they may want to learn from.

In addition to the immediate and longer-term consequences, we also want clients to gather information on the *interpersonal* and *intrapersonal* impact of their actions. These questions can include:

- How did my actions impact others? How did others react to my valued actions? Is it possible I'm making assumptions about how my actions impacted them and do I need to ask them directly to find out?

- Did engaging in this valued action contribute to a better quality of life for myself or for others around me? If so, in what ways? Do I need to ask others to find out?

- How do I feel about myself having engaged in this valued action? Did I like the person I was when I was engaging in this action?

- What thoughts, feelings, or bodily sensations occurred while I was engaging in this valued action? What thoughts, feelings, or sensations showed up after I did the prototype experiment? What do these reactions tell me about what might be important to me?

- How might my relationships be different a year from now if I continued enacting this prototype? What might be possible in future relationships if I continued this way of living?

- How might I feel about myself one year from now if I continued to consistently live out this way of valuing over a whole year?

STEP 3: REVIEW, REVISE, REPEAT

Prototyping is an iterative process. We need to take the data we gather along the way and revise our prototype accordingly. Sometimes clients will decide to completely throw out a prototype. For example, they may learn that while they *thought* living playfully would be extremely important to them, after prototyping "playful" for a while, they realized that being playful wasn't actually very meaningful to them. Maybe it turns out that it was their partner who wanted them to be more playful. Or maybe they realized playful was a "should" they had learned somewhere along the way, but when they freely chose to experiment with their related prototypes, living playfully didn't really float their boat (in other words, it wasn't intrinsically reinforcing, which if you remember back to chapter 1 is part of the definition of a value). That's great information! Alternately, it may be that the specific prototypes they tried weren't workable or engaging for one reason or another. In that case, they may need to try out other versions of "playful" or develop more skill at it before it becomes reinforcing.

Creating larger patterns of valued living. Values are fundamentally about the link between what someone is doing here-and-now and a larger context of purpose in which these actions are embedded. Small actions devoid of context are meaningless, and some meaning only develops over time. Thus, clients are supported in revising and extending the reach of their prototypes in order to create increasingly larger patterns of valued living. This means that onetime actions are often not enough to test out a prototype. The prototype itself might be a sustained activity, such as taking a class or joining a group of people engaging in a hobby as part of making new friends. Clients could also repeat a prototype across different contexts or in different valued domains while collecting data. Prototypes can also build upon one another, taking one valued step after another to eventually create a prototype for a whole pattern of valued living. However you do it, your task is to help your client continue to review, repeat, and expand their prototypes based on the data they collect until they have a more complete picture of what living a rich, vibrant, meaning-filled life would be for them.

TROUBLESHOOTING VALUES PROTOTYPING

Because prototyping is all about experimenting in order to gather information, there aren't many ways for it to go "wrong." All data tell us something. The main stumbling blocks tend to come from failing to effectively collect data. Sometimes this is a simple matter of a client forgetting what they were supposed to collect data on. Many of us have had the experience of walking out of some appointment, whether with a therapist, a physician, or your personal trainer, with all the intention in the world to follow through on the actions you discussed, only to completely forget about it until your next appointment. Thus, a written reminder is key. I almost always write down whatever my client has committed to for their prototype experiment, giving it to them to take as a reminder, perhaps with questions to consider.

Some clients will try to just recall their experience of the prototype experiment from memory. While they might like to think they will remember all the details, memory just doesn't work that way, especially when it comes to some of the detailed information we're looking to capture in our data collection. So, I always encourage my clients to *write it down!* They can do this through daily journaling, or they can create a simple tracking form where they record the results of their "experiments" at the end of each day. You may even want to create a tracking form to give your clients to help them record the results of their prototyping experiment. Whatever it is, have your client bring their completed "data collection" back to the next session so the two of you can review it together.

The other trouble spot that can arise during the prototyping process is when clients encounter what they interpret as "failure." Some prototypes are inevitably going to turn out different than anticipated. If they didn't, then what's the point of experimenting? Clients will often interpret these unexpected outcomes as failures. If your client becomes entangled with the belief that their experiment "failed," it can derail the prototyping process. So, if these kinds of barriers arise, it's important for the therapist to remind the client that prototypes are experiments for the purposes of learning and aren't about trying to get anywhere in particular. The therapist might reframe these "failures" as useful data. Or, this may be an opportunity to work with willingness and defusion repertoires that allow the client to step back and make room for these thoughts as part of the journey toward more clarity about what they want their life to stand for.

Pitfalls to Learning Through Doing

This chapter has been all about the reality that sometimes the best way to explore values is experientially through engaging in valued action. Below are a couple of the most common difficulties people have when utilizing this strategy in values exploration.

Too Much Talk, Not Enough Action

The point of prototyping is to help your client learn about what would make for a more meaningful, purposeful, vital life for them. That requires action. All the values exploration in the world doesn't make a lick of difference if you don't start acting on your ideas. I've seen a lot of therapists spend too many sessions talking about values exploration, doing Values Card Sorts, Sweet Spot exercises, Eulogy exercises, and others, only to leave out the part about trying out those values. Remember, clients don't need to "figure it all out" before taking action. Sometimes taking action and tracking consequences is the best way to further explore one's values.

Buying into Barriers

Internal barriers, such as difficult and entangling thoughts and feelings, will inevitably arise on the path toward a meaningful, values-based life. A psychological flexibility model tells us that rather than buying into or trying to problem solve away these difficult thoughts and feelings, which usually takes us down the EA route, we can take the power out of mental and emotional barriers through developing defusion skills, practicing willingness, learning to be present, and becoming more flexible in our perspective taking. Thus, throughout this process, make sure you are also tracking your client's overall psychological flexibility, as it is those repertoires that will allow for more sustained valued living.

Takeaways

- Valuing is happening right now. Helping clients track what they are valuing allows them to disengage the autopilot and gives them a choice about what they would choose to value.

- Reinforce the act of intentional valuing.

- Some of the best learning comes through doing. Values prototyping is an excellent way to continue the values exploration process.

- Values prototyping allows clients to get practice with intentional valuing while gathering important data in the process.

- Prototyping is an iterative and expanding process. Revise, repeat, and extend prototypes to create larger patterns of valued living.

Next Steps

- When a client is telling you about an activity they engaged in this week, ask them to notice what that action was valuing. You can either use some of the example questions in this chapter or come up with your own to explore this with your client.

- Use the Daily Valuing Tracking Form with one of your clients.

- Develop a values prototyping data collection form you could use with a client. Include information you think would be helpful for the client to track in their ongoing values exploration.

- Identify a client who might be ready for some values prototyping and introduce the idea to them to see if they are open to exploring it.

- **Inside-out learning:** Design and execute your own values prototype. Start with a question you want to answer about what you are valuing or would like to try valuing. Generate one prototype to experiment with. Implement that prototype and record the relevant data. What did you learn? How might you want to revise the prototype?

CHAPTER 7

When Inflexibility Creates Barriers to Values

Obstacles do not block the path. Obstacles are the path. —Zen proverb

It's often hard to know what is most important. It's harder still to hold on to that knowledge, especially in times of fear and suffering, when the call to avoid the pain of life pulls most strongly. Understandably, it is often during these times that psychological inflexibility creeps in and, like the Sirens' song, threatens to pull us off course from what truly matters. This is a normal and inevitable part of valued living and something we need to anticipate as therapists working with values.

In this chapter we will look at some of the common barriers that arise as clients begin exploring their values and identify ways to help clients develop the tools needed to effectively deal with these challenges when they emerge. When barriers arise, clients may need assistance in stepping outside of the stories they have about themselves, others, and the world (flexible perspective taking); seeing those thoughts as thoughts rather than "truths" (defusion); making space for the painful thoughts, sensations, and emotions that those stories are often trying to protect us from (willingness); and attending to what is important in the here-and-now (present moment). Our job is to travel the path with them for a while, helping them develop those capabilities so that they have the tools needed to live a life in line with what is most important to them even after therapy has ended.

Sometimes the Best Answer Is a Good Question

Human minds have evolved to be exquisite problem-solving machines. This goes for therapists' minds as well. When difficulties arise, when clients present us with stumpers, or when we feel stuck, it's natural for us to want to immediately find the solution. Our minds tend to frame these events as problems, and we go to work on solving them. However, sometimes this knee-jerk urge to solve the problem is part of what keeps us (both client and therapist) stuck. Sometimes, clients themselves can even appear to us as problems. In these situations, it's important to allow yourself the space to slow down, step back, and consider new perspectives that might help you see what you as the therapist may need to learn or how you might access new ways of being that you didn't even know were available to you. It's also important to keep in mind that 1. all of us have more to learn and 2. none of us has all the answers. If there are facts about what it means to be human, I contend that those are two of them. So, when difficulties arise, see if you can give yourself the grace to not know and to learn what is needed to be learned, together, with your client.

Tool: Values-Focused Psychological Flexibility Exploration

Sometimes a good question is better than a good answer. From a psychological flexibility standpoint, willingness, defusion, flexible perspective taking, and the ability to attend to what is present are what make sustained valued living possible. Your client may be stuck in any or all of these areas. Committed action is also an essential component of psychological flexibility, but I am not emphasizing it in this section on barriers to values exploration because committed action comes after some clarity is gained around values, not before. Committed action, by definition, involves instantiating values, or in other words, putting values into action. Instead, I'll be focusing on the other four flexibility repertoires (willingness, defusion, flexible perspective taking/self-as-context, and present-moment awareness) as those are the areas that often need strengthening in order for flexible values exploration to occur.

Below is a five-step process I encourage you to try out when you find yourself stuck or having difficulty in your values work with a client. It involves asking yourself good questions that might help you learn something about your client's psychological flexibility and those flexibility repertoires you might need to work on together.

Step 1: Identify a client who is having difficulty or whom you are having difficulty with. Remind yourself that none of us has all the answers and that this very act of reflecting can be a valued action. What value would you want this reflection process to put into action?

Step 2: Read through the Values-Focused Psychological Flexibility Reflection Questions that follow and identify the ones you want to reflect on based on two criteria: 1. pick questions that seem the most intriguing or seem to hold the most possibility and 2. pick questions that you most *don't* want to explore. It's often in the places we don't want go where we have the most to learn.

Step 3: Write a brief response to each question. Don't simply think about them. It's often only when we write down what we think and feel that we get clarity on our perspective or see gaps in our thinking.

Step 4: Give your client a rating on each of the four psychological flexibility rating scales that accompany the Values-Focused Psychological Flexibility Questions.

Step 5: Given your responses to the questions you selected and your ratings of your client's psychological flexibility, how can this inform your values work with the client? What action might you take? What might you need to learn or read up on to help this client? Would getting consultation from a colleague be helpful? If so, who? Did specific strategies emerge that you can test out in future sessions with this client?

Questions About Experiential Avoidance/Willingness

- Does my client see difficult experiences as a normal part of life, or do they tend to see painful thoughts, feelings, memories, and sensations as problems to be solved? What kind of behavior does this lead to? How does this tendency manifest as we start to talk about what matters to them?

- What feelings and/or thoughts is my client most motivated to avoid (for example, anger, sadness, jealousy, boredom, shame, hopelessness, anxiety, loneliness, "I'm damaged," "I should have...")? What longing/desire/need/value might these painful emotions be related to?

- What does my client do when we begin to talk about something painful or difficult (including values exploration)? Do they explore it openly? Do they acknowledge that it is painful? Do they rationalize or minimize the discomfort? How might I address these behaviors?

- What is one emotion/thought/memory/sensation that, if I could help my client make space for it, would free them up to take meaningful action in their life?

- Is there a sense of struggle, either within the client or between the client and me, in relation to a particular valued domain? Is there a sense of resignation? What might this tell me about what I need to explore?

- What difficult feelings, thoughts, memories, or sensations do I think come up for my client when we engage in values conversations? If I don't know, what could I do to find out?

Based on the above questions, rate your client's current level of willingness to experience painful thoughts, feelings, sensations, and memories in the service of what is important to them.

1	2	3	4	5	?
Not at all willing	Slightly willing	Somewhat willing	Significantly willing	Completely willing	Don't know

Questions About Defusion

- Does my client rely on a set of rules (should/shouldn't, must/can't, right/wrong) to guide their behavior? Where do these rules lead to the most constraints? What can I do to help my client loosen their attachment to these rules?

- Does my client rigidly hold to certain principles as being correct/right/moral in all contexts regardless of their workability? How much do they engage in dichotomous thinking? Do these seem to get in the way of their ability to openly explore what they might choose for their life? If so, how can I help my client notice the effects of holding so strongly to these principles or acting on dichotomous thinking?

- Does it feel like my client is often trying to convince me or argue for the rightness of a principle or value? Are there times when "Yes, but…" tends to come up a lot? What might my client be believing (fused with) at these times? If I don't know, how can my client and I both become more aware of some of the thoughts they might be most fused with?

- Are there areas of values conversation that elicit high levels of certainty from my client? Does that certainty limit my client's openness, curiosity, or values exploration in unhelpful ways? What do my client and I need to learn about that?

- Are there times when my client and I are discussing values when the conversation becomes busy, complex, or filled with comparison? If so, what tends to trigger this?

- What strategies might I use to help this client become more able to notice their thoughts as thoughts and get less caught up in their evaluations?

- What thought, belief, or story most holds this client back from being in contact with what matters most to them? What could I do to help this thought have less control over my client?

Based on the above questions, rate your client's current level of defusion (i.e., their ability to see thoughts as thoughts and not be rigidly attached to thoughts/beliefs).

1	2	3	4	5	?
Not at all defused	Slightly defused	Somewhat defused	Significantly defused	Completely defused	Don't know

Questions About Flexible Perspective Taking

- Does my client tend to get caught up in categorical and judgmental thoughts about themself or others?

- How much is my client able to view situations from alternate perspectives? What alternate perspectives might this client benefit from being able to take and in what situations?

- How much is my client able to engage in empathy or self-compassion? Do deficits in these areas impair my client from knowing what really matters to them? If so, how can I help my client develop these capacities?

- Does my client frequently appeal to their history as a way to understand, rationalize, or justify their responses or unworkable behavior (for example, "I can't trust people because I was abused")?

- What story (or stories) does my client tell about themself or others that most gets in the way of them having a sense of choice in their life? What can I do to help them step outside that story or be able to see it as a story?

- Has my client narrowed their life to only having one or two identities or roles (for example, mother, father, professional, "mentally ill," "addict")? If so, is this causing difficulties? What might I do to address this narrowing?

- Do our values conversations feel old and stuck? If so, when does this happen? How can I use perspective taking to bring more life to the conversation?

Based on the above questions, rate your client's current ability to step outside the stories they have about themself and others and engage in flexible perspective taking.

1	2	3	4	5	?
No ability to take alternate perspectives	Limited ability to take alternate perspectives	Some ability to take alternate perspectives	Significant ability to take alternate perspectives	Completely able to take alternate perspectives	Don't know

Questions About Present-Moment Contact

- Does my client ruminate (either out loud or internally) on past events or worry about imagined future events while in session? What strategies can I use to shift our values conversations from abstract discussions or discussions about the future/past to active valuing in the present moment?

- How well is my client able to shift from focusing on events outside the session to what is occurring in the present moment in therapy? How might I help them to do so more effectively?

- Do I often feel like my client isn't really engaged with me, but rather, is talking *at* me? Do we need to revisit the "why" underlying therapy itself or the values that might be relevant to our relationship?

- Does my client tend to tell stories that feel lifeless and old, like they have told them a hundred times before? Is it in my client's best interest for me to allow that to continue? Do I need to learn how to interrupt the client during these times? If so, what do I need to learn or be willing to experience in order to do that?

- Is my client often focused on getting someplace else in their life or achieving/accomplishing the next thing? How might this interfere with their moment-to-moment valuing?

- How can I make our values conversations more experiential and less "heady"?

- At what points in session does this client tend to stray into the future and get caught up in worry or move into the past and get stuck in rumination? What tends to trigger this? When this happens, how can I help my client return to the present moment?

- Are there times when values talk triggers intense problem solving (in other words, a focus on getting to some future point)? Is this interfering with the curious and expansive quality needed for values exploration?

Based on the above questions, rate your client's current ability to be in contact with the present moment.

1	2	3	4	5	?
No ability to be in the present	Limited ability to be in the present	Some ability to be in the present	Significant ability to be in the present	Completely able to be in the present	Don't know

Common Values Challenges Linked to Psychological Inflexibility

Through reflecting on the questions above, you have had a chance to take a step back to look at the bigger picture of how your client's psychological inflexibility may be interfering with values work. Below, I review some of the most common stuck points that often arise in values work, viewing them through the lens of psychological flexibility theory, and what this might suggest about how you might help.

When Avoidance Dominates Values (Deficits in Willingness Repertoires)

Pain inevitably emerges along the road to what matters most. When painful thoughts or feelings arise, many of our clients rely on ineffective and rigid avoidance strategies because that is the only "answer" that their learning history has taught them. Many of our clients' lives have become oriented around getting rid of what they *don't* want in the hope that doing so will eventually lead them to a life that they *do* want. They may use drugs, alcohol, sex, food, overexercise, or work to numb out their feelings. They may put off valued action, either struggling with procrastination and/or failing to follow through on commitments, including agreed-upon therapy commitments, such as homework assignments and not missing appointments. They may also feel hopeless about ever being able to live a life of meaning and purpose. And so, understandably, they respond to that pain in the way that most of us have learned to do when faced with pain—by trying to reduce it somehow.

Because values are inextricably linked to pain, you will often see this avoidance show up in the therapy room as soon as you initiate discussions about values. Below are some common ways this can happen.

CLIENT IS FOCUSED ON FEELING (OR NOT FEELING) A CERTAIN WAY

It's common for clients to respond to questions about their values with feeling states. For example, when asked what they would choose to value, clients might respond with statements such as, "I want to be less anxious," "I want to feel confident," or "I want to feel better about myself." We call these "process goals." If values, by definition, represent the outcome of a life well lived, then feeling better is a process goal if it is seen as a necessary precursor to that well-lived life. The unspoken implication of "I want to feel more self-confident," for example, is usually "I don't want to feel this self-doubt that I currently feel" and often "I need to feel more confident in order to do x, y, or z." While it is common and understandable to prioritize feeling good, a rigid focus on feeling good can distract us from the larger purposes of our life. The result is that a rigid focus on "feeling good" comes at the cost of living well.

Strategy to try: Focus on behaviors. When clients are rigidly focused on experiencing (or not experiencing) a particular feeling state, it can be useful to have them reconnect with the idea that values are about qualities of action. As outlined in chapter 1, values are about how we want to behave as we go through this life, not how we want to feel or not feel. The following is a brief example of how you might describe this to a client focused on feeling or not feeling a certain way:

Therapist: Values are the ways of living that would be most meaningful and important to you, the kinds of things you would want your life to have stood for when you get to the end of it. Feelings, on the other hand, are sensations that come and go. Sometimes feelings seem to be directly tied to what we are doing, but other times they seem like they come out of nowhere. They are often out of our control. With values, we're focusing on what you *do* have choice over—how you live this life, what you put your energy in the service of, and the actions you take in your life. People often report that they feel "better," maybe more proud, satisfied, or happy, when they are living a life that is meaningful and important, but that is more like a positive side effect. It isn't the goal. Living a valued life is the goal. When feelings become the primary goal of our life, we can lose sight of what really matters in the bigger picture.

Since values are about how we want to behave, not how we want to feel, you can also shift the focus to behavior by asking clients to imagine what they would do if they already had the feeling they are chasing. For example:

- If you were an actor playing a character who was feeling "confident/happy/good about themself," how would that character behave? What do you imagine that character would be able to do that you don't feel is possible in your life as it is now?

- If you could take a pill that would mean you would feel good all of the time without ever feeling anxiety, sadness, worry, self-doubt, or anger, then how do you think you would spend your time?

- What are you able to do when you are feeling happy/self-confident/at peace that you don't feel able to do at other times?

CLIENT IS FOCUSED ON "PEAK EXPERIENCES" OR EMOTIONAL INTENSITY

Some clients are rigidly focused on experiencing emotional intensity in general. These clients are constantly chasing the next "peak experience," whether that is climbing the next tallest mountain, starting the next fantastic business, finding the drug to give them the next highest high, or even having a child in the hope that doing so will bring meaning to their life. Upon closer investigation, you may unearth that this intense pursuit is centrally about obtaining a particular feeling (such as excitement, "the rush," confidence, or power) and avoiding other feelings (such as self-doubt, boredom, loneliness, insignificance, or vulnerability) that are hard to be with. As is often the case when trying to grasp on to any feeling, their conquests tend to feel hollow or empty and they quickly move on to the next "peak experience" in the hope that that will be the one to offer a more lasting and authentic sense of meaning or satisfaction.

Clinical example: Jerome. My client Jerome was what some people would refer to as an "adrenaline chaser." His rigid focus on having "peak experiences" initially caused some difficulties in our values exploration. Whenever I would ask him about times when he felt a sense of vitality or times he felt he was living in a way that was important or meaningful to him, he would talk about some extreme sporting activity or adventure. However, there was always something hollow in his description of these experiences. These conversations lacked the vitality (though they were certainly exciting) and willing vulnerability that lets me know I'm on the right track in terms of values. So, we kept exploring. The following is what came up during one of these conversations when he was relaying how "awesome" the previous weekend's base jumping adventure had been.

Therapist: Can you tell me a little more about what is meaningful or important to you about being someone who base jumps? (*Note here that I am shifting the conversation away from the elements of the specific activity toward focusing on him personally as he was engaging in that behavior, by focusing him on "being someone who base jumps." My hope was that doing so would get him closer to talking about the qualities of action that were meaningful, rather than just the activity itself.*)

Client: Well, to be honest, I guess it's not really all that meaningful or even that important to me. In fact, I usually feel really let down or disappointed after something like that, like it wasn't quite intense enough. I guess I do it for the rush. The rush I get when I'm about to jump is the only time when I don't feel utterly bored in my life. It's better than that.

Through this conversation, Jerome began to see that, for him, seeking peak experiences wasn't really about moving *toward* something as much as it was about moving *away* from boredom. In addition, it seemed that his rigid and persistent pursuit of increasingly intense emotional experiences had desensitized him to the sources of meaning and purpose that might be available to him in more emotionally nuanced or subtle experiences. He hadn't taken the time to explore what might be of value to him in things like relationships or nature, for example, because he was only in pursuit of "the rush" rather than values. Thus, while he had frequent but fleeting moments of intense pleasure, his lack of contact with his values resulted in a pervasive lack of meaning and purpose in his life.

Strategy to try: Explore the subtle. For clients like Jerome who seem to equate values with emotional intensity, I'd recommend focusing values exploration on more subtle, lower intensity experiences, particularly relational experiences involving bonding, connection, or intimacy. This may be in a relationship they have, or even the therapeutic relationship itself. These clients often have difficulty seeing the potential for contacting values in their everyday lives. Their rigid focus on emotionally intense experiences means that they often miss the lower intensity relational experiences related to bonding, a sense of belonging, or intimacy that are a rich source of meaning and satisfaction for many. The Sweet Spot exercise (see chapter 4) can be useful in this situation, as long as you guide the exercise in such a way that the client is able to explore a moment of tenderness, connection, or belonging rather than simply remembering some grand accomplishment.

When Fusion Obscures Values (Deficits in Defusion Repertoires)

The freedom to choose our values requires the ability to step outside the tyranny of our thoughts. When we are only able to see the world through the confines of our thinking, the possibilities for our life become limited. Below are some behaviors you might see when a client's fusion obscures their ability to contact or fully explore values.

CLIENT DENIES OR MINIMIZES VALUES

"What's the point?"
"Nothing matters in the end anyway."
"I don't really care about anything."
All of these may be examples of fusion that serves to deny or minimize values. When you bring up the idea of what matters most to them, these clients might change the topic, make jokes, or dismiss it in some way. Some clients may report that they once used to care about something but have now lost touch with anything that matters. For example, a client might say something like, "Yeah, I used to care about being kind and trusting in my relationships with others. But I've been burned too many times and realized it's just not worth it."

Strategy to try: "If you could choose." It's important to not feed fusion by trying to convince your client of anything. Instead, you can circumvent the mindiness that drives fusion by asking the client to imagine a world that was not bound by the rules imposed by their fusion, a world in which they could choose. For example, you might respond to a client's fused statement of "Nothing really matters anyway" with:

Therapist: If it *were* possible that you could choose, would you choose to have something or someone that was important in your life, or would you choose to have nothing that was important to you? Which one would you choose in your ideal world, assuming you could choose? *(Most people will acknowledge that they would choose wanting to have something/someone.)* Okay then, if that is what you would choose, how about if we make identifying what and who you would want to make important to you a part of what we do? We'll need to carve out some space and it might take some time for us to really explore this, but would that be something you'd be willing to do with me?

CLIENT RESPONDS WITH PLIANCE/COUNTER-PLIANCE

Any time you are exploring values with a client and you hear the words "should" or "shouldn't," your pliance radar should be going off. If you recall back to chapter 3, pliance is when a person's response is based on what they have learned will please (pliance) or displease (counter-pliance) someone else based on how others have responded to their behavior in the past. Clients oriented toward pliance may obsessively seek out the approval of others. Alternatively, clients may make decisions that are the opposite of what they have been told they "should" do (a "He said I have to go right so I'm taking a hard left" kind of counter-pliance response). Clients whose values exploration is dominated by pliance or counter-pliance tend to artificially constrain their behavior based on how it will impact others. They disregard or may not even be aware of their own preferences, priorities, or what might be most meaningful to them personally. Clients may even feel coerced by their own chosen values, shifting what might otherwise be values-based actions into "shoulds" that lose a sense of being freely chosen and instead come under aversive control.

Values conversations that are dominated by pliance/counter-pliance can feel dry, rote, and constrained. There can also be a sense of resignation or even shame to them. One of the most common examples I see of this is when my clients say, "I know I *should* value my health…" Although this statement poses as something about values, more often than not, I've found this to simply be another way my clients are trying to coerce or shame themselves into exercising more, quitting smoking, losing weight, or eating differently. Any of these goals may be ones that the client would like to pursue (or maybe not), but as soon as that goal becomes tied to a "should" rather than a freely chosen, intrinsically reinforcing value, the likelihood of sustaining motivation toward that goal decreases. This is a great example of why you want to pay attention to the *qualities* of the values conversation, rather than just the words that are being said. Does the client's statement come with a sense of free choice and vitality, or is it rooted in pliance, internalized rules, or expectations? Use the four qualities of effective values conversations as your guide and see if you can move the conversation in a direction that elicits those qualities.

Strategy to try: Create a different context. One of the best ways to help a client break free from the confines of their external rules is to take them outside the context in which those rules dominate. Because pliance is generally interpersonally based (the "rules" are perceived to come from others such as parents, a spouse, a larger cultural group, or a religion), a key strategy is to help the client explore what they might choose to value if no one else was around to observe them. You can ask your client:

- What do you think you'd choose to make important if no one would ever know what you chose?

- How would it be for you if everything you did in the service of valuing X was done anonymously so no know would ever know you valued X?

- Let's pretend you are transported through time and space into a totally different culture, one that had a completely different set of rules about what is and is not socially acceptable. Everything about what you've learned from your current upbringing and culture is completely opposite here. (*Give some apt examples like, "In this culture, generosity is considered the highest value. Wealthy individuals are stereotyped as being not generous and therefore have a lower status." Or, "In this culture, women are taught to value mastery and assertiveness and displays of kindness or nurturing by women are viewed negatively."*) How do you think that might change what you would choose to make important? Are there some things from your current culture you'd want to hold on to as important regardless of the new context? Are there some things that may feel a little freeing to let go of?

When Attachment to Stories Limits Values Exploration (Deficits in Flexible Perspective-Taking Repertoires)

Often values lay buried under layers of stories our minds provide us about who we are or should be, what we should care about or do, what is possible or what we're capable of, and what we are not capable of experiencing. Sometimes we get so caught up in our stories that we miss that our view is only from one perspective; we're only looking out through one window. Without the ability to step outside those stories and assumptions and take on alternate perspectives that expand our world beyond their confines, we cannot fully engage in values exploration. Below are some values challenges you might see that could indicate that a client has difficulty stepping outside what they believe to be "true" about themselves or others.

"I'M THE KIND OF PERSON" STORIES

Clients can truncate their values exploration when they restrict themselves (or others or the world) to certain ostensibly immutable classes or types. The words they use to confine themselves can come, for example, in the form of personality descriptors, histories, or diagnoses. They may say things like:

- I'm not the kind of person who is _____ (e.g., bold, courageous, nurturing).

- I wish I were someone who was more _____ (e.g., loving, kind, playful), but that's just not me.

- It isn't okay/safe to be _____ (e.g., vulnerable, intimate, compassionate) in this world.

- Other people are just not _____ (e.g., trustworthy, reliable, caring).

Each of these statements is an objectification of themselves, others, or the world that may reflect a rigid attachment to a narrow story as opposed to a more nuanced and flexible experience with themselves/others/the world. These clients may use values words (or their opposites) as identity labels rather than as ways to describe their behavior. For example, they might say "I am a loyal/reliable/nice/mean/selfish person" in a way that functions more as a kind of objectification of themselves rather than describing the qualities of their actions. In order to see the full spectrum of possible valued lives that could be available to them, we need to help clients take a step back from their restricted perspective. In doing this we are not trying to dispute our client's perspective; they may indeed not frequently act as lovingly or boldly as they would want. We're not trying to convince them that their perspective is wrong, inaccurate, or irrational. It's simply limited because it's only one perspective. Being able to help our clients open up to considering other perspectives may open up different ways of being that would result in a more meaningful and values-consistent life for them.

Strategy to try: Use perspective-taking exercises. Perspective-taking exercises are a bit like magic time machines capable of transcending the boundaries of any preconceived story by transporting a client to a different time or place, or even to being a different person. From this alternate perspective, they may be able to explore a possibility that isn't limited by what they already believe to be "true" about themselves, others, or the world. You can turn simple questions you might already be asking clients (such as "What did you used to care about/value?") into perspective-taking exercises by making slight changes to how you word the questions. In order to do this, you want to shift from simply asking the client to provide information to wording the question in such a way that the client is asked to respond from a different time, place, or person perspective. Below are some examples of perspective-taking questions that you might ask a client whose attachment to the stories they have about themself, others, or the world is limiting their values exploration:

- Can you picture how things were for you before life taught you there wasn't anything worth caring about? If I were talking to the "you" back then, what would that person say they care about?

- Think back to when you were younger and you had more hope for what your life could be. What would that younger, more hopeful you say you longed for back then?

- Is this what you would hope for your children some day? If it were possible, what would you want them to most care about? What would you want to matter to them?

- See if you can extend the trajectory of your current life out a bit. Imagine you continued to live exactly as you are. What do you imagine life might be like for you if you continued on this same trajectory for another five years, ten years, for the rest of your life? Looking back ten years from now, what do you think that the you at that time might say they lost out on by having continued to live in this way? What would they say they had missed out on?

Each of these questions above could be made into an experiential exercise by having the client close their eyes and visualize the scene described in the question. In addition, you can use more structured and extensive perspective-taking exercises such as the Feared Eulogy exercise (chapter 5) that can transport the client into an imagined future from which they may be able to connect with what might have made for a well-lived life. For a more thorough exploration of the ways in which perspective-taking strategies can help foster a more flexible sense of self, I would recommend *The Self and Perspective Taking* (McHugh & Stewart, 2012), "Building a Flexible Sense of Self" (chapter 6 in Villatte, Villatte, & Hayes, 2015), and "Building Flexible Perspective Taking Through Self-as-Context" (chapter 5 in Luoma et al., 2017) as excellent resources.

CLIENT HAS DIFFICULTY DIFFERENTIATING SELF AND OTHER

Some difficulties are rooted in problems of self—namely having difficulties in differentiating self from other. This can be especially true for clients with a history of abuse or chronic invalidation. They may have never had the opportunity to recognize their own perspective. They may confuse others' wants, desires, feelings, or experiences with their own. They may chronically and habitually defer to others when making decisions. As discussed in chapter 6, tracking the consequences of trying out different ways of valuing can be a very helpful way for clients to learn more about what they would choose to value based on their lived experience. However, if a client doesn't have the ability to reflect on their own experience, that is, to take their own perspective, they miss out on this important information source. Clients who have difficulty knowing their own experiences and preferences will often give chronically vague or noncommittal responses to values questions. For example, when asked what would be most important to them, they might give responses like:

- I guess I'd like people to think I was nice, I suppose.

- I just want to be a good person.

- I don't know.

Alternatively, they may give responses that are dependent on others, such as:

- You seem really patient. I would like to be more like that, I guess.

- My mom always said the most important thing is to be kind, so that's what I would value.

Solution to try: Practice noticing. Because these clients often confuse their own experiences with others' and thus often have a hard time making decisions based on their own experience, you may need to start with helping them build mindful awareness of their experience. You may need to start small, with very simple noticing exercises. For example, you might start sessions with a basic mindfulness exercise of noticing their five senses, maybe adding a cue for them to think about one thing *they* might want to discuss in that day's session. You can also incorporate simple mindful eating exercises (see Follette, Heffner, & Pearson, 2010) to help your client notice their own sensations.

Once your client is able to be aware of their ongoing experience, you can begin to help them practice choosing based on those experiences and preferences. The idea here is to build up the ability to choose between different things they want (as opposed to what others want or what they don't want) using initially more micro-level, situation-to-situation preferences and desires, eventually building to broader values. The Values Card Sort (chapter 4) is an excellent exercise to serve this function. Using the predetermined set of values cards in relation to a particular situation gives clients the chance to practice choosing from a more limited set of options. See http://www.newharbinger.com/43218 for a clinical example of how my client Charlotte and I worked toward helping her notice her own preferences as an initial step on the path toward having a sense of personal ownership over her values choices.

When Being Stuck in the Past or Future Conceals Values (Deficits in Present-Moment Repertoire)

Valuing occurs in the present moment. Values aren't things we used to care about or hope to care about one day. They are the ways of living today, in this moment, that are most important and provide us with a sense of meaning and purpose. Thus, rumination about the past or worry about the future can take people away from opportunities to contact values that are available in the here-and-now.

CLIENT IS CAUGHT IN RUMINATION OR WORRY

Sometimes clients respond to values conversations by falling into rumination about past regrets or hurts, or hopelessness about an imagined future. Some clients can be overly attached to their past and their stories about how it has shaped them, thus unduly restricting their future options. It's as if they believe the story of their lives has already been written and they are just going through the motions of living it out to its inevitable conclusion. Others can be so focused on getting someplace else that they miss the possibilities for meaning and purpose in the life they have now. They may be preoccupied with getting to some imagined future, as if something about their history, themselves, or their current circumstances must change before they can live their values. These clients frequently use if-then statements with regard to their values, such as:

- If I felt less depressed, I would be more engaged with my kids and partner.

- I would like to be more open and vulnerable if I could just find the right person.

- If I hadn't been abused, then I would be able to be more trusting and loving.

- If only I hadn't been such a workaholic when my kids were young, I would have been a good parent to them.

- Once I am more confident, I'd like to be more outgoing and fun.

Strategy to try: Write the Character of You exercise or Superhero Alter Ego metaphor. If a client is caught up in the past or future, sometimes the best thing to do is start from scratch. One way to do this is with the Write the Character of You exercise. In this exercise, the client is asked to imagine that they are developing the main character for a screenplay or novel they are writing. The character they are developing is an alternate version of themselves. This character has no predetermined backstory, no habits that define them, no history that limits them. The character should represent who they would most want to be, in their ideal world. This tends to be a more extensive homework assignment that the client can work on over the course of days or weeks.

A briefer exercise that is similar but can be done in session is the Superhero Alter Ego metaphor. Here clients are asked to consider what they might choose if they could create a secret alter ego. Here's how you might introduce this to a client:

Therapist: Imagine you woke up this morning and all of a sudden you learned your ordinary life was actually an alter ego for a superhero. Like you are Clark Kent for Superman or Diana Prince for Wonder Woman. Imagine this superhero who is your other half got to live a life unrestrained by your history or experience, starting right now. What qualities would you choose to endow that superhero with? What would that character's behavior be in the service of? What would your inner superhero stand for if you got to choose anything?

This exercise can help clients break out of rumination about their past or worries about some imagined future to connect with what they would choose in the here-and-now if they could choose anything. Many clients also have fun with it. I even had a client once create their own personal crest like the S on Superman's costume. They ended up putting that crest on a T-shirt that they wore under their normal clothes on days that were going to be especially challenging as a way to help them remember what they wanted to be about underneath all the struggle. Their values became their superpower.

CLIENT IS RIGIDLY ATTACHED TO PARTICULAR GOALS

Many of us have grown up in contexts that focus on and reinforce goal achievement or productivity. It's not surprising, then, that many people become identified by their goals or achievements. While this is not inherently problematic, unfortunately, these goals are all too often disconnected from a larger source of meaning; that is, the goals are disconnected from the person's values. Goals also have the downside of pulling us out of the present and into the future because they are always something off in the distance that you are hoping to get to. If clients have difficulty seeing how being rigidly focused on goals can pull them out of the present moment, the Goal Rope exercise is a simple experiential exercise that can help clients connect with this sense of goals always being in the past or future. You can find a detailed description of that exercise at http://www.newharbinger.com/43218.

Examples of goal-focused responses clients frequently give when asked about values include:

- I value having a family.

- I value being a mom/dad.

- I value my job.

- I value being beautiful and wealthy.

- I value money.

Each of the above examples are goals because they reflect something that can be attained or accomplished as opposed to describing an ongoing quality of action.

Sometimes goals are focused on others' behavior. These can include things like:

- It would be really important to me to have my kids visit me more.

- I would choose to have a more passionate spouse.

- I value having other people like me.

Again, each of these is a statement about a desired outcome to be achieved rather than a way of living.

Clients' goals may also focus on changing certain life circumstances. For example, a client who would value living adventurously might become fused with the idea that they need to first be wealthy in order to travel and have the grand adventures they dream of. Their life becomes focused on an imagined future in which they have achieved some financial status in the hopes that *then* they can start living adventurously. Alternatively, a client might say that they would have liked to live adventurously, but having kids has made that impossible now. There is fusion with the idea that attaining something (like attaining wealth) is either necessary or prohibits (in the example of having children) living out a value. In these cases, it's as if the goal precedes and supersedes the value as opposed to the goal emerging out of a value. Life becomes oriented around an endpoint of the goal rather than the goal serving as a marker en route to a valued direction.

Strategy to try: Link the Goals exercise. When clients have difficulty connecting the larger pattern or values behind their goal pursuits, I often use the Link the Goal exercise. For this exercise, clients are asked to write down the top five or ten things they feel most proud of having achieved or accomplished. If you have a younger client or someone who perceives themselves to be less accomplished, then you can ask them to list the top five to ten things they would feel proud to have achieved in their life if they could choose anything. Then ask the client to look at the list and say whatever words come to mind that relate to or link all of the things on the list. Working backward from already achieved goals can be a way to explore the common values that may underlie them. Alternatively, the exercise may result in the client seeing that the underlying purpose of their goals doesn't reflect what they would choose to value. From there, you can help the client see that the opportunity to live their values is always in the present by saying something like, "So right now, in this session, if this session were going to be in the service of helping you move toward _____ [name value that emerged from the exercise], what might you be doing?"

Sometimes More Focused Work Is Required

Even with all the above strategies, sometimes the barriers to connecting with values are so entrenched that you need to target the inflexibility more directly, setting aside in-depth values work until the client can find a more flexible place from which to approach it. There are numerous more general ACT books that provide comprehensive and detailed ways to target other flexibility processes beyond values (see Harris, 2009; Hayes et al., 2012; Luoma et al., 2017). Sometimes, doing a more thorough case conceptualization focused on psychological flexibility repertoires can be helpful in determining areas that might need more targeted focus. The case conceptualization model I use most frequently can be found in chapter 8 of *Learning ACT* (Luoma et al., 2017).

But What About "Values Conflicts"?

"What do you do about values conflicts?" is a common question I hear from therapists learning about values work. Framing it in this way, it can appear that the client is caught in a seemingly unwinnable conflict, and your job as therapist is to help them navigate it. However, as I see it, values aren't "things" that can be mutually exclusive or in conflict. Values are how you are living when you are living a meaningful life. If you are living in a way that is meaningful and full of purpose, then by definition you are living a life in line with your values.

As I see it, most of the time what people call "values conflicts" aren't really about values at all, but rather can be seen as a combination of avoidance and cognitive fusion, often on the part of the therapist as well as the client. When a therapist is referring to a "values conflict," they are often referring to a situation in which there are two things the client wants but can't do at the same time. In these cases, it often seems to the client (and sometimes the therapist as well) that one choice must be right/better and the other wrong/worse and they are struggling to try to figure out which is which. Rather than making a choice based on their values, the client becomes entangled with getting it right, not making a mistake, or avoiding the inevitable pain that comes with choosing. Their behavior may be driven by fear of failure, fear of being a bad person, or fear of missing out. All of this turns the person away from values and they get sucked into an experiential avoidance loop. The sense of choice and vitality slips away. They may be fused with conceptualizations of themself—that they don't deserve to make certain choices in their lives, that a particular choice is selfish, or that they "should" choose one decision over the other. They may be fearful of how others will perceive their choices and the fallout they will experience. Life energy is consumed in rumination and inaction. They become lost in complexity and lose contact with deeper, more connected, larger, or bolder purposes.

Instead of getting further mired in trying to find the "right" solution to these so-called "values conflicts," the answer may be to help your client develop greater psychological flexibility so that they can get on with living the meaningful, values-based life that is available to them. Clients may need to develop a broader, more compassionate perspective on themselves so that they are less bound up in narrowing rules or self-evaluations and can more easily make choices and face the consequences of their actions. They may benefit from developing more acceptance so they are less pushed and pulled by their fears or other emotions that are dominating their decisions. They may need to learn to be more in contact with the present moment so that they are able to use their own preferences and personal experience of what works for them to inform their choices, as opposed to solely being dependent upon internalized rules of others or society. Or they may need to develop the ability to defuse from their rumination or worry so that they do not lose themself in the virtual reality of this thinking and are more able to make the moment-to-moment choices that are part of a life well lived. And finally, they may need support in taking committed action and thereby experiencing the reinforcement that comes from enacting their values.

Another thing to consider when it comes to so-called "values conflicts" is: who is the one perceiving the conflict? I have never actually had a client use the term "values conflict." Maybe other people's clients do, but mine don't. Rather, it seems that it is frequently the therapist who frames things in this way. Clients often report feeling a struggle of competing demands between two valued domains, such as wanting to spend more time with their family and also wanting to spend time developing their career. Or, they may be struggling with choosing between two paths that would allow them to enact their values in different ways, such as having children or not having children. However, in my experience, clients rarely frame these struggles as "values conflicts." If you feel a client is struggling with something that you are seeing as a potential "values conflict," consider reflecting on the following questions:

1. Is it possible that I am seeing this as a values conflict when other ways of viewing this might be more helpful? If so, how might I conceptualize what is happening differently?

2. If my client could completely accept themselves for who they are, with all their emotions, thoughts, feelings, and history, would they still be held up by this seeming conflict? How might I help them develop this capacity?

3. Is my client focused on the outcome of this choice versus engaging in a process of choosing that has integrity for them? How could I help them to choose well and let go of the outcome?

4. Is my client able to contact their experience in the moment as it relates to this seeming conflict, or do they persistently get caught up in rumination or worry as it relates to this? What does this say about what I might need to help them develop?

5. Is it possible that my client may not have the skills or life context needed to effectively follow through on the specific goals or actions they are considering, and that is contributing to this difficulty? How could we address this deficit together?

When viewed this way, perceived values conflicts shift from being unwinnable binds to simply another example of how our normal language and cognition processes can get us stuck. Thus, we approach these as we would with any other difficulty; we help the client get better at making choices, in the present moment, aware that their thinking is only that, their thinking, while embracing their whole experience in a conscious manner, and being guided by what is most important. We don't need to play King Solomon; we just need to know how to help our clients (and often ourselves) develop more psychological flexibility.

Takeaways

- Asking ourselves good questions can help us take a step back and gain a broader view of how psychological inflexibility may be leading to barriers.

- We can be like moths circling around the flame of emotional and physical pain. Lives can become disconnected from what is most important as avoidance takes over and living becomes oriented around feeling better.

- Fusion often obscures values. Clients can be fused with thoughts about nothing mattering or the hopelessness of caring about anything. They can also be fused with "shoulds" or "shouldn'ts," as they confuse what they think others want them to do with their own freely chosen values.

- Clients can feel trapped by stories about who they are or feel defined by their past behavior. Helping your client take on alternate perspectives that are not bound by those limiting stories can free them up to create the values-based life they would choose to live.

- When clients are ruminating about the past or caught up in worry about the future, they miss the opportunity to contact the values that would create meaning and purpose in the present.

- Consider whether seeming "values conflicts" may actually be forms of psychological inflexibility. It may be more workable to let go of trying to resolve these apparent "conflicts" and instead help the client develop the capacity to make effective values choices.

Next Steps

- Select one client who is struggling with barriers to connecting with their values. Use the five-step process outlined at the start of this chapter to come up with a psychological flexibility–based conceptualization of the difficulties and possible next steps.

- Identify a client whom you perceive to be experiencing a "values conflict." Reflect on the questions posed at the end of that section in the chapter. If you were going to take a different perspective, what would be an alternate framework from which to view the difficulty? Test out that way of speaking about the difficulty with your client and see what happens.

- **Inside-out learning:** Identify an area of your life that matters to you and where you've felt stuck for a while, where you find yourself procrastinating, or where you've given up. Then review the questions from the five-step process at the start of the chapter, but with yourself as the focus. Journal about what you learn and any ideas of what you might test out in your own life.

CHAPTER 8

Context Matters:
Culture and Values Beyond the Individual

Community is first of all a quality of the heart. It grows from the spiritual knowledge that we are alive not for ourselves but for one another.
—Henri J. M. Nouwen

At the heart of any values-guided therapy is a desire to help those we serve live lives of their own choosing, lives of meaning and purpose. But none of us is an island. We are all dependent upon others and deeply influenced by the people around us and the cultures in which we have been embedded. Culture shapes both therapist and client alike. It influences how we engage with the world, including how we engage with psychotherapy (Owen, 2018). Our values themselves are closely tied to our culture, life experiences, and the people with whom we share those experiences. Therefore, an important part of helping our clients connect with their values is understanding the historical and current sociocultural contexts in which they are situated.

But in order to learn about different cultural perspectives, we first need to be aware of our own, including the ways in which our perspective might influence our work. Thus, this chapter includes opportunities for you to reflect on and become more aware of your own cultural lens and potential biases. There are ideas on what to do when values and culture collide, both inside the therapy room and beyond, and also ideas on how you might adapt your values interventions based upon certain contextual variables. Finally, we broaden our lens to explore the ripple effect of values as it extends into our communities, whether those are communities of two in a couple, a family, or broader societal communities. But let's begin with what we mean by this word "culture," including all the variables that intersect to create each of our unique and beautifully complex contexts.

Culture: Flexible, Evolving, and Broadly Defined

As it is often used in common parlance, "culture" is frequently very narrowly defined. Terms like "Black culture" or "Asian culture" or "gay culture" are common examples of how we can use the word "culture" to categorize an entire group of people based on some singular aspect of identity. Narrow cultural descriptions of this sort are often applied to devalued or minority groups, and frequently imply a homogeneity or over-simplification of the richness of culture. In reality, our cultural identities are incredibly multifaceted, and our identities around gender, race, ability and health (including mental health) status, class, age, ethnicity, religion, politics, family, history, and sexual-ity interact in complex ways.

From a contextual behavioral science perspective, culture refers to ideas, practices, and behaviors, as well as the contingencies that maintain them, which occur inside groups and vary from group to group (Masuda, 2014). This view of culture emphasizes the unique and constantly evolving ways in which our cultural contexts shape how we perceive and interact in the world. It also means that we cannot assume that cultural competence with one client, group, or identity will necessarily generalize to others or that generalized knowledge about a group will apply to the experience of any one member.

This broad and multifaceted view of culture is consistent with the concept of intersectionality (Crenshaw, 1989). Intersectionality theory maintains that the various ways we categorize each other and ourselves cannot be viewed in isolation, but rather intersect with one another (McCall, 2005). It is a way to understand how intercon-nected systems of power and oppression differentially impact individuals with various and often multiple marginalized identities, and potentially marginalized values (Cooper, 2016). When exploring how an individual's various identities interact, we need to make efforts to learn about the cultures in which our clients reside, especially nondominant cultures. At the same time, it is important that we not overgeneralize or make sweeping assumptions about our clients based on a limited selection of cultural variables (Luoma et al., 2017).

It's also important to keep in mind that our cultural identities are not fixed, but rather are fluid and ever evolving. Our sociohistorical identities interact with our ever-changing current context. Thus, when exploring ways in which culture may influence values, we need to recognize how these contexts evolve. For example, people facing the challenges of acculturation may benefit from a values focus that helps them as they struggle to integrate or separate their various cultural identities.

Finally, when considering culture, it is important to note that cultural practices that are good for the group may not be good for all individuals within the group. For example, a culture may maintain that certain behaviors, ideals, values, or identities are morally superior and may punish deviations from those moral guidelines. Those whose values differ from the moral guidelines of the majority may thus be harmed by this aspect of their culture. The result is that for some people, certain culturally based practices and ideas may also be the source of much pain through objectification, invali-dation, discrimination, and stigmatization.

The Importance of Humility: Know What You Don't Know

I choose to believe that most therapists would want to be culturally competent and welcoming of the rich diversity of contexts and perspectives of those we serve. If you aspire to those ideals, it can be uncomfortable or even painful to look at the places where we fall short. But an unwillingness to explore our own blind spots, ignorance, or cultural arrogance moves us further away from the ideals that many of us would aspire to. I learned this lesson the hard way.

For the first twenty-five years of my life, I lived in highly homogenous contexts in which my views and values were at least seen as valid, if not shared, by virtually everyone I interacted with. While I believed strongly in ideals such as inclusivity and equality, toward the end of graduate school it dawned on me: claiming to value inclusivity and equality is a whole lot easier if you're always surrounded by people who are just like you. So, for my last year of graduate school, I decided to put my values to the test. I moved out of my apartment in the heart of the liberal Dupont Circle neighborhood of Washington, D.C., to take an internship in a rural, conservative, highly religious town in the middle of the country where I knew the vast majority of people would hold different viewpoints from me. The problem was, while my intentions may have been good, I brought my cultural arrogance with me. I didn't bother to learn anything about the cultures I would be stepping into before I arrived. As a result, on the very first day of my internship, I said something that was incredibly ignorant and deeply, even if unintentionally, offensive to my new colleagues and supervisors. As soon as I realized my mistake, I felt tremendous shame. Unfortunately, though, rather than prompting me toward curiosity and humility, that shame led me to further try to hide my ignorance. As a result of my avoidance, I continued to "step in it" over and over and over again throughout that year.

I know what the "correct" ending of this story should be, the happily ever after ending. I wish I could say that over the course of my internship year I opened up to learning about my biases and that I was able to fully embrace this culture that was vastly different from my own. But, alas, this isn't Hollywood and I was a twenty-something-year-old without a lot of practice in either perspective taking or self-compassion. And so, the reality is, I just hunkered down in my ignorance and shame and distanced myself from those I perceived as "other" in the hopes of trying to minimize my shame-inducing mistakes. The result was a very painful year for me and for those around me who had to pay the price for my cultural arrogance and my unwillingness to look at what I didn't know.

It's been many years now since that first day of my internship. The repeated mistakes I have made (and continue to make more frequently than I would like) have taught me a great deal about the limitations of my knowledge and of my inherently limited cultural perspective. I now at least know there is a lot I don't know. And so now

I try to start from a place of assuming I do not know when it comes to my clients' unique and multifaceted cultural context. This posture of humility and acknowledged ignorance has helped me, over time, explore my own biases and blind spots and how these affect my work with clients, though of course, I still have a long way to go.

Even now as I write this story of my internship year, I still feel some shame, which I think is probably helpful in this case. Shame can serve to remind us of what matters to us, which in my case is the ability to relate meaningfully with others, and my behaviors had undermined that. But in addition to that shame, I now also feel some compassion that I didn't have for myself on that first day of my internship. I have compassion for how hard it is to be willing to explore our biases and ignorance in the service of our values. I have compassion for how difficult it is to be open to the limits of our own perspective. Acknowledging these things often brings judgment from others (maybe you are even having judgments right now as you read this about me) and very often from ourselves (indeed, my mind is busy judging away even as I type). But rather than retreating into avoidance that only perpetuates ignorance, we can choose to offer ourselves and others compassion that allows for ongoing learning and growth. And so, as you work through the rest of this chapter, including exploring your own cultural perspectives and biases, I hope that you will do so with a sense of compassion. This isn't easy stuff. We are bound to make mistakes and have blind spots. But by approaching the richly unique cultural context that shapes our clients' experience in the world with a profound sense of humility and curiosity for what we do not know, we are more equipped to be able to honor that context and behave in ways that are both helpful to our clients and in line with our values.

Exploring Your Own Cultural Context and Biases

We all, regardless of our sociocultural backgrounds, come from our own perspective. We all have personal biases that we carry into all the situations of our lives. We make assumptions about others, including about our clients, based on particular aspects of their apparent or stated identities. When these reactions based on categories such as gender, race, age, belief system, class, body shape, ability, ethnicity, or sexual orientation dominate over other aspects of a client's experience, we can lose sight of the richness of that client's lived experience. We can consciously or unconsciously impose our values, priorities, or moral codes on our clients. Each of these are natural, inevitable parts of being human. Attempting to ignore current and historical contexts or pretend that we can be "neutral" and not impacted by our own perspective only serves to perpetuate biases. The data suggest that simply trying to deny or suppress prejudicial thoughts typically backfires, often leading to increased stigmatization and stereotyping of others (Macrae, Bodenhausen, Milne, & Jetten, 1994; Newman, Caldwall, Chamberlin, & Griffin, 2005). Instead, in order to counteract this pervasive tendency to respond to others in terms of our evaluations and categorizations of them, we, as therapists, must develop the repertoires that will allow us to gain some psychological distance from and awareness of our personal conceptualizations of self and other and connect with a sense of conscious awareness that is a shared part of being human. For when we are unable to recognize that we see from only one perspective, we fail to fully consider others' perspectives. By acknowledging our different perspectives, we have the opportunity to honor and respect the diversity of contexts in which we all live.

TOOL: QUESTIONS FOR EXPLORING YOUR CULTURAL CONTEXT

One way to begin to consider the ways in which our cultural context has shaped our experience of the world is by exploring issues of privilege and power. In general, the more a person identifies with dominant cultures, the more difficult it can be to recognize the ways in which that context, and the privileges associated with it, shapes their experience of the world. If you've rarely suffered negative consequences because of the color of your skin, it's harder to recognize all the ways that race changes how others interact with you. If you've rarely been questioned about or disadvantaged by your gender identity, you are less likely to be aware of how that variable impacts your experience of the world. If you've always lived in a place where you feel you "fit in," it can be hard to know all the myriad ways people might be excluded or oppressed due to being perceived as "different." Our cultural background necessarily restricts our experiences and perceptions.

Those who identify with marginalized identities or nondominant cultures also have their own biases, both toward privileged and nonprivileged identities. Because our sociocultural identities are so multifaceted, even those of us who have large aspects of our identity that have been marginalized or oppressed by the dominant society may not be aware of some of the sources of privilege or power from which we do benefit. Conversely, we may have unwittingly internalized devaluing messages but not be fully aware of how that has impacted us in terms of how we relate to both ourselves and others. We all have biases. That is part of what it means to be human.

To examine these issues and their potential impact on your values work, I encourage you to pause here and go to http://www.newharbinger.com/43218, where you can find a list of questions designed to help you explore your own cultural context and potentially associated privileges.

Dialectic Between Humility and Boldness

As a therapist, I often feel the tension between a desire to stand in a place of humility and, at the same time, embrace boldness in the service of helping my clients experience the freedom to choose their own meaningful values-based path in this world. Sometimes out of a desire to be respectful or avoid painful mistakes, we, regardless of our sociocultural backgrounds, can become overly deferential to culture, treating it as some kind of third rail that cannot be touched. This avoidance of openly exploring our client's cultural perspective, including how well a client's own cultural perspective and biases may be serving them, is no less problematic than avoiding acknowledging our own cultural biases as therapists. And yet, I know at least I have fallen into this trap many times.

During that same internship year that started out with my offensive statements, I worked with a client who was struggling with feelings of attraction to members of the same sex. This young man was living in a context in which homosexuality was seen as a "sin" and was grounds for exile from the only community he had ever known. The cultural lens through which he was viewing his difficulties included the belief that if he could not somehow get "cured," he was doomed to eternal damnation. While this view was vastly different from what my own learning history (and my values) had taught me, I was also aware that this was the dominant view promoted by the culture in which this client and I were both living. I was so afraid of being perceived as disrespectful of his cultural and religious beliefs that I never even offered him the opportunity to explore the workability of those beliefs. I can't know whether the beliefs he expressed were consistent with freely chosen values or whether they were simply the result of fusion and social pressure. But because of my avoidance and fear, I'll never know because I never offered him the opportunity to explore those beliefs. In this way, I failed my client.

When exploring the ways in which a client's cultural context may have influenced their perspective, it is essential that you do so in an open and curious rather than prescriptive or judgmental manner. We are all influenced by our current and historical cultural contexts. This is not inherently problematic. However, because people's values may be at odds with those of the cultures in which they are embedded, we must be willing to navigate this dialectic between cultural humility and boldness. In doing so, we help our clients differentiate between those values that they would stake personal claim to, that they would freely choose, versus those cultural values that may be constricting their ability to live a life that would be most meaningful and vital to them (Luoma et al., 2017).

Culturally Informed Values-Guided Therapy

The flexibility processes that underlie and support valued living (see chapter 2) appear to be relevant across different contexts and cultural groups (Masuda, 2014; Skinta & Curtin, 2016). As Hayes and colleagues write, "Values may differ from culture to culture, but the idea of therapy serving the client values in the client's social context does not" (Hayes, Pistorello, & Levin, 2012, p. 992). The question isn't whether or not values-focused work is applicable to people in a particular population, but rather *how* we can take context into consideration in order to make our values work more effective with a given client.

Values Are Applicable to All

One of the reasons I love having values guide my work is that, the way I see it, values are the great equalizer in this all-too-often inequitable world. It doesn't matter who we are, where we live, what forms of suffering life has given us, what we have done or what has been done to us, living whatever life we have been given in a way that is personally meaningful and has integrity is possible for every one of us. Thus, as a values-guided therapist, there is no one for whom this work is not applicable. Of course, we need to tailor our interventions to be apt and workable for particular clients and their unique life contexts. However, the general premise of a values-guided approach to therapy is still the same: help clients explore what a well-lived, meaningful life would be for them through fostering conversations that engender a sense of choice, vitality, and willing vulnerability, and that are alive in the present moment.

When therapists first learn about working with values, there is often an implicit (or sometimes even explicit) assumption that this work only applies to certain kinds of clients. Often trainees will ask me questions like, "Aren't you just talking about highly verbal clients?" or "Can kids or adolescents really know what they value?" or "Isn't this all about the individual? What about clients who come from more interdependent cultures?" While an adequate exploration of all the unique variables involved in working with various populations is beyond the scope of this book (and, in the spirit of humility, beyond the scope of my expertise!), my fundamental answer to the question "Does this apply to X clients?" is always the same: "I sure hope so! How might you tailor it so that it does?"

When looking for ways to incorporate various cultural perspectives into your values-guided therapy, consider seeking consultation from a trusted colleague who has a rich knowledge of the cultural group or identity in question. These one-on-one consultations can help provide a nuanced and individualized approach to working with a particular client. In addition, consider reading a more comprehensive book on the topic. Two excellent resources for how to work with cultural factors from within a psychological flexibility model are *Mindfulness and Acceptance in Multicultural Competency* (Masuda, 2014) and *Mindfulness and Acceptance for Gender and Sexual Minorities* (Skinta & Curtin, 2016). Finally, your clients are the best experts on their own unique cultural context, so be sure to attend to how your values interventions are landing for them. Assume that you do not know. And above all else, abide by the platinum rule: "Do unto others as they would have done unto themselves."

General guidelines for culturally competent therapy, of course, also apply to values-guided therapy, such as making sure exercises and metaphors are culturally apt, considering linguistic and reading abilities for any exercises or forms that involve written text, and keeping financial barriers in mind when suggesting therapy-related assignments. Therapists should consult with other more comprehensive resources for more general recommendations (such as Sue, Sue, Neville, & Smith, 2019). While this book could never hope to cover all the ways in which values work can be tailored to all possible cultural contexts and identities, I want to briefly address some ideas related to three populations that I tend to get the most questions about. What follows are considerations when working with values with clients who are: 1. intellectually impaired or lower functioning, 2. of a particular age or phase of life (kids/adolescents or those at the end of their life), and 3. from more interdependent cultures. However, when reading the information below, please keep in mind that any discussion of whole classes of people will be incomplete and stereotyped and cannot do justice to the rich, multifaceted cultural identities that make up each of the individuals within a given group. In addition, consider how these categories intersect with other aspects of identity and context. For example, adolescents are not only dealing with peer, family, and school influences, but may also be dealing with issues related to gender or race or almost any other aspect of identity. People with cognitive impairments may be dealing with stigma related to their mental health status. Those facing the end of life may be encountering challenges related to how religion interfaces with values. These are but a few examples that point to the importance of attending to the intersecting nature of your particular client's sociocultural identities.

INTELLECTUALLY IMPAIRED OR LOWER FUNCTIONING CLIENTS

One of the most common myths I hear about doing values work is that it's only appropriate for more verbal, intelligent, and high-functioning clients. This is such an unfortunate and erroneous assumption. Getting to live a life of meaning and purpose is not reserved for those with a high IQ or for "higher functioning" clients. We all want to have a sense of choice and personal autonomy about what is important in our lives. Theoretical models of optimal functioning for people with intellectual disabilities emphasize that personally chosen values are an essential element of a good life for all individuals regardless of intellectual or cognitive capacity (Felce, 1997).

Not only are values applicable to individuals with more limited intellectual or verbal abilities, but the approach outlined in this book may be particularly well suited for that population. In this model, values are not some lofty intellectual ideal to be pondered and philosophized about. Values are a way of living; they are qualities of behavior. While a person with more limited intellectual abilities may not engage in the same behaviors as someone with more advanced cognitive abilities, values are not dependent upon the abilities people have, but rather are about how they choose to utilize the abilities they have. Regardless of whether someone is a NASA engineer solving complex physics problems or an individual with a developmental disability working at Goodwill, they have the ability to choose what they would want those endeavors to be about and what valued qualities they want to bring to their actions.

Some of the factors to consider when engaging in values-guided therapy, or any type of psychotherapy, with individuals with intellectual disabilities may include (Oliver, 2017):

- Their ability to comprehend metaphors is likely reduced and their overall verbal ability may be more limited. As such, relying on more concrete and potentially nonverbal means of communicating key concepts might be more effective.

- Exercises that rely on extended visualizations may be difficult due to potentially limited attention span.

- Their ability to engage in metacognitions and other perspective-taking tasks may be impaired.

- Their influence over what they do with their lives is likely significantly restricted. Therefore, the ways in which they are able to live out their values may be more limited than they are for some others.

When working with individuals operating in these contexts, it is essential to help them connect with *their* preferences, something that is often overlooked as others may frequently make decisions for them. For example, Miselli (2017) presents a case study of working with an intellectually disabled client in which he notes that the simple act of the therapist expressing interest in and asking the client about their own personal values became highly reinforcing for the individual. The client found exploring their values so rewarding that the values conversations themselves became the reinforcer, enriching the client's life through contacting what was most meaningful and important to them.

While people with intellectual and cognitive disabilities may have fewer options available to them with regard to how they might choose to live out their values, that in no way means a values-based life is not possible for them. They deserve interventions that focus not solely on how to help them with the fundamentals of living (such as case management, skills training, and activities of daily living) but also on what would make that life meaningful and worth living.

ADOLESCENTS

The literature on values work with adolescents is notably limited (Casas, Figuer, González, & Malo, 2007; Halliburton & Cooper, 2015). However, given that adolescence is a time when much identity exploration is happening and many important life decisions are being made, this may be an ideal time to focus on how values might serve as a guide for those decisions (Stattin & Kerr, 2001). In addition, freely chosen personal values may offer an alternative guiding force to the social pressures that adolescents are likely to feel from peers and the media (Halliburton & Cooper, 2015).

Multiple developmental factors should be considered when exploring values with adolescents. Language and examples should be age appropriate (Halliburton & Cooper, 2015). Asking an adolescent to imagine their own funeral or even their 80th birthday (chapter 5), for example, may feel too remote to make for an effective exercise. You may instead need to use another less distant milestone, such as an important graduation or school reunion. In addition, you may need to describe what values are in ways that feel more applicable to an adolescent. Rather than describing values as "those qualities that, when you get to the end of everything, you want to have embodied in your life," you might instead describe them as "how you are acting when life is most meaningful to you" or even more simply "the kind of person you want to be if you could choose." While these simplified descriptions may not capture all the nuances of what we mean by values, they are a good starting place and probably more approachable for adolescent clients.

Another contextual variable to consider when working with adolescents is that they are likely to still be living with their family or other adult guardians who have their own set of values that they may be trying to instill in their child. Adolescents may be keen to develop their own sense of morals and values as they push back against their parents (Halliburton & Cooper, 2015). Thus, it is important for the therapist to track whether an adolescent's stated values are indeed freely chosen, or whether they may be more the result of pliance or counter-pliance (see chapter 7).

Connecting with and feeling a part of a friend or peer group is often particularly salient for adolescents (Brown, Eicher, & Petrie, 1986). Thus, focusing on social or friendship valued domains may be a particularly relevant and effective avenue to explore values more broadly. Indeed, the Social Values Survey (Blackledge & Ciarrochi, 2006), which was developed for use with adolescents, focuses on values within social, family, and romantic relationships.

While some elements of values work will likely need to be adapted to be best suited to an adolescent population, the same four qualities that guide our values conversations with adults still apply. This includes a focus on valuing in the present moment. Adolescents are often asked about what they want to be or do at some future point. However, when engaging in values work with adolescents, it is important to help them contact the values that they would choose to embrace in the here-and-now.

These are just a few of the variables to consider when engaging in values work with adolescents. If you work with adolescents, *The Thriving Adolescent* (Hayes & Ciarrochi, 2015) is an excellent resource based on a psychological flexibility model. In it, you will find a wealth of information and resources, including a set of values cards that has been specifically adapted for use with adolescents.

THE ELDERLY AND THOSE FACING THE END OF LIFE

The final stages of life have been called the "legacy-creating stage" (Schaie & Willis, 2000). During this stage, people often become acutely aware of the limited time they have left. With that may come an increased motivation or even urgency to connect with what really matters, making values work particularly apt (Roberts & Sedley, 2016). In addition, those nearing the end of their life are often facing major health concerns and/or physical pain. Numerous studies have demonstrated the beneficial effects of connecting with and living out one's values for a wide variety of health and pain-related difficulties (Falk et al., 2015; Gregg et al., 2007; McCracken & Yang, 2006; Vowels & McCracken, 2008). For example, Davison and colleagues (2017) showed that an ACT intervention that had a strong emphasis on values work decreased symptoms of depression and anxiety among elderly adults in long-term care facilities.

More broadly, elderly adults are often faced with a loss of roles that may have been a source of identity and purpose for much of their lives. Many are transitioning from being caregivers to being the ones receiving care. There may be a loss of meaning or purpose as they leave the workforce and its accompanying sense of professional identity. Values work can be helpful in identifying ways of maintaining consistency with long-held values, while simultaneously being flexible in how those values are lived out.

One of the major transitions that happens as we age relates to our body and health. Many of us identify with our bodies and what they can do for us. We see ourselves as "runners," "gardeners," "adventurous," or "active." As our bodies begin to decline and eventually fail, many of these sources of identity and pleasure may start to fade as well. Helping clients explore the ongoing values that may underlie these sources of identity can give a sense of continuity and continued purpose in life. For example, the client who has always valued living life fully and adventurously may now begin exploring what living these final stages and going through the dying process "fully" and "adventurously" would mean for them.

Fusion with ageist stereotypes may be a significant barrier to effective values work with older adults. Although the specific form of the negative stereotypes may vary, most people across cultures hold strong, largely negative beliefs toward aging (Boduroglu, Yoon, Luo, & Park, 2006; North & Fiske, 2013; Yun & Lachman, 2006). In fact, the data suggest that, in general, people exhibit stronger ageist stereotypes than they do sexist or racist beliefs (Banaji, 1999; Rupp, Vodanovich, & Credé, 2006). This holds true even for those who are elderly themselves, with internalized self-stigma around aging being extremely common among older adults (Cherry et al., 2016), although this too may vary across cultures. As is frequently the case with fusion, though, we often aren't even aware of our implicit biases about aging or how those impact our behavior (Levy, Hausdorff, Hencke, & Wei, 2000).

Because of the pervasiveness of anti-aging biases, many of which are implicit, it is essential that therapists working with elderly populations and those facing the end of life examine their own biases and also their clients' potential self-stigmatizing biases. For example, therapists tend to have lower expectations for elderly clients' ability to change (Koder & Ferguson, 1998), which may result in those therapists being less inclined to consider addressing values with their older clients given the potentially life-changing nature of that work. In addition, given the prevalence of self-stigma among the elderly (Cherry et al., 2016), you may need to start your values work with older clients by exploring some of the thoughts with which they might be fused that could be a barrier to fully exploring the possibilities of living a values-based life at this phase of their journey.

CLIENTS FROM INTERDEPENDENT CULTURES

Unfortunately, values are often presented in a highly individualistic manner, with an erroneous assumption that values as "freely chosen" necessarily means only considering the individual. It is no wonder, then, that I often hear a concern from trainees that this approach to values work is not applicable to individuals from more interdependence-focused cultures or for those with more communal values. While values, from the perspective I am using in this book, are by definition experienced as freely chosen rather than imposed upon an individual by some external mandate, that in no way means that they cannot be sensitive to and inclusive of community. As Luoma and colleagues write, "Avoiding pliance doesn't mean ignoring socialization. Therefore, when working with clients from cultures that emphasize greater social interdependence, it's important not to use excessively individualistic rationales" (2017, p. 361).

Our cultural context shapes our most basic understandings of who we are and who others are, and even that distinction is culturally influenced. For example, while in many Anglo/Western languages there is a pronounced distinction between self and others, that is not the case in many Asian languages, where the distinction between "I" and "you" is more fluid (Nagayama Hall, Hong, Zane, & Meyer, 2011). From this perspective, the "self" is contextually dependent. As Markus and Kitayama (2010) state:

> Selves are always situated and, as a consequence, they always reflect their contexts in significant ways. Just as one cannot be an unsituated or general self, one also cannot be a self by one's self. Selves develop through symbolically mediated, collaborative interaction with others and the social environment. (p. 421)

Thus, how we view our "self" depends upon our cultural context. For some, including most dominant North American, Australian, and Western European cultures, "I" is a largely autonomous, independent, and unique entity. However, for others from more interdependence-focused cultures, such as much of Asia, Africa, and South and Central America, the "self" is seen as "inextricably and fundamentally embedded within a larger social network" (Gardner, Gabriel, & Lee, 1999, p. 321). In other words, for people from more interdependence-focused cultures, there is often more "we" in their sense of "I."

In addition, the extent to which you use the language of "free choice" might depend upon the relative independent versus interdependent self-identity of your client. As noted in chapter 1, the concept of values as "freely chosen" isn't a statement of a "truth," but rather our desire for individuals to experience the freedom to choose whatever would be most important and meaningful for them, which may be more self-focused or more communally focused depending on your client. We have also defined values as being "intrinsically motivating." Again, though, what may be intrinsically reinforcing depends on one's cultural context. For example, in two studies, Iyengar and Lepper (1999) found that Anglo-American children exhibited more intrinsic motivation for activities that they personally chose, whereas Asian-American children showed more intrinsic motivation for activities that had been chosen for them by an authority figure (either their mother or the experimenter). Thus, your interventions must be flexible and account for your individual client's cultural context. Values exploration exercises that rely heavily on individual pronouns or wholly autonomous decision-making processes may need to be adapted for individuals from more interdependent cultures, and such explorations likely need to incorporate a sense of "we" in the values exploration for those with more of an interdependent orientation.

Finally, it is important to remember that the ways in which values are enacted are contextually dependent. What is personally and socially adaptive in one cultural context may not be so in a different cultural context. For example, the ways in which someone coming from a Western culture would enact their value of intimately connecting with their partner might be more overt or public (such as saying "I love you" or public displays of affection), whereas this same behavior may not serve the function of relational intimacy for those from non-Western cultures (Masuda, in press). Similarly, it is common for individuals from more interdependence-focused cultures to reference relational variables when exploring their personal values (for example, "I am pursuing a particular career path in the service of honoring and caring well for my family"; Masuda, 2019). While therapists from more independence-focused cultures might, because of their own cultural biases, be suspect of such statements as potential evidence of pliance, this attitude may be ignoring important cultural variables that would lead to this being an adaptive way of enacting values.

What to Do When Values and Culture Collide

Because the variables that make up culture are so multifaceted, our values will inevitably collide with the moral views or judgments promoted by at least some in that culture. We all have things that are important to us that seem to conflict with the messages we get about what we should care about. The internalized messages we receive from our cultural contexts can obscure our awareness of what is most important to us. While this is an issue for all of us, the more a person's values do not align with those of the majority or when their valued paths are judged negatively by the dominant culture, the more distressing those conflicts are likely to be and the more difficult it may be for those individuals to be able to express their values.

When Valued Living Is Difficult or Dangerous

While values are always immediately available, certain ways of living out one's values may be less workable in particular contexts. What is valued in one cultural context may not be valued, or may even be expressly condemned, in another cultural setting. And yet, because our cultural identities are multifaceted and complex, it is possible that both cultural contexts may be important to the client. For example, a

Latinx client who is a first-generation American may struggle with how best they can live out their values in a way that is personally meaningful to them as they navigate between an American culture that values certain ideals and their familial culture that may prioritize other values. While the individual's values remain consistent, the ways they choose to enact those values will likely need to adapt depending on what cultural setting they are currently operating in. And, of course, all of this will be influenced by the client's relative level of acculturation.

Structural or institutional oppression and marginalization can present real-world barriers to how a person might be able to express their values in any given context. It may be unworkable, dangerous, or even deadly for clients to live out their values in particular ways. For example, living authentically may need to look different to an LBGTQ client living in a context hostile to their gender or sexual identity. Worshiping joyously may take a different form for the individual whose religious practices are forbidden in their current cultural context. A woman living in a highly misogynistic context may, for her own safety, manage carefully where or how she lives boldly. A client living in a poor, inner-city setting may need to enact values relating to respect differently on the street, in order to stay alive, versus at work, in order to retain their job. It is important for therapists to validate these real-world barriers and consider them when working on how the person will actually put their values into action. It's essential to engage in an open, ongoing, and nondefensive dialogue with our clients, especially those who have one or more marginalized identities, about how prejudice, discrimination, and stigmatization may impact their ability to freely choose how they would enact their values. Notice, however, that prejudice or oppression does not need to affect the *values* that person chooses, just how they are *expressed*.

Validating these painful limitations of the individual's current context does not preclude the therapist from honoring the client's freely chosen values. You and your client might need to explore workable ways that they can live in accordance with their values given their current context. But remember, values are always immediately available in the present moment. While your client may choose to (or become able to) eventually change their context to one that poses fewer barriers to valued living, as a values-guided therapist your job is to help your client embrace the opportunities that are *currently* available to them to live in line with their values. Though the form of valued living may look different in different contexts, living a life in line with our values is available to us all regardless of context.

When Therapist and Client Values Conflict

Many therapists express concerns about working with clients who appear to endorse values that the therapist does not agree with. I would argue that most often, these perceived values conflicts are not fundamentally values conflicts, but instead emerge from psychological inflexibility on the part of the therapist, the client, or, often, both.

As human beings, we all internalize aspects of the social norms, judgments, stereotypes, and moral guidelines of the cultures in which we have participated. Perceived values conflicts can be powerfully emotional for therapists, sometimes eliciting moral disgust, contempt, or righteous anger (Luoma et al., 2017). These are powerful emotions that can feed entanglement with judgments about our clients, and we may lose sight of the conscious human being we are working with. We may lack perspective taking, assuming that our moral views or values are the best, right, or true ones. Rigid fusion with one's own cultural perspective may be so strong that we (client and therapist alike) may not notice that we are viewing a situation from *a* perspective, but instead see it as "the" perspective.

Values as freely chosen means, in part, that they are chosen without coercion or even perceived coercion from the therapist. Judgments, expressed implicitly or explicitly, about whether certain qualities of living or behaviors are "right" or "wrong" can interfere with a client's sense of free choice. Thus, if you find yourself judging a client's value choices, the first place to look may be your own psychological flexibility—or inflexibility, as the case may be. Often the source of the perceived conflict is in us and our context, not the client. Thus, the first step is to turn the mirror on ourselves. As I said at the outset of this chapter, this isn't easy. But if you consider the potential of your own psychological inflexibility with humility, curiosity, compassion, and a connection to humanity as a collective whole, you may just find the solution to the supposed values conflict.

Many perceived values conflicts can also be seen as conflicts between cultural practices, not between individuals. Thus, an important strategy is to obtain consultation from colleagues who have knowledge of the group, cultural practice, or behavior that you feel you can't support. Often this can help you see the behavior or practice in a new way that can allow you to support your client in a manner that has integrity for you. In addition, perceived values conflicts often overlap with identity or group-based conflicts involving power differences, racism, marginalization, objectification, and prejudice. Thus, when perceived values conflicts arise, the therapist should consider whether any of these factors may also be relevant to the therapy.

Our personal cultural experiences and multifaceted identities can create blind spots and constrict our vision for what values may look like when lived inside particular contexts. Thus, when perceived values conflicts arise, it can be important to explore the following:

1. Consider the more abstract or broader values that might underlie the client's goal or values statement you are struggling with. This can often identify something that you can wholeheartedly align with.

2. What life experiences may have influenced your client's desire to pursue a particular goal or value? This can often help you step into the client's shoes and transform how you view their choices.

Below are some questions to consider as you reflect on whether your own inflexible perspective taking, experiential avoidance, or fusion with your own cultural context (both historical and current) or conceptualized self may be contributing to the perceived conflict.

- Are you experiencing disgust, contempt, anger, or fear toward this client or any of their behavior? What might this tell you about what you need to learn?

- In what ways might your upbringing, history, or culture have influenced your beliefs related to the value your client is endorsing? Is it possible that you would have different beliefs if you had a different upbringing, history, or cultural context?

- Do you have a story that the client's value or way of living out a value is somehow wrong, incorrect, or inadequate?

- Consider a time when you were a member of an out-group, where what you believed or held dear differed from the dominant view. What was that experience like for you? How would you have wanted others, especially those in the dominant group, to respond to what was most important to you?

- How do you think your client might feel if they perceived you did not approve of a way of being that they value? How might they want you to treat them with regard to this discrepancy?

- Given your values, how would you want to be toward this person who values something different than what you would choose to value? If you had children, how would you want them to be toward others who may have different values? What could you do that would help you behave more in line with your values in this way?

- What do you fear would happen if you supported your client in living out this value?

- What thoughts, feelings, or sensations would you need to be willing to experience in order to treat your client's values with the same respect, dignity, and worth as your own values?

Just as our own inflexibility as therapists can lead to perceived conflicts with what a client may choose to value, so too can a client's inflexibility contribute to values difficulties. Such psychological inflexibility isn't the result of being in the role of a therapist or the role of a client; it is the result of having a human mind that has evolved to solve problems and minimize pain. Without having had the opportunity to fully explore and freely choose what would be most important to us, many of us, including our clients, end up valuing things because of deeply ingrained habits and adaptations that we have made to deal with the challenges of life. In this way, what we end up valuing may be more the result of psychological inflexibility than it is the result of free choice.

If you are struggling with a client who is currently valuing something you find difficult to support, such as exerting power over people or dominating others in a way that harms them, consider whether it is possible that this behavior may be born out of psychological inflexibility as opposed to the person freely choosing to be antisocial as a way of living. The client may feel that this is a way they *have* to be, a fallback because they think they can't really value what they would choose because it is too dangerous, unacceptable, or not possible for them. This is likely a more effective and compassionate stance to take as a therapist in this situation. In their work with sexual offenders, for example, Quayle and colleagues have argued that it is typically experiential avoidance rather than inherently antisocial values that drives antisocial sexual behavior (Quayle, Vaughan, & Taylor, 2006). Thus, they suggest that effective treatment should include a strong focus on helping the individual connect with their values while simultaneously working to strengthen their psychological flexibility repertoires that will enable them to make space for the unpleasant thoughts, feelings, and sensations that will occur as they move toward those values.

If you are questioning whether what a client is proclaiming to value is truly what they would choose, look back to the four qualities of effective values statements to guide you. If values statements are made without a sense of choice, vitality, present moment, or willing vulnerability, then that is likely a clue that they are born out of inflexibility and avoidance. If that is the case, you may need to do more work on increasing the client's psychological flexibility before they are able to have a sense of choice over their values.

When doing values-guided work, it is your job to help your client connect with and live a life in line with their own freely chosen values. Ultimately, if you are unable to do this, then you will need to refer your client to someone who can serve them. However, referring out should be a last resort. Through working on increasing psychological flexibility, your client's and/or your own, it is likely that any perceived conflicts will dissipate, and you can get back to the important work of helping others have their life be in the service of what would be most important to them if they were free to choose.

The Values Ripple Effect: Couples, Families, and Organizations

Humans are highly social creatures and our actions or inactions impact countless others whose lives we touch, for better or worse. I am an individual therapist. I don't work with couples, families, or larger groups of people. And yet, one of the most rewarding parts of my work is to see the ways in which helping one person connect with their values can have a powerful ripple effect on so many others. Based on our individual work together, I have had clients use values to guide their family estate planning discussions, organize a "values retreat" for themselves and their partner, and even swap their family chores calendar out for a family values calendar. Loved ones can also be some of the best sources of support and motivation for clients in living out and staying true to their values. Whether you work with individuals, couples, families, or groups, consider how your client's relational context can be included in your values work together.

Including Loved Ones in Values Work

One way to extend the reach of your values work with clients is to include loved ones in values homework. For example, after a Values Card Sort exercise (chapter 3), I will often have my client go home and talk with their spouse or partner about what they discovered in the exercise. I have even given clients a set of values cards to take home. Sometimes my client's partner also does their own card sort and then the couple has a values conversation sparked by each of their discoveries. Other clients, who want to get a different perspective on what they have been valuing, have asked their partner or trusted friend to sort the cards by what they thought the client valued based on their behaviors. Before suggesting such an exercise, you will, of course, want to consider your client's individual situation. It's important to have a sense that the loved one is likely to respond in a supportive, constructive manner when presented with such a task. It is common for clients to want to share the values work they have been doing in therapy with their family. What follows is one of my favorite examples of when I got to see the values ripple effect in action with a client who brought her values work home to her kids.

CLINICAL EXAMPLE AND TOOL: VALUE OF THE DAY EXERCISE

Having recently gone through a nasty divorce, my client Jasmin was now raising her two daughters on her own. She was trying to make some changes to the family culture in their new life together. Before the divorce, Jasmin's household prized achievement over all else. Every evening her eight- and ten-year-old daughters were grilled by their father about what they accomplished at school and their latest test scores. Jasmin described these interactions as intimidating and very unpleasant for her kids.

One of the values exercises I had Jasmin practice was the Value of the Day exercise. The Value of the Day exercise, which is based, in part, on the Trying on a Value exercise (Dahl et al., 2009), is designed to give clients an opportunity to practice enacting a potential value for a short period of time and collect some data to see what living a life in the service of certain values would be like. As part of this exercise, every morning Jasmin would randomly choose one of the handful of values she had previously identified in the Values Card Sort exercise as being very important to her. She put seven of her most important values in a jar and whichever one she pulled out that morning would be her "value of the day." Then she would look for ways to live out that value during the day while tracking the results. For a detailed description of the Value of the Day exercise, see http://www.newharbinger.com/43218.

Jasmin started sharing what she was doing with her kids. She would tell them things like, "Today I was practicing treating others with kindness, and you know what

I found? I found that when I treated my client who was being kind of a jerk to me with kindness, I walked away from our interactions feeling really proud of myself and even less mad at her. Isn't that kind of cool?" Her daughters were very interested in what their mom was working on and would ask her what her "value of the day" was as they sat down for dinner. Pretty soon, her kids also shifted what they were sharing around the dinner table, moving from only focusing on what they had accomplished at school to how they were behaving at school, and even using some values-type words. Eventually, the family decided to create a "Family Values Calendar" where each week Jasmin and her two daughters would write down the values they each wanted to practice living out that week. Dinner conversations turned from just "What grade did you get on the spelling test?" to "Hey, how did it go today as you were practicing that value of patience?" They helped support each other in their values and checked in with each other about what they noticed as they were living out their values. How cool is that?!? Just imagine the potential trajectory shift that could result for those young eight- and ten-year-old girls as they got to start practicing values-based living at such an early age.

The Family Values Calendar, which was actually Jasmin's idea, is just one of the ways that you can begin to incorporate family members into values work. Many of the values exercises outlined earlier in this book can be modified for use with couples or families. For example, a couple can go through the Values Prototyping process (chapter 6) together as a way to explore what values they would want their relationship to embody and stand for. A family can explore a Family Sweet Spot together much in the same way it is described in chapter 4 but this time with all family members contributing their own perspective on the scene. And groups can act out the Feared Eulogy exercise (chapter 5) together.

Takeaways

- We all come from our own unique perspective and have our own cultural biases. Be aware of yours, but do so with compassion, as that is likely to foster the openness needed for learning.

- Practicing cultural humility doesn't mean avoiding exploring the workability of a client's cultural perspective.

- Consider how your values work can be adapted to best suit the needs and cultural context of your individual client.

- If your values seem to conflict with a client's values, first look at your psychological inflexibility related to your own cultural context.

- Values aren't really about an individual. They are about an individual in context, which includes lots of other people and relationships.

Next Steps

- Identify one client who has a cultural identity different from your own. It could be their race, ethnicity, socioeconomic status, ability status, gender or sexual identity, or any other aspect of culture. How might your values work with this client best be adapted to take into account this cultural context? What assumptions or biases might you have with regard to their cultural perspective? What resources can you access (colleagues, books, etc.) to learn more about that aspect of your client's identity? Take one specific action to learn more about that client's cultural perspective.

- Adapt one of the following exercises from previous chapters of this book to incorporate someone other than just your individual client.

    - Content on Cards (chapter 2)

    - Values Card Sort (chapter 3)

    - Sweet Spot exercise (chapter 4)

    - Two Sides of a Coin/Photo (chapter 5)

    - Exploring an Unsweet Spot (chapter 5)

    - Feared Eulogy (chapter 5)

    - Daily Valuing Tracking Form (chapter 6)

    - Values Prototyping (chapter 6)

    - Write the Character of You exercise or Superhero Alter Ego metaphor (chapter 7)

    - Goal Rope exercise (chapter 7)

    - Value of the Day (chapter 8)

  If you run groups, adapt any of the above exercises for the group context. If you do couples or family therapy, adapt an exercise to use with a couple or family. If you only work with individuals, find some way to include your client's partner, child, friend, or other loved one in the exercise.

- **Inside-out learning:** Spend some time reflecting on the ways in which your own historical and current cultural context shapes and supports (or doesn't support) your values. Use the questions found at http://www.newharbinger.com/43218 to reflect on your own cultural context and potential privileges. How might this influence your values work with clients? Consider a time when your cultural biases resulted in a blind spot or had a negative impact on your work with a client. What might you want to do differently in that situation in the future?

CHAPTER 9

We're in This Together:
Your Values as a Therapist

We work on ourselves in order to help others, but also we help others in order to work on ourselves. —Pema Chödrön

Being a therapist is hard. It can be lonely. Often clients come to us wanting the impossible, for us to take away their suffering, and we long to give them that impossible. We can feel helpless at times in the face of such pain. And even when we have been useful in helping ease some of the suffering for one person, there's more right around the corner, during the next session. Yet, we keep going. Why? Most of us did not decide to do this work because it was the most comfortable, pain-free, or financially lucrative path. For most of us, there is a larger value behind our decision to dedicate our lives to sitting with those who are suffering. Yet in the day-to-day grind of work, it can be easy to lose contact with that larger picture. We start seeing clients as problems to be solved and lose sight of what is most important to us in this work.

Staying connected to what matters most can help make this often difficult work more rewarding and meaningful. Connection with a larger sense of purpose gives us a container for holding the suffering of those with whom we work. By sharing our values with others, we can also connect with the common humanity that links us with those we serve and with our colleagues. And so, as we wrap up this book, we turn inward to consider our own values as therapists, what would make this work we do honorable and meaningful to us, and how to remain connected with those values on a day-to-day basis.

Exploring Your Values as a Therapist

Many therapies utilize various values clarification exercises, but in values-guided therapy, the entire therapy process is grounded in values. This includes having values guide how we are as therapists in the room with those we serve. So, unless you are clear on your values and connected with them as you do your work, you are missing something essential. What follows are several tools designed to help you get some clarity on the values you would choose to guide your work as a clinician.

Tool: Inside-Out Learning

Throughout this book, there have been opportunities for you to do some "inside-out learning" with regard to your own values. Hopefully, those exercises have given you a chance to do some values exploration of your own. If you have done those inside-out learning exercises, take a moment now to review them and any notes you might have taken when you did them. Consider the following:

- What have I learned so far about the values I want to bring to my work?

- Are there any themes that have emerged in my responses to the inside-out learning exercises?

- Is there anything I would want to follow up on or revisit in terms of these exercises?

If you have not taken the time to work through all the inside-out learning exercises, you might take a moment now to consider why. But as you are doing so, see if you can approach this from a place of curiosity, rather than judgment or self-criticism, so that even this act of considering why you haven't done the values exploration exercises might be guided by your values. From a place of self-compassion and genuine curiosity, you might consider the following:

- If I were to choose to spend the time to do the inside-out learning exercises in this book, what value would that be in the service of? Is that something I would choose to value?

  · If so, what is my plan for setting aside the time to do those exercises?

  · If not, what might be a next step I could take instead to help me articulate or help me stay in touch with my values?

Tool: Values Self-Reflection Questions

In addition to the inside-out learning exercises found in the previous chapters, the following are some questions you can reflect on to help further explore your values as you might enact them in your work. Select one or two of the questions below that either seem most apt or that you feel discomfort when thinking about. You might choose to journal about your responses and/or share your responses with a trusted colleague or loved one.

- If someone were going to describe how you are on your very best days at work, how might they describe you?

- What is it like when you are really engrossed with your work, when you're not doing something because you have to, but rather because you're captivated by it? What are those times about for you?

- When no one knows what you are doing, what kind of person do you feel most proud of being at work?

- Imagine you could start all over again and reinvent yourself in your job. It's a clean slate and you can embody any qualities you want as a new you. How would you ideally want to be if you could start over? What qualities would you want this reinvented self to embody?

- Imagine that you are in your office sitting across from the very last client you are ever going to see in your entire career. This is it, the last session of your career. How would you want to be in this session with this last client that you'll ever work with? What might that tell you about what is important to you in terms of how you would want to be with all your clients?

- What kinds of things are most difficult for you in terms of your work? What situations bring up the most pain or suffering for you? What might this pain tell you about what matters most to you?

- If you knew that every day you could come home from your job and know that all those hours had been spent in the service of _____, what would you want to be in that blank? Would that be a worthwhile day at work? What is it like thinking of having days like that?

After you have spent some time reflecting on a couple of the questions above, use the following to debrief your experience:

- What thoughts, feelings, urges, or judgments came up as you did this exercise?

- What might those tell you about what is important to you?

- Do those thoughts, feelings, urges, or judgments ever get in the way of you being the person you want to be? If so, how would your values inform how you would want to respond when those potential barriers come up?

Tool: How Would You Choose to Serve

As with our clients, moving our values exploration away from the theoretical and intellectual and toward something personal and specific can often be the best way to connect with what really matters to us. The How Would You Choose to Serve exercise is an eyes-closed exercise designed to help therapists connect with their values in relation to their work. This five- to ten-minute exercise focuses on someone you work with. There is also a writing portion to the exercise in which you can reflect on what came up for you during the visualization and what that might mean for you in terms of your values. This can be an especially helpful exercise if you have a particular client you are struggling with or who is experiencing a type or intensity of pain that it is hard for you to remain present to. If this seems like something that might be helpful for you, go to http://www.newharbinger.com/43218 and listen to the How Would You Choose to Serve exercise. You will also find a written copy of the exercise there.

How to Infuse Your Day-to-Day Work with Values

Helping our clients live a values-based life isn't solely a matter of doing a few values clarification exercises. We need to help them have ways to reconnect in an ongoing way with what is most important to them, especially in times of difficulty. The same thing goes for us as therapists. Even if you have gone through all the exercises in this book and have a solid sense of what values you would want to bring to your work, it is important to have ways to remain in contact with those values in day-to-day life. So, we end this chapter and this book with a variety of strategies and exercises designed to help you bring values into your daily life on an ongoing basis.

Doing Things Differently Rather Than Doing Different Things

This job can take a toll on us. The data suggest that anywhere from 21 to 67 percent of mental health professionals are experiencing high levels of burnout at any given time (Morse, Salyers, Rollins, Monroe-DeVita, & Pfahler, 2012). When burnout sets in and we begin to feel helpless, hopeless, or just plain exhausted, it's very common to think about ways we can change what we are doing in our work. Maybe I should see fewer clients? Maybe I should leave my current job setting and try some other work environment? Maybe I should leave clinical work altogether? All of these might be useful options to consider. But while cutting back or changing your work might be a useful goal, I again want to suggest putting values before goals. What if the solution isn't so much about changing *what* you do, but rather *how* you do the things you do? In other words, how could values help you do things differently rather than just focusing on doing different things? There is data to support the idea that helping therapists reconnect with their values, along with strengthening other psychological flexibility repertoires, can decrease burnout among mental health workers (Brinkborg, Michanek, Hesser, & Berglund, 2011; Hayes et al., 2004; Vilardaga et al., 2011).

I work with many people who are ambivalent about the relationships they are in. They come to therapy wanting to figure out whether or not they should leave the relationship, get a divorce, break up, or have an affair. I often tell them something like this:

Therapist: You may choose to leave, and that may be the right choice in the end in terms of your values. We can explore all those options together. And, right now, today, you are in this relationship. So how about if we start by figuring out how you would most want to be in this relationship if you were free to choose, given that, at least right at this moment, you are in it.

This helps clients orient to their values in the here-and-now. Many people find that when they begin living in line with their values, being the kind of partner/spouse/ friend they want to be, they find the relationship much more meaningful and fulfilling. Sometimes they still decide to leave the relationship in the end. But even if that is what they end up choosing, it is their values guiding that decision. That is a very different place than choosing to leave someone or something because you just can't stand it anymore.

This same strategy can apply to your work life. If you are feeling dissatisfied with your work, it's very common to focus on what different things you could do that you might enjoy more. But what if you started by considering what ways of being in this current job might be more meaningful or have a sense of purpose to them? For example, rather than assuming that the solution is to see different clients (or fewer clients or no clients), how could you bring a different quality to your work (enact your values) with the same clients that may result in you being more satisfied or fulfilled by the time you're spending at work? Do you think you would have the same feelings of discontent if you were somehow able to embody more compassion, curiosity, play, or whatever values you would want to guide your work with these same clients? If you are in a place of discontent in your work, you might consider the following as ways to help you orient to the values you want to guide who you are in this work, given that, at least for right now, this is the work you are choosing to do:

- Try the Value of the Day exercise from chapter 8 (see http://www.newharbinger.com/43218) with five to seven values you would ideally want to have be a part of your work life. Be sure to track the results. What did you learn from this exercise about potential ways of living that were most meaningful or rewarding to you?

- Finish this statement: If I could be more _____ (some quality of your behavior, as opposed to some feeling you might experience) at work, that would be rewarding or important to me.

- Think back to when you first started this job. What were your hopes at that time? How did you imagine being (in other words, what qualities did you hope to embody) as you began this new stage of your career? Now, even as you may be reaching the end of this particular part of your career, what would it be like to still embody those same qualities? How might you do this?

- Imagine that you have decided to leave your work and are wrapping up this week. How would you want to spend this last week of your job? How would you interact with your clients, colleagues, and yourself? How might that change your experience of your workday? What would it be like for you if you could bring those same qualities to your job every day?

- When you think about having a different job or changing your work in some significant way, how do you imagine yourself behaving in that new context? What qualities would you ideally want your new colleagues or clients to see in you? How could you bring those qualities to your work now?

In addition to turning to values to help guide you during times of more pervasive discontent or burnout, it's also important know how to stay in contact with your values throughout your workday on a daily basis, so as to benefit from the motivation and clarity of direction they can provide.

Reconnecting with Values Throughout Your Day

One of the things that I find difficult about doing therapy is the amount of emotional investment it takes for me to be the kind of therapist I want to be. I am a very introverted person. Spending hour after hour intensely connecting with my clients can be difficult and emotionally exhausting. There are times, honestly many times, when I feel overwhelmed, inadequate, worried, or just utterly spent. We all feel discouraged, emotionally exhausted or disconnected, apathetic, or frustrated at times. These are all common and understandable side effects of spending our days sitting with those who are suffering. During these times we might have the urge to "check out," trying to distance ourselves from the suffering that is in front of us. It's also common for therapists to try to just "push through," to ignore our feelings and power on. But in my experience, these strategies don't really do anything to help me reconnect with a sense of meaning or vitality in my work. They may help me simply get through the day, but if I want it to have been a worthwhile day, a day in which the difficulties I encountered were worth something important in the end, then I need to do more than just try to minimize or push through my distress. I need to reconnect with my values and what I most want to be about in this work.

TOOL: BEFORE-SESSION VALUES PRACTICE

I have been incredibly fortunate to have had many amazing professors, mentors, supervisors, and colleagues from whom I have learned a great deal. And yet, if I had to choose just one thing that helps me be the therapist I want to be, it isn't something I learned in a book or in the classroom. It is the practice I do before each of my sessions. I really mean it when I tell my supervisees that the single most important thing I do as a therapist is how I spend the two to three minutes before every session. Being someone who likes ritual, I wanted a very simple practice I could do before every single session to facilitate the transition and reconnect with what matters most to me. This doesn't need to take more than a minute if that's all the time you have, but I have found it helpful to make it a part of my routine that I always do before seeing someone. Here is what I do, though of course feel free to modify it in whatever way to fit your own situation. You can also find a written description of this at http://www.newharbinger.com/43218:

1. I sit down in my therapy chair and close my eyes, letting all the busyness and preparation I have been doing fade away. I allow myself to picture the client I am about to meet with. I see them in my mind's eye as they are sitting there in the waiting room just outside my door.

2. I then imagine what that client might be feeling or thinking as they are waiting to meet with me. I reflect on the idea that there is something important in this next hour for the client, something they are hoping for.

3. Then, I take a moment to connect with this person as a larger conscious being and the common humanity we share. I usually do this by picturing someone else who cares for this client. It could be their partner, their child, their pet, a friend, or their parent. I try to picture what that loved one looks like as they are looking at my client, and what they would wish for my client, this person they care about.

4. Finally, I come back to the present moment and recognize that I have this one hour to be with this individual person, this person who thinks and feels and suffers and loves and is loved, just like me. Then, I reflect on this: *Given this opportunity, how do I want to be toward this person over the next hour?* This is the key part for me. I am not reflecting on what I want to do or any particular agenda I want to cover in the session. Rather, I am reflecting on who I want to be with this person, what qualities I would choose to embody in this one hour that I have. At the end of the hour, even if all my interventions fall flat, even if there is little objective "progress" made, what kind of person would I most want to be with this individual? What way of being would have made this hour worthwhile regardless of the outcome? Then, I go out and get my client and we begin the session.

I find that when I am able to connect with my client as a human being and also my values for how I want to be with this fellow human being, I become more energized and present to the task at hand. I also find the work much more meaningful and satisfying for me personally. At times, I have shared my before-session practice with clients. Those clients know that even before they walk into the room, I am taking steps toward the values I want to guide my work with them. Sometimes, I've even had clients adopt this practice for themselves. They sit in the waiting room not just thinking about what they want to say, but also about the values they want our work together to be in the service of. Sometimes we'll even begin the session by sharing with each other what came up for us in our before-session practice and what values we each want to embody in our hour together. Sharing in this way may not be helpful or appropriate for all clients, of course, but in the right contexts, it can be a powerful way to ground your work together in values.

TOOL: BEFORE-SESSION COMPASSION EXERCISE

Another way of reconnecting with what matters most throughout your day is the Before-Session Compassion exercise. The act of extending compassion and empathy toward your client and yourself before therapy sessions can help you stay as connected with your values for your 6 p.m. client as your 9 a.m. client. The Before-Session Compassion exercise, which is based on an empathy exercise originally developed by Vilardaga, Levin, and Hayes (2007), is a quick perspective-taking exercise you can use between sessions that can help you reconnect with what matters most to you in your work. This is similar, in many ways, to the Before-Session Values practice I described above, and like that practice, this exercise only needs to take a few minutes. You don't necessarily need to give a response to the questions in the exercise, just give yourself a few minutes to reflect on them. There is also an audio version of the exercise available at http://www.newharbinger.com/43218 if you prefer to use this as an eyes-closed guided exercise.

To do the exercise, before you go out to the waiting room to pick up your client, have a seat, put down your agenda, and set aside trying to figure out what you're going to do in the session. Then allow yourself a few minutes to reflect on the following:

1. Imagine that you are your client waiting outside for the session. What might they see, hear, or smell as they are waiting for their appointment? Really try to experience things from their perspective. Imagine the thoughts, feelings, and judgments this person might be having right now as they are sitting in the waiting room. Notice any anxieties or fears they might be feeling as they antic-ipate the session. Notice any hopes or longings they might have about the session. Even though some of what they are experiencing right now may be uncomfortable, notice that they are still choosing to be here, to do this work with you. Could it be that there is something in this work that is about more than simply their comfort, something important to them? What might that be?

2. Now, become aware of any feelings, thoughts, or judgments you have about the client, their problems, or the upcoming session. Notice your own urges, anxiety, or hopes for the client as you connect to their fears. Take a moment to reflect on the fact that even though some of the experiences you are having right now may be uncomfortable, by taking this action of pausing to reflect on your values, you are taking a step toward something that is important to you. What might that be? If you could choose, what would you have this next hour with this client be in the service of?

3. If you were transported in time to the end of therapy with this client, what would you like this client to have taken from this time with you? Imagine this were the very last time you were going to see this client. What would be the most important thing you would have wanted them to take from your work together?

4. Now bring your attention back to your physical presence in this room. Notice your body…and the sounds around you…and go greet this person you will be sharing the next bit of your life with in the service of something that matters.

Therapist Self-Disclosure of Values

Now that you have thought about your own values that relate to your work, a relevant consideration is how much to share of your values with your clients. Regardless of theoretical orientation, a large part of what makes therapy effective or not has to do with the therapist-client relationship (Lambert & Barley, 2001). Having our behavior guided by those values we hold most dear is a key part of being authentic in those relationships. Sharing our values with our clients can have a powerful impact on the work, both for our clients and for us as therapists.

Various theoretical orientations advocate differing positions on whether, when, and how much a therapist should reveal about themselves to their clients. It is also important to take into account any relevant cultural considerations when thinking about how much and why you might self-disclose to clients. For example, clients from some cultural backgrounds may only find therapist self-disclosure (TSD) helpful later in therapy, after a secure therapeutic relationship has been established (Masuda, 2019). However, in general, the data suggest that clients across sociocultural backgrounds tend to benefit from certain types of TSD (Constantine & Kwan, 2003; Hill, Knox, & Pinto-Coelho, 2018). In fact, data suggest that TSD, when done in a culturally sensitive and client-focused manner, can bridge some of the perceived gaps often felt by clients who are working with therapists who are racially or culturally dissimilar to them (Burkard, Knox, Groen, Perez, & Hess, 2006; Constantine & Kwan, 2003). From an ACT perspective, some amount of TSD is generally considered to be not only acceptable but an essential component of competent ACT. TSD is even included in the ACT core competency guidelines (see Luoma et al., 2017, Appendix A), which explicitly state, "The therapist is willing to self-disclose when it serves the interest of the client."

But how do you know what is in the best interest of your client? In addition to cultural considerations (Mahalik, Van Ormer, & Simi, 2000), scientific research does provide some guidelines for what is likely to be more or less effective in terms of TSD (Henretty & Levitt, 2010). For example, self-disclosures that are specifically related to the client, such as sharing feelings or reactions to the client, are generally preferred by clients compared to disclosures about the therapist that are not directly focused on the client, such as information about the therapist's life outside of therapy (Henretty & Levitt, 2010). In addition, data show that clients are more likely to return to therapy after a therapist has shared positive reactions to them personally as compared to when the disclosure is either negative or not directly focused on the client (Watkins & Schneider, 1989).

Regarding TSD around values, it is often helpful to directly state your *therapy-relevant* values to your clients. "Therapy-relevant" values refer to those values that specifically guide your work with a client and how you would choose to be in the room with them specifically. In contrast, statements about more general personal values that are not about how you want to be with that specific client tend to be riskier or potentially problematic. Sharing therapy-relevant values may also entail sharing a positive reaction to the client as you are specifically sharing who you want to be in relation to that particular client. These kinds of disclosures, if timed appropriately, are likely to solidify the therapeutic relationship and reinforce a sense of therapist authenticity. In addition, by explicitly declaring our therapy-relevant values, we are modeling the kind of values-guided behavior we are encouraging our clients to engage in.

It is important to note that these should be your *therapy-relevant* values that you are sharing. There may be times when what you would choose to value outside of the therapy room may differ from what your client chooses to value in their lives. In these cases, it is usually a safer bet to keep these differences to yourself. The primary reason is that, whether intentional or not, these disclosures may function to coerce the client to act in line with the therapist's values. If you've made it this far in the book, you probably know that values are meant to be freely chosen and therapist coercion runs counter to creating a sense of free choice. Thus, if you find yourself tempted to disclose personal values beyond those specifically related to your actions with this client, I would encourage you to first do some introspection about your motivation for doing so, specifically whether a part of you might be wanting to convince your client that a certain way of living is superior, teach them the "right" way to live, or indirectly attempt to control your client. In addition, you might also get consultation from colleagues before making exceptions to these guidelines around TSD.

Here are some examples of self-disclosure related to values that are likely to be more or less effective:

Likely Ineffective or Problematic Therapist Self-Disclosure	Likely Effective and Therapy-Relevant Self-Disclosure
I personally think honesty is an essential value, so I think you need to tell your partner about your affair. (*Probably functions as an attempt to coerce or convince a client regarding what they should value*)	I care deeply about you and our work together. I will be here with you, by your side, as we work through all this pain. (*Values-related, present-focused, and disclosing feelings about the client*)
I choose to value compassion for all living beings and so I am a vegetarian. (*Sharing non-therapy-related or client-focused values*)	I am committed to doing whatever I can to help you live a life that is meaningful to you. That is what I want to be about in our relationship. (*Therapist modeling how their therapy-related values are guiding their behavior*)
What about your spiritual values? I find so much meaning in connecting with something greater than myself. I know you have said spirituality isn't that important to you, but I think it would be helpful for you to reconsider and explore that more. (*Imposing your own personal values on your client. Note you could encourage exploration of spirituality if you felt that was therapeutically important without sharing your values.*)	It is hard for me to see you hurting in this way because I really care for you. So, just like you, part of me wants to move away from talking about this stuff because I can see how painful it is. But, because I choose to value being courageous and bold here with you, I will not turn away from your pain. I will instead choose to act with faith in you and what your life can be. (*Declaration of therapy-related values that also emphasizes a common humanity between therapist and client*)

You're a Person Too!

Hopefully, throughout this book you have been thinking about the values you would want to guide your work. You have likely thought about how you want to be with your clients and may have also considered what qualities you want to bring to your interactions with colleagues. You may have even considered how these values might impact your loved ones and others you may interact with when you get home from work at the end of the day. But what about the person you spend the most time with at work—yourself? Have you considered how your values could guide how you want to be with yourself? Are the qualities you would choose to bring to your interactions with others different than how you would ideally choose to be in your interactions with yourself? If you would choose to value things like kindness or compassion or playfulness or openness or whatever else it might be, would you ideally want to live out those values not just with others, but with yourself as well? If not, what makes you so different that you would exclude yourself from the ways that you'd ideally want to treat all the other people you have a relationship with?

You might be thinking I'm about to launch into a treatise about the importance of "self-care," the one most of us have heard so many times. I'm not. In fact, I'm going to come right out and say it…I really don't like the concept of self-care, at least not how it is usually thought of. The problem I have with self-care is that it is usually described as being somehow distinct from how we normally behave in the rest of our lives. It is the exception rather than the rule. Self-care, as normally understood, is analogous to what my mother would call a "Disneyland parent." The "Disneyland parent" is the one who is never really present in their child's day-to-day life. They might show up for the big game, but they don't bother to take their kid to practice. They are absent for the thankless tasks of driving their kid to the dentist or sitting with them as they cry their way through their first breakup. Instead, once a year, they swoop in and take their kid to Disneyland, as if that's what will make them be a "good" parent. But how you care for your child or your partner or yourself isn't really about the big exceptional things you do. Our values are lived out in the day-to-day moments, how we treat ourselves and others on an ongoing basis.

Rather than trying to carve out time from the normal way of caring for yourself to engage in some one-off "self-care," you might consider using values to guide the way you interact with yourself on an ongoing basis. Values have a consistency and integrity to them that intermittent self-care breaks lack. So, go ahead and take that Wednesday afternoon yoga break. Get a massage once a month. Take that annual ski trip with the guys or gals. And by all means, take your kids to Disneyland if you want. But if you really want to care well for yourself, consider what your values might tell you about how you would interact with yourself on a daily basis.

TOOL: SELF-RELATED VALUES REFLECTION QUESTIONS

To consider the idea of a values-based way of caring for yourself, take some time to write down your responses to the following:

- How would I choose to treat others I care about? If those are important values to me, would I also choose to embody them in all my relationships, including my relationship with myself? How would this look in terms of my relationship with myself and how I treat myself?

- What would my values tell me about how I would want to respond to myself when I feel I have failed or fallen short in some way? What would this look like when I am struggling with a client or having difficulty at work? What might be the impact of responding to my failures in a values-consistent manner rather than responding with self-criticism or some other punishment?

- If I were a client of mine, how would I encourage or support that client in using values to guide how they treat themselves?

- If I wanted to have values guide how I treat myself, how could I put that into practice? How could I use the skills I know for initiating and sustaining behavior into action on this? What is one concrete next step I could take?

Just imagine what it would be like if you treated yourself the same way you treated your clients or those you love. This isn't a onetime "treat" you give yourself; it's a way of being in all your relationships, including your relationship with yourself. What kind of impact could this have on your life and on those you care about, including yourself?

Takeaways

- Values aren't just for clients. Being a values-guided therapist means that values guide your actions as well.

- Values clarification is not enough. We also need to have ways to remain connected with what matters most to us in this work on a day-to-day basis.

- Put values before goals. When considering potential changes you might want to make, sometimes it's helpful to start with doing things differently rather than trying to just do different things.

- It can be helpful to develop a regular practice that allows you to reconnect with your values throughout your day, something you can do before every session.

- By sharing our therapy-relevant values when appropriate, we model values-based behaving. Doing so can also strengthen the therapeutic relationship.

- Consider values as an alternative to self-care. When thinking about what values you want to guide your interactions with others, also consider how you want to interact with yourself.

Next Steps

- Using the guidelines outlined in this chapter, practice sharing your therapy-relevant values with a client this week. What was happening with the client that led you to share in that moment? What was the intended function of your self-disclosure? How well did it serve that function?

- Do either the Before-Session Values practice or the Before-Session Compassion exercise before each session one day this week. Track the consequences.

- Make a plan for how you can incorporate your self-related values into your life and give it a go!

Wrap-Up Steps

Now that you have come to the end of this book, I would encourage you to take the time to do the two following things to synthesize your learning and come up with a plan for how to continue what you have started here.

1. Fill out the Values-Guided Therapy Self-Assessment again (see Appendix A). Do you notice any differences between how you filled it out when reading chapter 1 and now? What does this tell you about next steps you'd want to take?

2. Fill out the Values-Guided Action Plan (Appendix B), focusing on next steps you would choose to take to continue this work of having values guide your therapy (and maybe your own life!).

Parting Thoughts

As we come to a close, consider taking a moment to pause. Notice the time and effort you put into reading this book and what that effort was in the service of. It has been such a joy and privilege for me to get to share my passion for values through writing this book. I truly hope you have found it useful both for yourself and for the people you serve.

Values-Guided Therapy Self-Assessment

Below are some questions to ask yourself regarding your values work with clients.

1	2	3	4	5	?
not true	mostly not true	somewhat true	mostly true	very true	don't know

Knowledge and Toolkit		Rating
1	I am competent at helping my clients explore and articulate their values.	
2	I have a solid understanding of theory that guides my use of values interventions and practices.	
3	I utilize a variety of different values-focused tools/exercises/ interventions in my work with clients.	
4	I utilize out-of-session exercises/homework to help my client practice more values-consistent living.	
5	I facilitate experiences in the therapy session that allow my client to connect with their values.	
General Values-Guided Therapy Practices		
6	I explicitly discuss values with my clients.	
7	Values are included in my informed consent process.	
8	My client's values inform our treatment plan.	
9	Values are an integral part of my case conceptualization.	
10	The ultimate purpose of my therapy interventions is to facilitate valued living.	

Knowledge and Toolkit	Rating
Awareness and Acceptance of Client's Values	
11	I usually know what my client would choose to value.	
12	I usually know what really matters to my client beyond alleviation of their pain.	
13	I often use my client's values to help motivate them during times of difficulty.	
14	I attempt to reinforce behavior that is consistent with my client's values.	
15	I am able to work effectively with someone who chooses to value something different than what I choose to value.	
Therapist's Values	
16	I am connected with what matters most to me about my work.	
17	My values guide how I interact with my clients.	
18	I explicitly share my therapy-relevant values with my clients.	
19	I am able to connect with my values to motivate me during times of difficulty in my work.	
20	My clients are aware of what matters to me in the work that we are doing together (i.e., they know what I value).	
Personal Strengths	
21	The following are some of the particular strengths and skills I bring to doing values work with clients:	

Knowledge and Toolkit	Rating
Personal Growth Areas	
22	The following are areas where I would like to grow in terms of my values work:
Potential Barriers	
23	The following are difficult thoughts and feelings that I experience as I pursue incorporating values into my work (e.g., "I don't know what I'm doing," "My clients won't get it," "anxiety," "feeling incompetent," etc.):
24	The following is how I would choose to respond if/when the above potential barriers arise (be sure to include how you would like to respond to/treat yourself in those times):

Values-Guided Action Plan

1. What is the single most important or meaningful thing I learned from working through this book?

2. What might this say about what I would choose to value?

3. How can I turn that into action (e.g., something to try out, apply, learn more about, or practice)?

4. What is one concrete goal I could complete that takes me in the direction of what I would choose to value?

5. What is the next smallest step I can take toward this goal?

6. The time, day, and date that I will take that first step is:

7. What thoughts, feelings, sensations, or urges am I willing to have in order to take this step in the service of my values?

    Thoughts:

    Feelings:

    Sensations:

    Urges:

8. When I encounter these thoughts, feelings, sensations, or urges, how would I choose to respond given my values? How would I want to treat myself when I experience these difficult thoughts, feelings, sensations, or urges?

References

Arch, J. J., & Craske, M. G. (2008). Acceptance and commitment therapy and cognitive behavioral therapy for anxiety disorders: Different treatments, similar mechanisms? *Clinical Psychology: Science and Practice, 15*(4), 263–279.

Arch, J. J., Eifert, G. H., Davies, C., Vilardaga, J. C. P., Rose, R. D., & Craske, M. G. (2012). Randomized clinical trial of cognitive behavioral therapy (CBT) versus acceptance and commitment therapy (ACT) for mixed anxiety disorders. *Journal of Consulting and Clinical Psychology, 80*(5), 750–765.

Banaji, M. R. (1999, October). *Unconscious isms: Examples from racism, sexism, and ageism.* Paper presented at The Way Women Lean Conference, New Haven, CT.

Bastian, B. (2018). *The other side of happiness: Embracing a more fearless approach to living.* London, UK: Penguin UK.

Bastian, B., Jetten, J., & Ferris, L. J. (2014). Pain as social glue: Shared pain increases cooperation. *Psychological Science, 25*(11), 2079–2085.

Bastian, B., Jetten, J., Hornsey, M. J., & Leknes, S. (2014). The positive consequences of pain: A biopsychosocial approach. *Personality and Social Psychology Review, 18*(3), 256–279.

Bell, K., Salmon, A., Bowers, M., Bell, J., & McCullough, L. (2010). Smoking, stigma and tobacco "denormalization": Further reflections on the use of stigma as a public health tool. A commentary on Social Science & Medicine's Stigma, Prejudice, Discrimination and Health Special Issue (67: 3). *Social Science & Medicine, 70*(6), 795–799.

Blackledge, J., & Ciarrochi, J. (2006). *Social values survey.* Unpublished manuscript, University of Wollongong, Wollongong, Australia.

Blackledge, J. T., Ciarrochi, J., & Bailey, A. (2006). *Personal Values Questionnaire.* Unpublished manuscript, University of Wollongong, Wollongong, Australia.

Boduroglu, A., Yoon, C., Luo, T., & Park, D. C. (2006). Age-related stereotypes: A comparison of American and Chinese cultures. *Gerontology, 52*(5), 324–333.

Bramwell, K., & Richardson, T. (2018). Improvements in depression and mental health after acceptance and commitment therapy are related to changes in defusion and values-based action. *Journal of Contemporary Psychotherapy, 48*(1), 9–14.

Brinkborg, H., Michanek, J., Hesser, H., & Berglund, G. (2011). Acceptance and commitment therapy for the treatment of stress among social workers: A randomized controlled trial. *Behaviour Research and Therapy, 49*(6–7), 389–398.

Brown, B. (2012). Brené Brown: Listening to shame [Video file]. Retrieved from https://www.ted.com/talks/brene_brown_listening_to_shame/up-next.

Brown, B. B., Eicher, S. A., & Petrie, S. (1986). The importance of peer group ("crowd") affiliation in adolescence. *Journal of Adolescence, 9*(1), 73–96.

Burkard, A. W., Knox, S., Groen, M., Perez, M., & Hess, S. A. (2006). European American therapist self-disclosure in cross-cultural counseling. *Journal of Counseling Psychology, 53*(1), 15–25.

Burnett, W., & Evans, D. J. (2016). *Designing your life: How to build a well-lived, joyful life.* New York: Knopf Publishing.

Cameron, A. Y., Reed, K. P., & Gaudiano, B. A. (2014). Addressing treatment motivation in borderline personality disorder: Rationale for incorporating values-based exercises into dialectical behavior therapy. *Journal of Contemporary Psychotherapy, 44*(2), 109–116.

Casas, F., Figuer, C., González, M., & Malo, S. (2007). The values adolescents aspire to, their well-being and the values parents aspire to for their children. *Social Indicators Research, 84*(3), 271–290.

Chapin, H. (1988). My grandfather. On *The gold medal collection* [CD]. New York: Elektra Records.

Chapman, A. L., Gratz, K. L., & Brown, M. Z. (2006). Solving the puzzle of deliberate self-harm: The experiential avoidance model. *Behaviour Research and Therapy, 44*(3), 371–394.

Chawla, N., & Ostafin, B. (2007). Experiential avoidance as a functional dimensional approach to psychopathology: An empirical review. *Journal of Clinical Psychology, 63*(9), 871–890.

Cherry, K. E., Brigman, S., Lyon, B. A., Blanchard, B., Walker, E. J., & Smitherman, E. A. (2016). Self-reported ageism across the lifespan: Role of aging knowledge. *The International Journal of Aging and Human Development, 83*(4), 366–380.

Christie, A. M., Atkins, P. W., & Donald, J. N. (2017). The meaning and doing of mindfulness: The role of values in the link between mindfulness and well-being. *Mindfulness, 8*(2), 368–378.

Ciarrochi, J., Blackledge, J. T., & Heaven, P. (2006, July). *Initial validation of the social values survey and personal values questionnaire.* Paper presented at the Second World Conference on ACT, RFT, and Contextual Behavioral Science, London, England.

Constantine, M. G., & Kwan, K. L. K. (2003). Cross-cultural considerations of therapist self-disclosure. *Journal of Clinical Psychology, 59*(5), 581–588.

Cooper, B. (2016). Intersectionality. In L. Disch & M. Hawkesworth (Eds.), *The Oxford handbook of feminist theory* (pp. 385–406). New York: Oxford University Press.

Crenshaw, K. (1989). Demarginalizing the intersection of race and sex: A black feminist critique of antidiscrimination doctrine, feminist theory and antiracist politics. *University of Chicago Legal Forum,* 139–167.

Creswell, J. D., Welch, W. T., Taylor, S. E., Sherman, D. K., Gruenewald, T. L., & Mann, T. (2005). Affirmation of personal values buffers neuroendocrine and psychological stress responses. *Psychological Science, 16*(11), 846–851.

Dahl, J., Lundgren, T., Plumb, J., & Stewart, I. (2009). *The art and science of valuing in psychotherapy: Helping clients discover, explore, and commit to valued action using acceptance and commitment therapy.* Oakland, CA: New Harbinger Publications.

Dahl, J., Wilson, K., Luciano, C., & Hayes, S. C. (2005). *ACT for chronic pain.* Oakland, CA: Context Press.

Davison, T. E., Eppingstall, B., Runci, S., & O'Connor, D. W. (2017). A pilot trial of acceptance and commitment therapy for symptoms of depression and anxiety in older adults residing in long-term care facilities. *Aging & Mental Health, 21*(7), 766–773.

Duarte, C., Stubbs, J., Pinto-Gouveia, J., Matos, M., Gale, C., Morris, L., & Gilbert, P. (2017). The impact of self-criticism and self-reassurance on weight-related affect and well-being in participants of a commercial weight management programme. *Obesity Facts, 10*(2), 65–75.

Durant, W. (1961). *The story of philosophy.* New York: Simon and Schuster.

Durso, G. R., Luttrell, A., & Way, B. M. (2015). Over-the-counter relief from pains and pleasures alike: Acetaminophen blunts evaluation sensitivity to both negative and positive stimuli. *Psychological Science, 26*(6), 750–758.

Falk, E. B., O'Donnell, M. B., Cascio, C. N., Tinney, F., Kang, Y., Lieberman, M. D., ... & Strecher, V. J. (2015). Self-affirmation alters the brain's response to health messages and subsequent behavior change. *Proceedings of the National Academy of Sciences, 112*(7), 1977–1982.

Felce, D. (1997). Defining and applying the concept of quality of life. *Journal of Intellectual Disability Research, 41*(2), 126–135.

Follette, V., Heffner, M., & Pearson, A. (2010). *Acceptance and commitment therapy for body image dissatisfaction: A practitioner's guide to using mindfulness, acceptance, and values-based behavior change strategies.* Oakland, CA: New Harbinger Publications.

Forman, E. M., Butryn, M. L., Hoffman, K. L., & Herbert, J. D. (2009). An open trial of an acceptance-based behavioral intervention for weight loss. *Cognitive and Behavioral Practice, 16*(2), 223–235.

Forsyth, J. P., & Forsyth, J. R. (2015, October). *The sphere-a-flex model.* Paper presented at Acceptance and Commitment Therapy: A Practical Introduction in Clinical Practice, Portland, OR.

Forsyth, J. P., Parker, J. D., & Finlay, C. G. (2003). Anxiety sensitivity, controllability, and experiential avoidance and their relation to drug of choice and addiction severity in a residential sample of substance-abusing veterans. *Addictive Behaviors, 28*(5), 851–870.

Frankl, V. E. (1946/1984). *Man's search for meaning: Revised and updated.* New York: Washington Square.

Gardner, W. L., Gabriel, S., & Lee, A. Y. (1999). "I" value freedom, but "we" value relationships: Self-construal priming mirrors cultural differences in judgment. *Psychological Science, 10*(4), 321–326.

Gibran, K. (1995). *The prophet.* New York: Knopf Publishing.

Gilbert, P. (2010). *Compassion focused therapy: Distinctive features.* London, UK: Routledge Press.

Gloster, A. T., Klotsche, J., Ciarrochi, J., Eifert, G., Sonntag, R., Wittchen, H. U., & Hoyer, J. (2017). Increasing valued behaviors precedes reduction in suffering: Findings from a randomized controlled trial using ACT. *Behaviour Research and Therapy, 91*, 64–71.

Goodall, J. (n.d.). Retrieved from http://team.janegoodall.org/site/PageServer?pagename=i eatmeatless_pledge.

Greenberg, L. S. (2015). *Emotion-focused therapy: Coaching clients to work through their feelings* (2nd ed.). Washington, DC: American Psychological Association.

Gregg, J. A., Callaghan, G. M., Hayes, S. C., & Glenn-Lawson, J. L. (2007). Improving diabetes self-management through acceptance, mindfulness, and values: A randomized controlled trial. *Journal of Consulting and Clinical Psychology, 75*(2), 336–334.

Grumet, R., & Fitzpatrick, M. (2016). A case for integrating values clarification work into cognitive behavioral therapy for social anxiety disorder. *Journal of Psychotherapy Integration, 26*(1), 11–21.

Hadjistavropoulos, T., Craig, K. D., Duck, S., Cano, A., Goubert, L., Jackson, P. L., Mogil, J. S., Rainville, P., Sullivan, M. J., Williams, A. C., & Vervoort, T. (2011). A biopsychosocial formulation of pain communication. *Psychological Bulletin, 137*(6), 910–939.

Halliburton, A. E., & Cooper, L. D. (2015). Applications and adaptations of acceptance and commitment therapy (ACT) for adolescents. *Journal of Contextual Behavioral Science, 4*(1), 1–11.

Harper, S. K., Webb, T. L., & Rayner, K. (2013). The effectiveness of mindfulness-based interventions for supporting people with intellectual disabilities: A narrative review. *Behavior Modification, 37*(3), 431–453.

Harris, R. (2009). *ACT made simple*. Oakland, CA: New Harbinger Publications.

Hayes, L. L., & Ciarrochi, J. V. (2015). *The thriving adolescent: Using acceptance and commitment therapy and positive psychology to help teens manage emotions, achieve goals, and build connection*. Oakland, CA: New Harbinger Publications.

Hayes, S. C. (2005). *Get out of your mind and into your life: The new acceptance and commitment therapy*. Oakland, CA: New Harbinger Publications.

Hayes, S. C., Barnes-Holmes, D., & Roche, B. (Eds.). (2001). *Relational frame theory: A Post-Skinnerian account of human language and cognition*. New York: Plenum Press.

Hayes, S. C., Bissett, R., Roget, N., Padilla, M., Kohlenberg, B. S., Fisher, G., … & Niccolls, R. (2004). The impact of acceptance and commitment training and multicultural training on the stigmatizing attitudes and professional burnout of substance abuse counselors. *Behavior Therapy, 35*(4), 821–835.

Hayes, S. C., Pistorello, J., & Levin, M. E. (2012). Acceptance and commitment therapy as a unified model of behavior change. *The Counseling Psychologist, 40*(7), 976–1002.

Hayes, S. C., Strosahl, K. D., & Wilson, K. G. (2012). *Acceptance and commitment therapy: The process and practice of mindful change* (2nd ed.). New York: Guilford Press.

Hayes, S. C., Strosahl, K., Wilson, K. G., Bissett, R. T., Pistorello, J., Toarmino, D., … & McCurry, S. M. (2004). Measuring experiential avoidance: A preliminary test of a working model. *The Psychological Record, 54*(4), 553–578.

Henretty, J. R., & Levitt, H. M. (2010). The role of therapist self-disclosure in psychotherapy: A qualitative review. *Clinical Psychology Review, 30*(1), 63–77.

Hill, C. E., Knox, S., & Pinto-Coelho, K. G. (2018). Therapist self-disclosure and immediacy: A qualitative meta-analysis. *Psychotherapy, 55*(4), 445–460.

Hinds, E., Jones, L. B., Gau, J. M., Forrester, K. K., & Biglan, A. (2015). Teacher distress and the role of experiential avoidance. *Psychology in the Schools, 52*(3), 284–297.

Holmes, J. (1996). *Attachment, intimacy, autonomy: Using attachment theory in adult psychotherapy*. Northvale, NJ: Jason Aronson.

hooks, b. (1992). Agent of change: An interview with bell hooks (H. Tworkov, Interviewer). *Tricycle: The Buddhist Review, 2*(1), 48–57.

Howe-Martin, L. S., Murrell, A. R., & Guarnaccia, C. A. (2012). Repetitive nonsuicidal self-injury as experiential avoidance among a community sample of adolescents. *Journal of Clinical Psychology, 68*(7), 809–829.

Iyengar, S. S., & Lepper, M. R. (1999). Rethinking the value of choice: A cultural perspective on intrinsic motivation. *Journal of Personality and Social Psychology, 76*(3), 349–366.

Janoff-Bulman, R. (1992). *Shattered assumptions: Towards a new psychology of trauma*. New York: Free Press.

Joseph, S., Linley, P. A., & Harris, G. J. (2004). Understanding positive change following trauma and adversity: Structural clarification. *Journal of Loss and Trauma, 10*(1), 83–96.

Katz, B. A., Catane, S., & Yovel, I. (2016). Pushed by symptoms, pulled by values: Promotion goals increase motivation in therapeutic tasks. *Behavior Therapy, 47*(2), 239–247.

Koder, D. A., & Ferguson, S. J. (1998). The status of geropsychology in Australia: Exploring why Australian psychologists are not working with elderly clients. *Australian Psychologist, 33*(2), 96–100.

Kohlenberg, R. J., & Tsai, M. (1991). *Functional analytic psychotherapy: Creating intense and curative therapeutic relationships.* New York: Springer Publishing.

Labelle, L. E., Campbell, T. S., & Carlson, L. E. (2010). Mindfulness-based stress reduction in oncology: Evaluating mindfulness and rumination as mediators of change in depressive symptoms. *Mindfulness, 1*(1), 28–40.

Lambert, M. J., & Barley, D. E. (2001). Research summary on the therapeutic relationship and psychotherapy outcome. *Psychotherapy: Theory, Research, Practice, Training, 38*(4), 357–361.

Levy, B. R., Hausdorff, J. M., Hencke, R., & Wei, J. Y. (2000). Reducing cardiovascular stress with positive self-stereotypes of aging. *The Journals of Gerontology Series B: Psychological Sciences and Social Sciences, 55*(4), P205–P213.

Lewis, C. S. (1960). *The four loves.* New York: Harcourt.

Lindsley, O. R. (1968). *Training parents and teachers to precisely manage children's behavior.* Paper presented at the C. S. Mott Foundation Children's Health Center, Flint, MI.

Liu, W. S., Liu, N. K., & Elliott, R. (2010). Ouch!–a logotherapeutic discourse of butch and tattooed in China. *Journal of Consumer Behaviour, 9*(4), 293–302.

Lundgren, A. T., Dahl, J., Melin, L., & Kees, B. (2006). Evaluation of acceptance and commitment therapy for drug refractory epilepsy: A randomized controlled trial in South Africa. *Epilepsia, 47*(12), 2173–2179.

Lundgren, T., Luoma, J. B., Dahl, J., Strosahl, K., & Melin, L. (2012). The bull's-eye values survey: A psychometric evaluation. *Cognitive and Behavioral Practice, 19*(4), 518–526.

Luoma, J. B., Hayes, S. C., & Walser, R. D. (2017). *Learning ACT: An acceptance & commitment therapy skills-training manual for therapists* (2nd ed.). Oakland, CA: New Harbinger Publications.

Macrae, C. N., Bodenhausen, G. V., Milne, A. B., & Jetten, J. (1994). Out of mind but back in sight: Stereotypes on the rebound. *Journal of Personality and Social Psychology, 67*(5), 808–817.

Mahalik, J. R., Van Ormer, E. A., & Simi, N. L. (2000). Ethical issues in using self-disclosure in feminist therapy. In M. M. Brabeck (Ed.), *Psychology of women book series. Practicing feminist ethics in psychology* (pp. 189–201). Washington, DC: American Psychological Association.

Markus, H. R., & Kitayama, S. (2010). Cultures and selves: A cycle of mutual constitution. *Perspectives on Psychological Science, 5*(4), 420–430.

Masuda, A. (accepted for publication). Adapting acceptance and commitment therapy to diverse cultures. In M. E. Levin, M. P. Twohig, & J. Krafft (Eds.), *Innovation in ACT* (tentative title). Oakland, CA: Context Press/New Harbinger Publications.

Masuda, A. (Ed.). (2014). *Mindfulness and acceptance in multicultural competency: A contextual approach to sociocultural diversity in theory and practice.* Oakland, CA: Context Press.

May, R. (1975). *The courage to create.* New York: W. W. Norton & Co.

McCall, L. (2005). The complexity of intersectionality. *Signs: Journal of Women in Culture and Society, 30*(3), 1771–1800.

McCracken, L. M., & Yang, S. Y. (2006). The role of values in a contextual cognitive-behavioral approach to chronic pain. *Pain, 123*(1–2), 137–145.

McHugh, L., & Stewart, I. (2012). *The self and perspective taking: Contributions and applications from modern behavioral science.* Oakland, CA: New Harbinger Publications.

Mellick, W., Vanwoerden, S., & Sharp, C. (2017). Experiential avoidance in the vulnerability to depression among adolescent females. *Journal of Affective Disorders, 208,* 497–502.

Miller, M. B., Meier, E., Lombardi, N., Leavens, E. L., Grant, D. M., & Leffingwell, T. R. (2016). The Valued Living Questionnaire for Alcohol Use: Measuring value-behavior discrepancy in college student drinking. *Psychological Assessment, 28*(9), 1051–1060.

Milton, J. (2007). *Paradise lost.* London: Pearson Education.

Miselli, G., Cavagnola, R., Leoni, M., & Corti, S. (2017, June). Altering the value of reinforcers: Values conversations for intellectual disabilities. In G. Miselli (Chair), *Working with values and values-consistent behavior.* Symposium conducted at the meeting of the Association for Contextual Behavioral Science, Seville, Spain.

Moran, D. J., Bach, P. A., & Batten, S. J. (2018). *Committed action in practice: A clinician's guide to assessing, planning, and supporting change in your client.* Oakland, CA: New Harbinger Publications.

Morse, G., Salyers, M. P., Rollins, A. L., Monroe-DeVita, M., & Pfahler, C. (2012). Burnout in mental health services: A review of the problem and its remediation. *Administration and Policy in Mental Health and Mental Health Services Research, 39*(5), 341–352.

Nagayama Hall, G. C., Hong, J. J., Zane, N. W., & Meyer, O. L. (2011). Culturally competent treatments for Asian Americans: The relevance of mindfulness and acceptance-based psychotherapies. *Clinical Psychology: Science and Practice, 18*(3), 215–231.

Neacsiu, A. D., Lungu, A., Harned, M. S., Rizvi, S. L., & Linehan, M. M. (2014). Impact of dialectical behavior therapy versus community treatment by experts on emotional experience, expression, and acceptance in borderline personality disorder. *Behaviour Research and Therapy, 53,* 47–54.

Neff, K. D., & Germer, C. K. (2013). A pilot study and randomized controlled trial of the mindful self-compassion program. *Journal of Clinical Psychology, 69*(1), 28–44.

Nesse, R. M. (1991). What good is feeling bad? The evolutionary benefits of psychic pain. *The Sciences, 31*(6), 30–37.

Newman, L. S., Caldwall, T. L., Chamberlin, B., & Griffin, T. (2005). Thought suppression, projection, and the development of stereotypes. *Basic and Applied Social Psychology, 27*(3), 259–266.

North, M. S., & Fiske, S. T. (2013). Act your (old) age: Prescriptive, ageist biases over succession, consumption, and identity. *Personality and Social Psychology Bulletin, 39*(6), 720–734.

O'Connor, M., Tennyson, A., Timmons, M., & McHugh, L. (2019). The development and preliminary psychometric properties of the Values Wheel. *Journal of Contextual Behavioral Science 12,* 39–46.

Oliver, M. (2017, June). *Working with ACT with people with intellectual disabilities: Lessons learned and areas for development.* Paper presented at the Association for Contextual Behavioral Science, Seville, Spain.

Osbon, D. K. (Ed.). (1995). *A Joseph Campbell companion: Reflections on the art of living.* New York: Harper Perennial.

Owen, J. (2018). Introduction to special issue: Cultural processes in psychotherapy. *Psychotherapy, 55*(1), 1–2.

Oxford Dictionary. Morals. (n.d.). Retrieved from https://en.oxforddictionaries.com/definition/moral.

Páez-Blarrina, M., Luciano, C., Gutiérrez-Martínez, O., Valdivia, S., Ortega, J., & Rodríguez-Valverde, M. (2008). The role of values with personal examples in altering the functions of pain: Comparison between acceptance-based and cognitive-control-based protocols. *Behaviour Research and Therapy, 46*(1), 84–97.

Pielech, M., Bailey, R. W., McEntee, M. L., Ashworth, J., Levell, J., Sowden, G., & Vowles, K. E. (2016). Preliminary evaluation of the Values Tracker: A two-item measure of engagement in valued activities in those with chronic pain. *Behavior Modification, 40*(1–2), 239–256.

Polk, K. (2014). The Psychological Flexibility Warm-Up. In K. L. Polk & B. Schoendorff (Eds.), *The ACT matrix: A new approach to building psychological flexibility across settings and populations*. Oakland, CA: New Harbinger Publications.

Porges, S. W. (2003). Social engagement and attachment. *Annals of the New York Academy of Sciences, 1008*(1), 31–47.

Powers, T. A., Koestner, R., Zuroff, D. C., Milyavskaya, M., & Gorin, A. A. (2011). The effects of self-criticism and self-oriented perfectionism on goal pursuit. *Personality and Social Psychology Bulletin, 37*(7), 964–975.

Quayle, E., Vaughan, M., & Taylor, M. (2006). Sex offenders, internet child abuse images and emotional avoidance: The importance of values. *Aggression and Violent Behavior, 11*(1), 1–11.

Roberts, S. L., & Sedley, B. (2016). Acceptance and commitment therapy with older adults: Rationale and case study of an 89-year-old with depression and generalized anxiety disorder. *Clinical Case Studies, 15*(1), 53–67.

Rogers, C. R. (1961). *On becoming a person*. Boston: Houghton Mifflin.

Rupp, D. E., Vodanovich, S. J., & Credé, M. (2006). Age bias in the workplace: The impact of ageism and causal attributions. *Journal of Applied Social Psychology, 36*(6), 1337–1364.

Schaie, K. W., & Willis, S. L. (2000). A stage theory model of adult cognitive development revisited. In B. Rubinstein, M. Moss, & M. Kleban (Eds.), *The many dimensions of aging: Essays in honor of M. Powell Lawton* (pp. 175–193). New York: Springer.

Sheldon, K. M., & Elliot, A. J. (1999). Goal striving, need satisfaction, and longitudinal well-being: The Self-Concordance Model. *Journal of Personality and Social Psychology, 76*(3), 482–497.

Skinta, M., & Curtin, A. (Eds.). (2016). *Mindfulness and acceptance for gender and sexual minorities: A clinician's guide to fostering compassion, connection, and equality using contextual strategies*. Oakland, CA: New Harbinger Publications.

Spinhoven, P., Drost, J., de Rooij, M., van Hemert, A. M., & Penninx, B. W. (2014). A longitudinal study of experiential avoidance in emotional disorders. *Behavior Therapy, 45*(6), 840–850.

Stattin, H., & Kerr, M. (2001). Adolescents' values matter. In J.-E. Nurmi (Ed.), *Navigating through adolescence: European perspectives* (pp. 21–58). London, UK: Routledge.

Stoddard, J. A., & Afari, N. (2014). *The big book of ACT metaphors: A practitioner's guide to experiential exercises and metaphors in acceptance and commitment therapy*. Oakland, CA: New Harbinger Publications.

Sue, D. W., Sue, D., Neville, H. A., & Smith, L. (2019). *Counseling the culturally diverse: Theory and practice* (8th ed.). Hoboken, NJ: Wiley & Sons.

Thompson, B. L., Luoma, J. B., & LeJeune, J. T. (2013). Using acceptance and commitment therapy to guide exposure-based interventions for posttraumatic stress disorder. *Journal of Contemporary Psychotherapy, 43*(3), 133–140.

Tull, M. T., Gratz, K. L., Salters, K., & Roemer, L. (2004). The role of experiential avoidance in posttraumatic stress symptoms and symptoms of depression, anxiety, and somatization. *The Journal of Nervous and Mental Disease, 192*(11), 754–761.

Twohig, M. P. (2009). Acceptance and commitment therapy for treatment-resistant posttraumatic stress disorder: A case study. *Cognitive and Behavioral Practice, 16*(3), 243–252.

Törneke, N. (2010). *Learning RFT: An introduction to relational frame theory and its clinical application.* Oakland, CA: New Harbinger Publications.

Vilardaga, R., Levin, M., & Hayes, S. C. (2007, November). A comprehensive review of perspective taking procedures in the psychological literature. In R. Vilardaga (chair), *A psychological analysis of perspective taking: Research and applications informed by relational frame theory.* Symposium presented at the 41st Annual Convention of the Association for Behavioral and Cognitive Therapies, Philadelphia, PA.

Vilardaga, R., Luoma, J. B., Hayes, S. C., Pistorello, J., Levin, M. E., Hildebrandt, M. J., Kohlenberg, B., Roget, N. A., & Bond, F. (2011). Burnout among the addiction counseling workforce: The differential roles of mindfulness and values-based processes and work-site factors. *Journal of Substance Abuse Treatment, 40*(4), 323–335.

Villatte, J. L., Vilardaga, R., Villatte, M., Vilardaga, J. C. P., Atkins, D. C., & Hayes, S. C. (2016). Acceptance and commitment therapy modules: Differential impact on treatment processes and outcomes. *Behaviour Research and Therapy, 77,* 52–61.

Villatte, M., Villatte, J. L., & Hayes, S. C. (2015). *Mastering the clinical conversation: Language as intervention.* New York: Guilford Press.

Vowles, K. E., & McCracken, L. M. (2008). Acceptance and values-based action in chronic pain: A study of treatment effectiveness and process. *Journal of Consulting and Clinical Psychology, 76*(3), 397–407.

Watkins Jr, C. E., & Schneider, L. J. (1989). Self-involving versus self-disclosing counselor statements during an initial interview. *Journal of Counseling & Development, 67*(6), 345–349.

Wilson, D. S. (2015). *Does altruism exist?: Culture, genes, and the welfare of others.* New Haven, CT: Yale University Press.

Wilson, K. G., & DuFrene, T. (2009). *Mindfulness for two: An acceptance and commitment therapy approach to mindfulness in psychotherapy.* Oakland, CA: New Harbinger Publications.

Wilson, K. G., & Sandoz, E. K. (2008). Mindfulness, values, and the therapeutic relationship in acceptance and commitment therapy. In S. Hick & T. Bien (Eds.), *Mindfulness and the therapeutic relationship* (pp. 89–106). New York, NY: Guildford Press.

Wilson, K., Sandoz, E. K., Flynn, M. K., Slater, R. M., & DuFrene, T. (2010). Understanding, assessing, and treating values processes in mindfulness-and acceptance-based therapies. In R. A. Baer (Ed.), *Assessing mindfulness and acceptance processes in clients: Illuminating the theory and practice of change* (pp. 77–106). Oakland, CA: New Harbinger Publications.

Wong, P. T. (1997). Meaning-centered counseling: A cognitive-behavioral approach to logotherapy. *The International Forum for Logotherapy, 20,* 85–94.

Woods, D. W., Wetterneck, C. T., & Flessner, C. A. (2006). A controlled evaluation of acceptance and commitment therapy plus habit reversal for trichotillomania. *Behaviour Research and Therapy, 44*(5), 639–656.

Yun, R. J., & Lachman, M. E. (2006). Perceptions of aging in two cultures: Korean and American views on old age. *Journal of Cross-Cultural Gerontology, 21*(1–2), 55–70.

Jenna LeJeune, PhD, is cofounder and president of Portland Psychotherapy Clinic, Research, and Training Center in Portland, OR. As a clinical psychologist, she is interested in helping people live lives of meaning and purpose even in the midst of suffering. In her clinical practice, Jenna specializes in working with clients struggling with relationship difficulties, including problems with intimacy and sexuality, trauma-related relationship challenges, and struggles people have in their relationship with their own bodies. She is also a peer-reviewed trainer in acceptance and commitment therapy (ACT), and provides trainings for professionals around the world.

Jason B. Luoma, PhD, is cofounder and CEO of Portland Psychotherapy Clinic, Research, and Training Center—a research and training clinic based on a social enterprise model that uses business revenue to fund scientific research—where he maintains a small clinical practice. As a researcher, Luoma studies shame, self-criticism, and the interpersonal effects of emotion, as well as related interventions. He is a peer-reviewed ACT trainer, former chair of the ACT Training Committee, and former president of the Association for Contextual Behavioral Science.

Index

A

about this book, 3–4

absence, pain of, 102–104

acceptance: misuse of term, 35. *See also* willingness

acceptance and commitment therapy (ACT): evoking and utilizing emotions in, 104; values component of, 4, 10

action: charting a new course of, 118–119; committed, 134; importance of in values work, 45; obstructed by psychological inflexibility, 47; prototypes and quality of, 121–122; tracking in daily life, 114–117; values as qualities of, 12–13

adolescent clients, 163–164

ageist stereotypes, 165

ambivalent clients, 69

anger, usefulness of, 95

anxiety, usefulness of, 98

appetitives, 18–20

assessing values: measures available for, 67–68; Values Card Sort tool for, 60–67. *See also* self-assessments

augmentals, 20

autopilot, 114

aversive control strategies, 23

avoidance. *See* experiential avoidance

awareness: of choice inside pain, 97–99; of cost of experiential avoidance, 69

"away" moves, 18

B

barriers to values: pitfall of buying into, 130; planning for potential, 125–126

Bastian, Brock, 102

Before-Session Compassion exercise, 182–183

Before-Session Values practice, 181–182

behaviors: based on values, 11, 21–22, 52; rule-governed, 70, 143–144; tracking in daily life, 114–117

biases, exploring your own, 158–159

boldness, humility vs., 159–160

Brown, Brené, 79

Bull's-Eye Values Survey (BEVS), 67

Bunch, Charlotte, 113

Burnett, Bill, 119–120

burnout, therapist, 52, 178–180

C

Campbell, Joseph, 21

Card Sort exercise. *See* Values Card Sort exercise

caring, vulnerability of, 99

case conceptualization model, 150

Chapin, Harry, 14, 16

Chödrön, Pema, 175

choice: conversations about, 80–81; inherent in pain, 97–99

chosen values, 11, 16–18, 80–81, 166

clients: ambivalent or unmotivated, 69; helping to access emotions, 104–110; orienting toward values, 51–71; reward-focused, 86–87; values conflicts with, 168–171

cognition, values and, 20–21

cognitive behavioral therapy (CBT), 43

cognitive defusion. *See* defusion

cognitive fusion. *See* fusion with thoughts

coin metaphor, 98–99, 112

committed action, 134

Committed Action in Practice (Moran, Bach, & Batten), 113

conceptualized self, 38–39

conflicting values. *See* values conflicts

consistency, provided by values, 22–23

contact with the present moment. *See* present-moment contact

MORE BOOKS *from*
NEW HARBINGER PUBLICATIONS

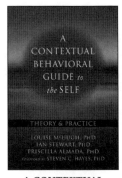
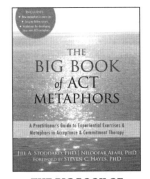
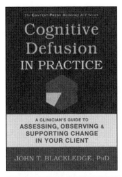
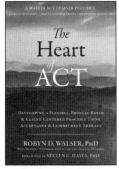
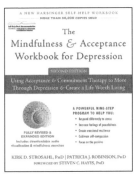
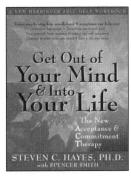

Register your **new harbinger** titles for additional benefits!

When you register your **new harbinger** title—purchased in any format, from any source—you get access to benefits like the following:

- Downloadable accessories like printable worksheets and extra content

- Instructional videos and audio files

- Information about updates, corrections, and new editions

Not every title has accessories, but we're adding new material all the time.

Access free accessories in 3 easy steps:

1. Sign in at NewHarbinger.com (or **register** to create an account).

2. Click on **register a book**. Search for your title and click the **register** button when it appears.

3. Click on the **book cover or title** to go to its details page. Click on **accessories** to view and access files.

That's all there is to it!

If you need help, visit:

NewHarbinger.com/accessories

new harbinger
CELEBRATING
40 YEARS